Food Cultures of France

**Recent Titles in
The Global Kitchen**

Food Cultures of the United States: Recipes, Customs, and Issues
Bruce Kraig

Food Cultures of Israel: Recipes, Customs, and Issues
Michael Ashkenazi

FOOD CULTURES OF FRANCE

Recipes, Customs, and Issues

Maryann Tebben

The Global Kitchen

BLOOMSBURY ACADEMIC
NEW YORK • LONDON • OXFORD • NEW DELHI • SYDNEY

BLOOMSBURY ACADEMIC
Bloomsbury Publishing Inc
1359 Broadway, New York, NY 10018, USA
50 Bedford Square, London, WC1B 3DP, UK
29 Earlsfort Terrace, Dublin 2, Ireland

BLOOMSBURY, BLOOMSBURY ACADEMIC and the Diana logo are trademarks of
Bloomsbury Publishing Plc

First published in the United States of America by ABC-CLIO 2021
Paperback edition published by Bloomsbury Academic 2025

Copyright © Bloomsbury Publishing Inc, 2021

COVER PHOTOS: Woman baking crêpes in a food cart at a funfair at St-Quentin in Picardie, France. (Hilke Maunder/Alamy Stock Photo); World flags vectors. (pop_jop/iStockphoto)

All rights reserved. No part of this publication may be reproduced or transmitted in any form or by any means, electronic or mechanical, including photocopying, recording, or any information storage or retrieval system, without prior permission in writing from the publishers.

Bloomsbury Publishing Inc does not have any control over, or responsibility for, any third-party websites referred to or in this book. All internet addresses given in this book were correct at the time of going to press. The author and publisher regret any inconvenience caused if addresses have changed or sites have ceased to exist, but can accept no responsibility for any such changes.

Library of Congress Cataloging-in-Publication Data
Names: Tebben, Maryann Bates, author.
Title: Food cultures of France : recipes, customs, and issues / Maryann Tebben.
Description: Santa Barbara : Greenwood, an imprint of ABC-CLIO, [2021] | Series: The global kitchen | Includes bibliographical references and index.
Identifiers: LCCN 2020035093 (print) | LCCN 2020035094 (ebook) | ISBN 9781440869655 (print) | ISBN 9781440869662 (ebook)
Subjects: LCSH: Cooking, French. | LCGFT: Cookbooks.
Classification: LCC TX719 .T4 2020 (print) | LCC TX719 (ebook) | DDC 641.5944—dc23
LC record available at https://lccn.loc.gov/2020035093
LC ebook record available at https://lccn.loc.gov/2020035094

ISBN: HB: 978-1-4408-6965-5
PB: 979-8-2163-8664-3
ePDF: 978-1-4408-6966-2
eBook: 979-8-2160-8574-4

Series: The Global Kitchen

To find out more about our authors and books visit www.bloomsbury.com and sign up for our newsletters.

Contents

Series Foreword		vii
Introduction		ix
Chronology		xv

Chapter One	Food History	1
Chapter Two	Influential Ingredients	19
Chapter Three	Appetizers and Side Dishes	41
Chapter Four	Main Dishes	61
Chapter Five	Desserts	81
Chapter Six	Beverages	99
Chapter Seven	Holidays and Special Occasions	119
Chapter Eight	Street Food and Snacks	137
Chapter Nine	Dining Out	155
Chapter Ten	Food Issues and Dietary Concerns	175

Glossary	195
Selected Bibliography	203
Index	213

Series Foreword

Imagine a typical American breakfast: bacon, eggs, toast, and home fries from the local diner. Or maybe a protein-packed smoothie, sipped on the go to class or work. In some countries in Europe, breakfast might just be a small cookie and a strong coffee, if anything at all. A South African breakfast might consist of a bowl of corn porridge with milk. In Japan, breakfast might look more like dinner, complete with rice, vegetables, and fish. What we eat varies from country to country, and even region to region. The Global Kitchen series explores the cuisines of different cultures around the world, from the history of food and food staples to main dishes and contemporary issues. Teeming with recipes to try at home, these volumes will delight readers by discovering other cultures through the lens of a treasured topic: food.

Each volume focuses on the culinary heritage of one country or one small group of countries, covering history and contemporary culture. Volumes begin with a chronology of major food-related milestones and events in the area, from prehistory to present. Chapters explore the key foods and meals in the country, covering the following topics:

- Food History;
- Influential Ingredients;
- Appetizers and Side Dishes;
- Main Dishes;
- Desserts;
- Beverages;
- Holidays and Special Occasions;
- Street Food and Snacks;
- Dining Out; and
- Food Issues and Dietary Concerns.

Chapters are textual, and each chapter is accompanied by numerous recipes, adding a hands-on component to the series. Sidebars, a glossary of important terms, and a selected bibliography round out each volume, providing readers with additional information and resources for their personal and scholarly research needs.

Whether readers are looking for recipes to use for classes or at home, or to explore the histories and traditions of world cuisines, the Global Kitchen series will allow readers to fully immerse themselves in other cultures, giving a taste of typical daily life and tradition.

Introduction

France as a territory has changed shape and size in its history from Gaul to the present day, beginning as a portion of the Roman Empire and subsequently annexing nearby territories to earn its nickname "the Hexagon" in the eighteenth century. France also colonized overseas territories in Asia, Africa, and the Caribbean to constitute its empire between the seventeenth and nineteenth centuries, before a series of revolutions led to decolonization in the 1960s. In the modern era, France sets its cuisine as the highest pinnacle of gastronomy, seeking to defend it against other established national cuisines and the threat of globalization. The food of present-day France is a product of this heritage, having changed and developed under each successive generation.

Presented as a monolith impervious to outside influences, French food has, of course, borrowed from outside influences and followed the fads and economic restrictions of each age. In the modern portrait of French food, it is possible to trace the heritage of France's earliest ancestors in Gaul, who adored meat and butter. Medieval and Renaissance banquets offered numerous dishes of meat and fish, and diners created a hierarchy of meats with poultry at the top, followed by fish and then butcher's meats. The Catholic Church in France also dictated when meals had to follow "lean" rules that excluded most meats and animal fats but allowed seafood. In France today, poultry is more popular than ever, and some holiday customs replicate the tradition of eating fish, even if fewer French practice Catholicism. As French citizens abandoned the church after the Revolution, they also abandoned the practice of observing Lenten (lean) days, and the demand for salt cod and herring declined, but *brandade de morue*, a first course of salt-cod hash and potatoes, still finds its way onto French tables. At Christmas Eve and New Year's Eve feasts, seafood takes center stage.

The medieval age of bread, when bread inspectors kept quality high and prices fair, resonates in France's current bread regulations and the *boulangeries* on every corner. The French public then demanded good bread at a fair price, and the government created and enforced statutes to ensure the supply, just as government decrees do now. Medieval bakers made different kinds of bread for different budgets: bread from fine white flour, bread from mixed flour (usually rye or millet), and dark bread made from coarse flour. Bread came in heavy, round loaves that were meant to last at least a week. After the Revolution, snow-white bread from soft wheat flour became the only desirable bread. Modern French baguettes came out of this change, driven by fads and public opinion.

Prior to the Renaissance vogue for fresh vegetables and seasonal fruit, the French cared little for greenery. Very few recipes for vegetables appeared in cookbooks, and the elite considered vegetables to be the food of the poor. The French today embrace freshness and seasonality in fruit and vegetables; they look for local produce at the market and are familiar with the different varieties of the produce they use. The French government publishes a monthly newsletter identifying the agricultural products at their best in each season. Respect for seasonality means that the French enjoy these foods at their peak of flavor and with care for the environment since local products require less packaging and shipping. Seasonal eating is also a cultural practice of many French families, passed on from generation to generation.

In the seventeenth century, cookbook authors set into print the name and the idea of "French cuisine," with a vocabulary that still stands. Ragouts of meat in sauce from François La Varenne's 1651 cookbook modernized elite cooking and created the template for the classic braised dishes of home cooking and the sauces that remain the hallmark of French cuisine. La Varenne and his fellows in the seventeenth century enabled the transition from medieval cooking that often paired sweet or spicy sauces with meat to a more refined style of cuisine that sought to match flavors rather than contrast them.

In the eighteenth century, French citizens clamored for good bread and some meat for all, in a sense applying the revolutionary slogan *liberté, égalité, fraternité* ("liberty, equality, brotherhood") to food. If not for the French Revolution, which sent private cooks looking for work when their aristocratic employers fled France (or met their end), and if not for a clever bouillon-shop owner who served soup to paying customers, the world would not have restaurants. By the eighteenth century, cookbooks for the middle classes became available; as such, less complicated recipes with less expensive ingredients became accessible to a wider public.

Introduction

Restaurants made foods previously only known to the wealthy available to anyone with enough money for a single meal. Gastronomic cuisine opened fine dining to the middle class, but it did not erase all connections to aristocratic banquets. The names of dishes and, particularly, sauces honored noble figures and royalty: cookbooks and menus featured sauces named for princes, princesses, dukes, and kings.

The nineteenth century brought a renewed interest in elite cuisine, and France once again claimed its place at the top, with Marie-Antoine Carême and his foundational cookbooks, which redefined French sauces and brought artistry to plated dishes. In the twentieth century, French cuisine revised itself again to meet new standards for healthier, less butter-heavy sauces and new flavors from overseas territories but did not abandon its comforting old classics like lamb stews and pot-au-feu (boiled beef). Finally, in the twenty-first century, faced with the growing popularity of industrial food and fast food, France has redoubled its efforts to remind its own citizens and the world that French cuisine still matters. French eating habits have adjusted to accommodate fusion cuisine and American imports like hamburgers and bagels, but the French still gather for lunch at 1:00 p.m., still eat a proper three-course meal most of the time, and never miss foie gras (goose liver) at Christmas. The French meal has always had a clear structure from beginning to end, with defined courses and the expectation that guests will spend a significant amount of time at the table. This tradition remains at French holiday tables and in restaurants, if not in everyday life.

The French have long been trendsetters when it comes to food. Nose-to-tail eating appeared in France well before the current wave of interest in it. Cookbooks beginning in the seventeenth century offer recipes for foie gras and veal liver as well as kidneys and sweetbreads (the thymus gland, usually of veal) and even pigs' tails in sauce. Current French menus, just like those from the seventeenth and eighteenth century, include frog legs, snails, and, less often, pigs' feet and beef tongue. French techniques are recognized as the standard for professional chefs even today. Most restaurant chefs learn French techniques in cooking school or at an apprenticeship in France. The center of fine dining has always been Paris, and the temples of gastronomy remain Parisian for the most part.

The evolution of French cuisine from the Middle Ages to the present can be documented in published cookbooks and other official works, but it must also take into account the eating habits of the French people at all levels. The Gauls and Franks, especially the wealthy, were principally meat eaters, supplied by rich hunting lands and domestic livestock. Wealthy aristocrats in the seventeenth and eighteenth centuries indulged in swans, herons, and peacocks, as well as large cuts of roasted meat. Before the nineteenth century, typical French diners ate mainly mutton or lamb and some beef, if they could afford meat at all. Laws and government decrees enabled all classes to have access to some type of meat but perhaps only a bit of pork to flavor the soup. After prices fell and fresh meat became more readily available, modern French consumers embraced beef and poultry. Poultry now represents an even larger percentage of meat consumption than beef does, and the French now eat mainly chicken and some rabbit, although the demand for rabbit has dropped by about half since the 1960s. Today the French consume less meat than ever before.

Before the eighteenth century, sugar was nearly exclusively reserved for the wealthy; it was so precious that it was used for decorations at banquets rather than for edible treats. As sugar became more available, individual cakes and pastries began to appear as the final course at banquets, and eventually pastry shops and chocolate shops opened during the nineteenth century to serve all those who could afford to buy a sweet treat. Dessert was no longer reserved for special occasions; it could be a daily treat for middle-class households and an occasional indulgence for almost everyone. French pastry shops still cater to those seeking a sweet treat, providing everything from high-end éclairs at Fauchon, in Paris, to the brownies and cheesecakes that imitate American desserts and are beloved by French teenagers.

French gastronomy has also met with challenges over its long history. French chefs who were determined to create a French culinary identity in the seventeenth century did so in order to defend France's status in Europe. Even though the French resist foreign influences, France has long borrowed from other culinary traditions. Those who take the long view point out that tomatoes and potatoes, both staples in French cuisine, originated in the Americas. French menus today reflect adopted spices and ingredients, some from the colonial era. Restaurant cuisine in particular represents a fusion of techniques and ingredients from all over the world, and commentators routinely wonder if French cuisine is out of date. Immigrants from current and former French territories who live and work in France are not always included in the French food landscape. These populations have met with indifference and outright hostility regarding their food practices, such as halal meat. The former colonies in the Caribbean, now French departments, provide agricultural exports to mainland France but struggle with the idea that they are not considered French.

Smaller towns, especially in far northern and southwestern France, have seen steep declines in the number of restaurants and small shops in their city centers, once the place for sharing culinary traditions and creating

Introduction xiii

community. With the growth of large supermarkets and discount chains on the outskirts of town and a persistently difficult economic climate, a number of family-run food stores and restaurants have closed. In their place, fast-food franchises and snack shops fill the void but are not always welcome. Kebab shops serving sandwiches and quick meals, often run by immigrant owners, fill a role once held by the local restaurants. The French have an uneasy relationship with immigrants, especially those from North Africa, and food is an especially touchy subject. In a less dramatic way, the invasion of American food and American-style restaurants stokes the fear that French traditions are being erased. The newest trends in French food are in fast food: French tacos (burritos filled with French fries, ground meat, and cheese), bagel sandwiches, and food trucks. A relatively new entry, the fast-food crepe filled with gummy bears and fresh fruit combines elements of old and new, with distinct American influences but French creativity and fresh ingredients. France has faced a number of challenges in its culinary history, and it continues to confront political and economic strife. But its citizens still embrace French gastronomy as a proud tradition that belongs to all of them. The French have enjoyed foie gras, a particularly French specialty, for nearly 400 years. Recent questions about animal cruelty have not deterred them. New worries about obesity and food safety have been met with government programs encouraging the French to eat local, to return to the old ways. Many French people have a fond memory of their grandmother's cooking even if more modern French households cook less and eat prepared foods more. The main courses in classic French home cooking are still immediately recognizable to the French and are connected to family and happy memories. In essence, French food represents a patchwork of tradition, borrowings, and inputs from immigrant cuisine that are resisted and then sometimes adopted, according to the will of the people. New trends will be incorporated alongside the classics, and French food will always be at once old and new.

Chronology

Known for its fine food as early as Roman Gaul, France has maintained its reputation as a country known for culinary excellence. In the official portrait of French cuisine beginning in the seventeenth century, chefs emphasized refinement and technique. Aristocratic tables created food trends by establishing a hierarchy of meats and introducing sugar as a luxury item. In the seventeenth century, cookbook authors set the rules for fine cuisine in print and defined this kind of cooking as French cuisine. The French model was disrupted by the French Revolution, which chased private chefs abroad and dismantled the aristocratic class that supported them. Classic French cuisine was revived in the nineteenth century by the great chefs of high-end, extravagant dishes, a model that was threatened in the twentieth century by outbreaks of food contamination and then unsettled in the twenty-first century by the influence of world cuisine along with the younger generation's embrace of fast food. A chronology of French food shows that French cuisine does not belong exclusively to the elites but to the people of France. It shifts and changes as its people do.

1–100 CE
Roman author Pliny in *Natural History* praises the young, fresh cheeses from Nîmes in the south of France, and Greek author Strabo, in *Geography* (written between 7 BCE and 23 CE), admires "the finest salted-pork" from the Franche-Comté in eastern France.

52
Roman invaders enter Gaul and mix with the native residents, producing the Gallo-Roman society.

371
A poem written by Ausonius, prefect of Gaul and native of Bordeaux, praises the many fish good for eating found in the Moselle River, in the eastern part of the territory.

476
The last Roman emperor is forced out of the Gallic territories, and King Clovis I begins his reign as king of the Franks.

771–814
Charlemagne is king of the Frankish Empire.

843
The three sons of Louis the Pious divide the empire after his death into West Francia, Middle Francia, and East Francia, creating the territories later known as France and Germany.

1163
Construction begins on the Cathedral of Notre Dame in Paris, a reconstruction of a former cathedral on the same site, to be completed in 1345.

1190
Construction begins on the fortress called the Louvre, on the right bank of the Seine, by King Philippe Auguste, who had earlier ordered the streets of Paris paved. The Louvre would become a stately castle and residence for French kings before its transformation into the current museum.

1226
Louis IX takes the throne and in 1297 is canonized, to be known as Saint Louis, the only French monarch to become a saint.

1263
The central fish market opens in Paris on orders from King Louis IX.

1309–1376
Catholic popes, beginning with French pope Clement V, take up residence in Avignon, France, rather than Rome, Italy, due to a dispute between the papacy and Philip IV, king of France. Members of the papal court of Pope Urban V in 1366 protest the idea of returning to Rome because they are enamored with Burgundy wines. Seven French popes reside in Avignon until Gregory XI returns the papacy to Rome in 1376.

1348–1349
The Black Plague reaches Paris.

c. 1380–1393
Le Viandier and *Le Ménagier de Paris*, composed in France, are recognized as the first printed cookbooks in Europe.

1381
Royal statutes for the Grande Boucherie (main butcher shop) in Paris order that only sons of members of the Grande Boucherie can become butchers in Paris.

1416
Charles VI demolishes the Grande Boucherie and revokes all legal privileges for butchers.

Chronology

1431
Joan of Arc is burned at the stake in Reims for heresy.

1532
François Rabelais publishes *Pantagruel*, the first of five novels of the adventures of gluttonous giants Pantagruel and Gargantua, his father, featuring numerous descriptions of food.

1598
Henri IV signs the Edict of Nantes, granting civil rights to Protestants in largely Catholic France.

1606
The Pont Neuf in Paris, on the west end of the Ile de la Cité, is the first bridge in the city constructed without houses or other structures on it.

1635
The Académie Française, an organization created to maintain the purity and standards of the French language, is established by Cardinal Richelieu, chief minister to King Louis XIII.

1651
La Varenne's *Le cuisinier français*, the first cookbook to identify French cuisine by name and the first cookbook to use a butter-flour roux to thicken sauce, is published.

1661–1715
Louis XIV (known as the Sun King), who will bring the court to Versailles in 1682, rules France.

1670
An act of Parliament allows bread makers to use brewer's yeast as a leavener in bread dough, but only if it comes from Paris and is mixed with the traditional natural starter.

1686
Café Procope is opened in Paris by an Italian; frequented by philosophers and writers like Voltaire and Diderot, it is the oldest continuously operating café in Paris.

1691
François Massialot's *Le cuisinier royal et bourgeois* contains the first published recipe to use chocolate, for wigeon (a kind of duck) in chocolate sauce.

1693
L.S.R. (Le sieur Robert) publishes his cookbook *Art de bien traiter*, criticizing the old-fashioned cooking in La Varenne's book.

1751–1772
The *Encyclopédie*, subtitled the *Reasoned Dictionary of Sciences, Arts, and Professions*, is published by Diderot and d'Alembert. As participants in the so-called Age

of Enlightenment (*Age des Lumières*), the authors attempt to apply science and reason to explain everyday phenomena.

1768
The first "restaurant" (bouillon shop) owner, Mathurin Roze de Chantoiseau, publishes a guide for travelers indicating where to find good food shops in Paris.

1774–1775
The so-called Flour War, a series of riots by the French people demanding fair prices for grain and flour to make bread affordable, stretches over several months. More than 300 riots take place in April 1775 alone.

1789
The storming of the Bastille prison marks the start of the French Revolution.

1791
The Allard Law definitively abolishes all professional guilds and ends the exclusive right of master butchers to slaughter animals and sell animal parts in Paris.

1792
A proclamation by the new National Assembly creates the French Republic.

1793
King Louis XVI and Queen Marie-Antoinette are executed by guillotine, which is thought to mark the end of the French monarchy.
The revolutionary government imposes the *maximum général* across the country; it refers to the maximum price for essential foods, including meat, butter, and fish.

1794
Robespierre, leader of the revolutionary Jacobins, is executed by guillotine.

1794
The Haitian Revolution is the first successful overthrow of a colonized country by an enslaved people. France's sugar plantations on Saint-Domingue (the former name for Haiti) allowed France to dominate the sugar trade in the eighteenth century. Haiti finally will gain its independence in 1804.

1795
France adopts the metric system.

1803
France sells territory in Louisiana (the Louisiana Purchase) to the United States, releasing its last North American colonial lands.

1804
Napoleon I declares himself emperor of France by coup d'état and remains in power during the first empire, 1804–1814.
Père Lachaise cemetery in Paris opens.
The Rocher de Cancale, known for its namesake oysters, opens and is one of the earliest fine dining restaurants in Paris.

Chronology

1806
The first stone is laid for the Arc de Triomphe at the Place de l'Etoile, intended to symbolize Napoleon's military power and honor his victories. The monument will finally be dedicated in 1836.

1808
Charles Louis Cadet de Gassicourt publishes the first gastronomic map of France, including regional specialties outside of Paris.

1810
Nicolas Appert publishes his technique for preserving food in glass jars, the first method for canning food for long-term preservation and transport. The French military carry "appertized" rations on their ships, and French companies deliver canned food to the colonies.

1815
The Battle of Waterloo brings Napoleon's greatest defeat and his exile to St. Helena. Louis XVIII becomes king of France, restoring the Bourbon monarchy.

1818
Five central slaughterhouses open in Paris, replacing the individual slaughterhouses run by butchers.

1833
Marie-Antoine Carême revolutionizes French elite cuisine with his cookbook *L'art de la cuisine française* (The art of French cooking).

1848
With the fall of the July Monarchy, slavery is finally abolished in French colonies.
Napoleon I's nephew Louis-Napoleon Bonaparte becomes the first elected president of France.

1853
Famed mustard company Grey Poupon (now owned by Kraft) opens for business in Dijon.

1853–1870
Les Halles, a covered market for fresh produce, meat, and other supplies, is constructed in Paris.

1854
One of the few French companies associated with tea, Mariage Frères (Mariage Brothers) wholesale tea company opens in Paris.

1855
Bordeaux winemakers establish the classification of *premier cru* (first-growth) wineries and rank Château Lafite, Margaux, Latour, and Haut-Brion as the best in the region.

1856
Gustave Flaubert publishes *Madame Bovary*, a novel about an unhappily married woman living in the countryside whose appetites lead her to scandalous and dangerous behavior.

1859
To enlarge Paris, Napoleon annexes nearby suburbs and endorses a decree creating 20 arrondissements in the capital.

1862
Victor Hugo writes *Les Misérables*. His novel *Notre Dame de Paris* (*The Hunchback of Notre Dame*) was published in 1831.
French vines are infected with the phylloxera aphid that destroys the roots of grapevines. The insect will devastate the fine-wine industry through the 1870s and 1880s.

1869
French chemist Hippolyte Mège-Mouriès invents margarine as a substitute for butter, which was in short supply.

1870–1871
The Franco-Prussian War results in the Prussian siege of Paris that causes widespread food shortages, illness, and destruction. Louis-Napoleon is captured, and the Commune (elected council of revolutionaries) rules Paris for a brief period before being crushed by the French army. The Tuileries Palace burns to the ground.

1873
Emile Zola publishes *Le Ventre de Paris* (*The Belly of Paris*), a novel set in the vast, open Les Halles market selling fruit, vegetables, meat, and everything else that feeds Paris.

1887
A court of appeals in Angers, France, rules that "champagne" is not a generic term but applies only to the wines from the Champagne region that become bubbly after a secondary fermentation. Legally, from this date, champagne can only be produced in Champagne.

1889
The Eiffel Tower is completed for the Exposition Universelle in Paris and opened to the public. Work on the tower began in 1887.

1895
Louis Lumière and his brother, Auguste, the inventors of the motion picture, present the first projection of a film to a public audience.

1900
The Michelin Guide is published for the first time, for the World's Fair of that year. The guide features names and addresses of gas stations and garages for

Chronology

automobile travelers, but in the 1920s it will begin to include restaurant recommendations.

1903
The first Tour de France bicycle race is held.
Auguste Escoffier, monumental chef, publishes *Le guide culinaire*, introducing tomato sauce as the fourth foundational sauce in French cuisine. Escoffier is also credited with inventing peach Melba and crêpes Suzette.

1904
Perrier water introduces its iconic green glass bottle with its signature shape.

1913
Marcel Proust publishes the first volume of his multivolume novel *A la recherche du temps perdu* (In Search of Lost Time). A foodie before his time, Proust makes numerous references to food in his novel, including the madeleine cookie and *boeuf en gelée* (beef with aspic).

1914–1918
In World War I, Germany declares war on France. In 1918 France regains the annexed regions of Alsace and Lorraine.

1915
France bans absinthe, the green liquor made from wormwood that was thought to cause hallucinogenic effects. It returns to circulation in the twentieth century in a new formula without wormwood.

1917
Due to wartime shortages, the government of Paris bans the sale of soft white bread, brioche, and croissants.

1919
The Basilica of Sacré-Coeur in Montmartre is consecrated. It is now the second most popular landmark in Paris, after the Eiffel Tower.

1924
The first Meilleur Ouvrier de France (best worker in France) award includes various categories, among them cooking and pastry making.

1925
Roquefort cheese earns the first AOC (Appellation d'Origine Contrôlée) label for cheese, mandating that Roquefort cheese may only be aged in the caves in the town of Roquefort.

1931
The Paris Colonial Exposition runs for six months; it is intended to showcase products and traditions from France's overseas colonies and encourage French citizens to use these products and adopt new foods (such as rice from Indochina and tropical fruits from African colonies).
The Michelin Guide begins to publish restaurant reviews using the star system.

1933
Famed chef Eugénie Brazier, of Lyon, becomes the first woman to win three Michelin stars at two different restaurants.

1935
The French government creates the Appellation and Dénomination d'Origine Contrôlée (AOC and DOC) designations for wine, legislating geographic areas and rules for production and guaranteeing authenticity and quality of wines with this label. The labels later will apply to many cheeses and other foods.

1936
Orangina, the soda made with orange juice, is created in Marseille by Algerian-born Léon Beton from a recipe developed by a Spanish pharmacist.

1939–1944
In World War II, France declares war on Germany. After the Maginot line fails to keep Germany from crossing France's borders, Germany rules the northern half of France and the Vichy government rules the southern half. The Allies liberate Paris on August 25, 1944.

1939
Rationing of bread, pasta, and sugar begins during the war. The list of rationed items expands in 1940 and 1941 to include butter, cheese, coffee, milk, and wine.

1944
French women gain the right to vote.

1949
Simone de Beauvoir, eminent philosopher and writer, publishes *Le Deuxième Sexe* (*The Second Sex*), a sociological and historical work about the place of women in society.

1954
The French conclude the Indochina War and leave Vietnam, beginning the wave of decolonization that results in the independence of most of France's former colonies after 1960. Some former colonies vote to remain overseas territories or departments of France, including Guadeloupe and Martinique.

1962
The long and bloody conflict between France and Algeria comes to an end, after eight years of war and terrorist attacks inside France. French citizens living in Algeria (called *pieds noirs*) are expelled from Algeria and return to France.

1979
McDonald's opens its first restaurant in France, but the fast-food chain does not gain nationwide popularity until the 1980s.

1981
The first TGV (*train à grande vitesse*, "very fast train") high-speed train travels from Paris to Lyon. TGVs now reach most of France and other nearby countries and travel at up to 200 miles per hour as commercial trains.

Chronology

1983
The Jules Verne restaurant on the second level of the Eiffel Tower opens to the public.

1986
The Musée d'Orsay, dedicated to nineteenth-century French art and an impressive collection of Impressionist paintings, opens in Paris.

1988
The pyramid in the courtyard of the Louvre museum, designed by architect I. M. Pei, is inaugurated.

1989
Domino's Pizza opens its first restaurant in France.

1996
An outbreak of *la vache folle* (mad cow disease) causes fears about the safety of French beef. The United States bans imports of French beef.

2002
The euro replaces the French franc as legal currency.

2003
La Tour d'Argent restaurant serves its one millionth pressed duck, its signature dish.

2010
UNESCO honors the "gastronomic meal of the French" as part of its Intangible Cultural Heritage of Humanity list.

2011
The French government creates the Fête de la gastronomie (day of gastronomy) on the last weekend in September, a national holiday to honor French cuisine.
Paris's first food truck, Le Camion qui fume ("the smoking truck") opens for business.

2015
Terrorist attacks on the magazine *Charlie Hebdo* and other venues in Paris result in nearly 150 deaths.

2017
The United States at last reinstates imports of French beef after mad cow outbreaks in 1996 and 2000.
France creates the Nutri-Score nutritional rating system for packaged foods, a label that rates a food's nutritional value on a scale from A to E, in order to help consumers choose healthier foods.

2018
Riots break out in some parts of France when the Intermarché supermarket chain offers a 70-percent-off sale on Nutella, a very popular chocolate-hazelnut spread for toast and crepes.

For the first time, the hamburger surpasses the *jambon-beurre* ("ham and butter") sandwich in overall sales in France.

2019

The French government's nutritional office for the first time recommends eating more nuts and whole grains and choosing environmentally friendly foods, such as local and organic produce.

Mirazur restaurant in Menton, France, near Nice, is named the top restaurant by The World's 50 Best Restaurants, a contest sponsored by S. Pellegrino and Acqua Panna water.

2020

Chef Mauro Colagreco at Mirazur, an Argentinian immigrant, is named best chef in the world by the World Summit of Chefs in Monaco; it is the first time a non-French chef has won the title.

CHAPTER ONE

Food History

French food began before France did, in the ancient Roman Empire. The territory now known as France was divided into three territories: Gaul in the northwest of what is now France, the Frankish Empire farther northeast, and the Visigoth territory to the southwest. In 52 CE the Romans invaded Gaul but did not conquer the native peoples, as they had in other parts of the Roman Empire. Rather, they established the Pax Romana ("Roman peace") and created a shared society of Gallo-Roman residents. By the fifth century the invading Huns pushed the Franks farther into Gaul and eventually disrupted the Roman hold on the territory. In 476 Clovis, king of the Franks, replaced the last Roman emperor with the Merovingian dynasty and united the kingdoms into one territory known as Francia. Gaul and its surrounding territories already had a reputation for good food, including the young, fresh cheeses from Nîmes in the south of France that were cited by Pliny in *Natural History* (first century CE) and "the finest salted-pork" from the Franche-Comté in eastern France that was cited in Greek author Strabo's *Geography* (composed between 7 BCE and 23 CE). The Gauls and Franks, especially the wealthy, were principally meat eaters; their supply came from rich hunting lands as well as domestic livestock, including cattle, pigs, sheep, and goats. The remainder of the Frankish diet consisted of bread and vegetables. In the Merovingian era the Franks began to cultivate wheat across the territory, but only the wealthy used wheat to make bread since they could pay for access to the mills and common ovens required for baking. Poorer classes turned grains into porridges and depended on lesser grains like rye, barley, and millet. Like their modern cousins, the Franks, unlike the invading Romans, appreciated butter.

Anthimus and Food

Much of our knowledge of Gallic and Frankish food comes from a Greek doctor named Anthimus, who lived in the Frankish Empire in the sixth century CE and wrote a catalog of the foods he experienced called *On the Observance of Foods*. He was particularly interested in the Franks' tradition of eating raw pork fat, believed to be the key to their robust health. Anthimus endorsed eating eggs (including a sort of meringue made of whipped eggs) if they were properly cooked. He differed from his contemporaries, who thought eggs were indigestible. His recipe for beef stew called for boiling and then roasting, and he suggested eating butter as a remedy for illness.

Lenticula (Lentils with Vinegar and Coriander)

In truth, lentils are good washed and thoroughly boiled in clean water. The first hot water is poured off, and then more hot water is added to good measure, not too much, and thus they are cooked slowly in the coals. When they are cooked, a moderate amount of vinegar is added for taste. The spice called Syrian sumac is added to them: a spoonful of this powder is sprinkled on the lentils while on the fire and mixed well. Then they are pulled off the fire and eaten. For taste, however, it is proper to add a good spoonful of olive oil while cooking, in the second round of hot water, and one or two spoons of coriander with the roots, not in small pieces but whole, and a modest amount of salt for flavor.

From Anthimus, *De observatione ciborum* [On the observance of foods] (c. 511 CE), edited by Valentinus Rose (Leipzig: Teubner, 1877), 18–19.

The Middle Ages and Renaissance

The medieval period in France inaugurated the country's dedication to fine bread. The French public demanded good bread at a fair price, and the government created and enforced statutes to ensure the supply. Bakers, in turn, joined professional associations and demanded protections for their industry. Between the fifth and the sixteenth centuries, debates about bread quality and price formed the national appreciation for bread that continues in the present day. In fourteenth-century Paris bakers were required to supply bread seven days per week at a standard weight determined by test bakes conducted by government officials to determine how much bread each batch of wheat would produce. By law, different kinds of shops produced different baked goods: *pâtissiers* ("pastry cooks") did not make cakes or pastries, as they do now, but meats wrapped in pastry; cake bakers were called *gâtelliers* (from the word *gâteau*, for "cake"); *oubloyers* made *oublies*, or unleavened wafers cooked between two hot iron plates. Before the fourteenth century, bakers were called *fourniers*, for *four* ("oven") because they baked bread prepared by others in their shop ovens; *pancossiers* bought grain and turned it into bread that they sold in their shops; Parisian bread bakers were called *talemeliers*. Bakers were also required to supply different kinds of bread for different budgets: bread from fine white flour, bread from mixed flour (usually rye or millet), and dark bread made from coarse flour. One estimate determined that each adult in France in the Middle Ages ate 600 grams of wheat per day, approximately one standard loaf of bread.

Meat production had similar regulations in the Middle Ages. King Charles VI ended the monopoly held by master butchers in Paris in 1416 by demolishing the Grande Boucherie (Central Butcher) and creating four royal butcheries, which were rented by butchers. For most of the French citizens in this period, meat was a luxury item eaten only on feast days or Sundays. Pork remained a meat of lower distinction, and those who could afford meat ate mainly mutton or lamb and some beef. The first printed cookbooks appeared in the Middle Ages, and since they were intended for wealthier classes, they contained a number of recipes for meat and fish dishes. The *Viandier* (from the word *viande*, for "meat"), written around 1380, is generally attributed to a chef named Taillevent but was likely a compilation of a number of different texts. The *Ménagier de Paris* (roughly, the Parisian household manual) appeared around 1393 and included a number of recipes plagiarized from the *Viandier*. The *Ménagier* was addressed to housewives and gave instructions on cooking, shopping, and managing a middle-class household.

Wealthier households in the Middle Ages and the Renaissance prized meat and viewed vegetables as food of the poor. Fresh vegetables and fruit were considered unhealthy as they upset the balance of bodily humors believed to exist in the body. Medical treatises in Renaissance France suggested that the poor, rural populations had hardier digestive systems than wealthy city-dwellers. It was believed that the poor could thrive on coarse grains and thick vegetable stews that would be indigestible for the wealthy classes. But at the court of King Henry II and Catherine de Médici (1547–1559), fresh vegetables graced banquet tables, and out-of-season vegetables such as asparagus and artichokes were especially in demand. When medical guidelines opposing fresh vegetables fell out of favor, elites gradually incorporated vegetables and fruit into their daily diets. Wine was too expensive for most budgets; in its place, cider; beer; or water boiled with honey, herbs, and vinegar were the beverages of choice.

The Classical Age

In the seventeenth century, France enjoyed an explosion of cookbooks, beginning with François Pierre La Varenne's *Le cuisinier françois* in 1651, the first cookbook to label a style of eating "French."

Of course, these printed books represented only the higher classes since only wealthy households could employ a cook and the literacy rate among the public was very low. The ingredients in cookbook recipes, particularly meat and spices, would have been out of reach for middle- and lower-class household budgets. By the eighteenth century, cookbooks for the middle class became popular, with less opulent ingredients and less complicated recipes that were accessible to a wider public.

Simplified recipes and cooking techniques led to the first wave of nouvelle cuisine in the eighteenth century, leaving behind the stews and thick sauces of the previous generation. Sauces that had been thickened with breadcrumbs or egg yolks used a *roux* of flour and butter, and the spicy vinegar flavors of the medieval and seventeenth-century periods gave way to a preference for shallots, fresh herbs, and lighter flavors. Fresh fruit and vegetables had earlier been seen as food for the poor, but in the early modern era, there was a vogue for fresh produce among the upper classes, including a passion for fresh peas at Versailles under Louis XIV.

Longe de Porc à la Sauce Robert
(Pork Loin with Sauce Robert)

Lard the meat with pork fat, then roast it, and baste it with verjuice and vinegar and a bouquet of sage. When the fat has rendered, use it to fry an onion, which once fried you will put under the loin with the sauce from basting. When the dish has simmered together a bit, being careful not to let it harden, serve. This sauce is called sauce Robert.

From Pierre François La Varenne, *Le cuisinier françois* (Paris, 1651), 51.

> ## Epaule de Veau à la Bourgeoise
> ### (Veal Shoulder Bourgeois-Style)
>
> Put a veal shoulder in a baking dish with two quarts (a *demi-septier*) of water, two tablespoons of vinegar, salt, pepper, parsley, spring onions, two cloves of garlic, one bay leaf, two onions, two root vegetables cut in slices, three whole cloves, a bit of butter. Cover the dish and seal the edges with flour mixed with a little water. Cook in the oven for three hours, then skim the fat from the sauce before passing it through a sieve. Serve the sauce on the veal shoulder.
>
> From François Massialot, *La Cuisinière bourgeoise* (Paris, 1752), 122.

Food Storage Origins

Nicolas Appert invented a process he called "appertization" to preserve food for long storage, first in glass containers and then in tinned iron cans. His technique, published in 1810, produced the first canned food and revolutionized food storage and food safety. Appert invented the precursor to the bouillon cube in 1814, and his technique of canning food was widely used for military rations. His first preserved products were bottled peas, milk, broth, and beef stew. Louis Pasteur improved on Appert's discovery by determining exact temperatures for killing harmful microorganisms in food, a process he patented in 1865 and called "pasteurization."

The Revolutionary Era

For most people, the story of food and the French Revolution begins with Marie Antoinette's "Let them eat cake!" reportedly her response to hungry Parisians claiming that there was no bread. It is easily the most famous anecdote about the doomed French monarchy and gives us an idea of the social factors that drove the Jacobins to seize the Bastille and guillotine the royal family. Unfortunately, it never happened. Bread was at the heart of the conflict between the government and the people in the late eighteenth century, but bread was only part of the story. In 1790 Chantrelle de Beaumont presented a treaty for consideration by the National Assembly (the lower house of the French parliament) to guarantee supplies of the four objects of "first necessity" for existence: bread, meat, firewood, and wine. The demand by the citizens of the French nation for legal intervention from the government to provide these foods (plus firewood) may seem unlikely for a people who had just taken to the streets to demand Liberté, égalité, fraternité, but when it came to food, the French upheld a long tradition of government protectionism.

Firewood was essential in several ways: for heating homes, cooking food in the hearth, and baking bread. Bread represented half the calories of the Parisian diet in 1789 and was the center of the diets of most French citizens, particularly members of the lower classes, who could rarely afford any significant quantity of meat. Rural families subsisted on vegetables they grew themselves and meat from the family pig, which was slaughtered and either smoked or salted to last the year. But everyone ate bread. Bread at a just price and reasonable weight and quality had long been promised to the French public as an object of necessity, subject to price protections and regulation by the police. Since the Middle Ages, the government had participated in market regulation of bread and meat, and the French consumers had come to expect such intervention. In the medieval marketplace and until the eighteenth century, the government and its officers policed the baking trade to set prices for different kinds of bread and their corresponding weights, so that all buyers had access to an affordable loaf. Starting in the seventeenth century, in times of scarcity or high grain prices, officials sometimes relaxed these rules.

In periods of crisis, the government allowed bakers to bring to market only dark, heavy bread made from mixed flours (*pain bis*), and it banned soft white bread, a rule that bakers freely ignored. The bakers claimed that few customers wanted *pain bis* and that they ended up with unsellable bread; consumers complained that the *pain bis* sold at market was of such poor quality that it was only fit for dogs. In good economic times, the rules were lightly enforced, but in times of stress, radical officials resorted to various forms of punishment against bakers who failed to heed the rules, including corporal punishment and even threats of hanging. A change to the way grain was distributed led to frequent grain riots throughout the eighteenth century.

Until the end of Louis XIV's reign (1661–1715), grain reached the market with heavy government intervention. In 1723 a royal declaration by Louis XVI ordered that all grain be sold in the public market, giving access first to individual buyers followed by professional bakers and then merchants. Prior to the reforms, when producers hoarded grain to wait for a better price, government officials ordered the stores to be taken to market, or occasionally (and secretly) they bought grain to sell to the public below market prices. When the government ceased these interventions in the mid-eighteenth century and the country was hit with severe grain shortages due to poor harvests, two types of bread riots resulted: riots in the markets by urban dwellers who stole bread in response to high prices and grain riots in rural areas in which the people seized stores of grain and sold them at a fair price, usually the going price in the market (Tilly 1971, 24). But grain was not the only issue; without flour, there was no bread, and the millers controlled the flour trade. After a number of grain crises in the early 1740s and the late 1760s, and flour shortages in the late 1760s and early 1770s, the price of bread grew steadily. But a 1763 law had removed all restrictions on grain sellers to keep them in the market, and the government could only attempt to control bread prices, not flour. After widespread market riots, officials revoked some of the free-market rules and returned some power to the bread makers' guilds.

Liberal reforms proposed in 1774 by Anne-Robert Jacques Turgot, controller general of finances under Louis XVI, attempted to take away all interventionist protections, with explosive results that came to be known as the Flour War. The philosophy of the physiocrats (called *économistes* in French), one to which Turgot subscribed, opposed guilds and market taxes. Physiocrats believed that a free market would lead at first to higher prices for consumers but that ultimately prices would stabilize and producers could reinvest profits into the land to promote better harvests. Turgot reinstated the older free-trade regulation for grain, eliminating restrictions and taxes on buying and selling grain. The government backed Turgot's desire to liberalize the market and allow it to be regulated by supply and demand. Grain prices rose and with them bread prices; grain shortages broke out, caused by speculators who hoarded grain to await a higher price. As a result, beginning in April 1775 angry customers (many of them women) carried out 300 riots in 22 days, sometimes using a tactic called *taxation populaire* (setting a fair price for grain, selling it, and returning the proceeds to the grain merchant) and sometimes looting grain, flour, or bread outright. Contrary to rumor, rioters did not confront Louis XVI at the palace at Versailles to demand lower prices for bread, but an angry crowd raided the flour market in the nearby town, and the military governor ordered bread prices lowered. By May 3 news of the successful raid on Versailles and another bread price hike led rioters to storm nearly 1,300 bakeries and the central bread market (Bouton 1993, 83–88). Bakers were ordered to observe a price ceiling for bread, and when bread prices nevertheless rose higher than they ever had before, rioters took to the streets and looted bread shops and markets. When authorities refused to intervene, the French people demanded their right to bread with continued violent uprisings. In the end, Turgot failed in his effort to liberalize the French grain market and was ousted in 1776. Grain skirmishes ended for a time, but the back-and-forth between liberal and interventionist policies continued.

The bloody Revolution of 1789 disrupted efforts to stabilize the market. Shortages recurred in Paris, and the government resorted to bread rationing for a time. Louis XVI met his end at the guillotine in January 1793, and Marie Antoinette followed in October. Without a king, the French nation lacked a central authority, and in the chaos of the new state, leadership was unclear. In 1793 the Jacobins imposed a maximum grain price across the country and a maximum price for a number of essential foods, but the policy lasted only for a year, until the Jacobins began to lose ground and their leader, Maximilien Robespierre, was guillotined in July 1794. The revolutionary movement, so prominent in Paris, slowly gave way elsewhere to the right-wing sentiment that would support Napoleon's coup d'état in 1804, and grain had much to do with politics. To provide the Paris grain market with the massive quantities it demanded, provinces were pushed to the limit. Normandy and Beauce (a region just west of Paris) had long been major suppliers of grain to Paris, and farmers who sent all of their stocks of grain to the capital were left without grain for their own bread. Regional officials in these areas refused to ship grain to Paris, and during the Flour War, the city was left practically empty of wheat, stoking the anger of the hungry, bread-loving citizens.

Changing food statutes affected butchers in Paris in the years before the Revolution but less dramatically than in the case of bread. To guarantee that all classes had access to some type of meat, a principle of the French nation even before the 1790 decree, legal statutes fixed prices for certain meats (usually organ meats or less desirable cuts) to within the reach of the lower classes. The wealthy paid a premium for steaks and roasts, allowing butchers to charge a minimum price for lower-quality meat and to avoid waste. Since the fifteenth century, a small number of families had held exclusive rights to the butcher trade in Paris, under authorization from King Charles VI. Butchers held property rights to their stalls and passed them down from father to son, excluding anyone who did not already belong to the guild and creating new members only by marriage. A letter from Louis XIII in 1637 renewed this privilege and granted stall ownership to the dynastic families in perpetuity.

The development of a major rail system was still more than a century away, which meant that animals were transported by wagon and only for short distances. To maintain standards of freshness and safety, authorities in Paris required that all animals for slaughter be purchased live from livestock markets within seven leagues (about 28 kilometers) from the center of Paris, and two livestock markets furnished the great demand for meat in Paris: one at Poissy, established in 1577, and one at Sceaux, created in 1667. Regulations extended to the days the market could be open: Thursday for Poissy and Monday for Sceaux. In 1735 increasing demand for meat expanded the limit to 20 leagues (80 kilometers), and new livestock markets joined the system. Each animal sold at these markets carried a tariff payable to the crown, a built-in revenue generator for the court and an incentive to keep the regulation in place but one that also raised meat prices for consumers. In principle, the requirement that all butchers buy livestock at the same place on the same day kept prices down since sellers had willing customers and pricing was transparent. The ever-increasing population of Paris and its geographic situation, with homes and buildings rapidly replacing grazing land, made intervention a necessity, but it was also part of a long-standing tradition.

In Paris, the butchers' work stalls created hazards for the urban population living side by side with live animals that sometimes escaped and ran through the streets of the city. The slaughter of animals produced waste products and potential water contamination, to say nothing of the smells and noise. As Paris grew, authorities in the eighteenth century attempted to take back some of the butchers' privileges, beginning with the location of their stalls. New spaces were created away from the center of the city, and officials attempted to isolate the slaughter of animals outside the city. Under this plan, butchers' stalls would be used only for cutting meat, not killing and skinning animals. The butchers' guild refused to accept the proposal to separate the two parts of their business, and their efforts were successful for a time. Ultimately the Allard Law in 1791 definitively abolished all guilds and ended the exclusive right of master butchers to slaughter animals and sell animal parts in Paris, dividing the trade into several professions. Without the restriction of guild membership, new butchers joined the profession in droves; the trade grew exponentially and included unlicensed meat sellers and butchers from outside the city limits. In an effort to open up free trade and lower prices, these policies also introduced unreliable producers and questionable sanitary practices since the butchers' guild no longer had the power to regulate the profession.

Under the revolutionary regime, Paris had difficulty supplying enough meat to its people. The government issued ration cards and instituted the *maximum général* (maximum price for food) in 1793 to cover fresh and cured meats, lard and butter, and ocean fish so that sellers could not charge more than an agreed-upon, "just" price. In March 1794 the government established the Boucherie générale (a municipal meat-processing market) to take over all animal slaughter at a centralized location and distribute meat to butchers, who were then authorized to sell it at a set price. After the Jacobin regime fell in July 1794 and the maximum price rule was abandoned in December, meat prices quadrupled in four months. The Boucherie générale closed in 1796, but in 1818 five central slaughterhouses opened in Paris, once and for all separating the butcher trade from the slaughter of live animals.

Birth of the Restaurant and Gastronomy

Those who could not afford cuts of butcher's meat could still purchase a cup of meat broth to substitute for a meal. The French word *restaurant* (literally, "restoring") meant a refreshing or restorative substance, and the term was later applied to highly condensed bouillons made from meat and served to the poor or the sick. Vendors of hot bouillon had a special place in the Parisian dining universe because hot broth was thought to help certain medical conditions and because there were few public places to dine in Paris in the late eighteenth century. Travelers could take a meal at a tavern or a boardinghouse, and certain shops (called *traiteurs*) offered cooked food to be taken home, but the restaurant as a business that offered private dining at an individual table did not yet exist. An entrepreneur named Mathurin Roze de Chantoiseau in 1768 set up a bouillon shop to sell hot broth to customers. He then wrote and published a guide for travelers that promoted his shop, calling himself the "first Restaurateur" (Spang 2001, 21–25). Chantoiseau's shop offered a social setting in which to sip a cup of bouillon just as one might savor a coffee in a café. With the addition of individual tables and small, cooked dishes to the menu, the restaurant as we now know it was born. By the 1790s, the term "restaurant" came to be used for any shop in Paris offering meals, although the restaurant (bouillon) sellers, *traiteurs* or cook-caterers, and taverns or inns served different kinds of meals and different kinds of patrons. Restaurants as businesses remained an exclusively Parisian phenomenon for some time; they were rarely encountered anywhere but Paris until the middle of the nineteenth century.

Paris was the capital of fine food, but the regions of France had their own well-known cheeses, wines, and other products that began to earn national recognition in the early nineteenth century. Charles Louis Cadet de Gassicourt created the first gastronomic map of France in 1808, identifying cities and regions with images of their culinary specialties: foie gras in Périgord, Camembert in Normandy, and sparkling wine in Champagne, among others. France had long maintained a reputation as a territory naturally gifted with excellent food and wine, and the wave of nationalism that arrived with Napoleon set the stage for patriotic pride and international promotion of French culinary superiority. After Napoleon's defeat at Waterloo in 1815, occupying armies from Prussia, Russia, Germany, and England (among others) dined in the Parisian restaurants and spread word of this new business (and the good food found there) in their home countries, forging a reputation that remains today. Restaurants made foods previously only known to the wealthy available to anyone with enough money for a single meal. Access bred appreciation, and a wave of gastronomic writers began to praise fine dining in Paris. Most famous among them was Alexandre Grimod de la Reynière, author of *Almanach des gourmands* (1803–1812), a journal dedicated to sharing the best addresses for restaurants, food shops, and other culinary delights. Grimod de la Reynière's *Almanach* contained the first-ever restaurant review.

Since Paris was the center of the food universe in France, it required a well-managed distribution center to bring food from all parts of France to feed the hungry capital. In 1811 Napoleon I originally envisioned a vast covered market of eight massive pavilions, called *les Halles*, in the center of Paris. Construction finally began in 1848 under King Louis-Philippe, in power during the brief constitutional monarchy, but the market did not reach its final form until 1870. With the leadership of Emperor Napoleon III and the design of Baron Haussmann, the architect of Paris, 10 of what eventually became 12 pavilions were constructed between 1853 and 1870. Haussmann redesigned the city of Paris, demolishing entire city blocks to create the vast boulevards, like the Champs-Élysées, that define modern Paris. His plans for the central market answered the need for food

---

Sauce à la Robert (Robert Sauce)

After having cut three large onions in small dice, brown them lightly in clarified butter, then drain them and simmer them with consommé and two large spoonsful of simmered Espagnole sauce.* When the sauce is perfectly reduced, mix in a little powdered sugar, a little pepper, a little vinegar, and a teaspoon of fine mustard.

*A brown sauce made from a roux of butter and flour; a mirepoix of carrot, celery, and onion; wine; and reduced meat essence.

From Marie-Antonin Carême, *L'art de la cuisine française au XIXe siècle* (Paris, 1833), 212.

provisioning for the exploding population of the city of Paris, even if his tactics were not always well received. He created new housing for waves of new residents of Paris but tore down beloved neighborhoods as well. Les Halles included pavilions for vegetables and fruit, fish and seafood, meat, poultry, butter and cheese, and even fresh flowers.

Even as Paris became a world capital for food, one of the greatest threats to French gastronomy came in the form of an insect. The Phylloxera aphid, an invasive pest, feasted on grapevine roots and caused widespread destruction in French winemaking regions in the late nineteenth century. The insect arrived on infected vines from the United States in 1862, and the infestation turned into an epidemic in first-growth (the most expensive and most highly acclaimed) vineyards in the 1870s. American vines had long been imported into France with no such problems. Scientists guessed that in the past the insects had not survived the weeks-long journey by boat from the United States to France but that new faster transport times by ship meant that the insects were still alive and ready to proliferate in the vulnerable French soils. Winemakers lost acre after acre of vines, and after attempts to burn infected vines and treat the soil with sulfur failed, the only solution found was to graft phylloxera-resistant American vines onto French vines. The proud French winemakers resisted what they saw as an American corruption of their wine, but in the end, they had no choice but to accept it. Slowly the French wine trade recovered, but many expert winemakers had been driven out of the profession, and their expertise was lost. New techniques introduced by botanists, such as arranging vines in rows rather than in round groupings and using machines for harvest, forever changed the practice of making

---

Brochet à la Sausse Allemande (Pike in German Sauce)

Take a pike that you have dressed properly. Cut it in two and cook it in water but not completely. Having removed it, scale it so that it is very white and place it in a casserole dish with white wine, chopped capers, anchovies, thyme, fresh herbs and chopped mushrooms, and also truffles and morels. Bring it to the boil and cook gently so that it does not break. Put in a piece of good butter so that it is well thickened, and a little parmesan. When ready to serve, dress your platter and garnish with whatever you like.

From François Massialot, Le Cuisinier royal et bourgeois (Paris, 1691), 161.

wine in France. Producers who had survived the phylloxera epidemic focused on fine wines, and ordinary table wines became less and less financially viable.

Wars and the Modern Era

In the twentieth century, food in France was profoundly changed by the two world wars. The French had suffered deprivation and shortages regularly before, as during the siege of Paris by the Prussians in 1870 and episodes of famine caused by poor harvests. In addition to the disruption of supplies caused by France's entry into World War I (1914–1918), French wheat production declined dramatically during the war. In 1916 France produced only a third as much wheat as it had before the war, in 1913 (Hautcoeur 2005, 171). With much of the available food dedicated to provisioning soldiers on the front lines, the French people experienced rationing and shortages but only in the later years of the war. Soldiers' rations included canned meat and soup (using the technique developed by Nicolas Appert a century before), hard bread, instant coffee, chocolate, sugar, and wine. When cooked food was available for soldiers, it often consisted of soup made from rice or beans. In fact, the generic term for soldiers' meals was not "lunch" or "dinner" but *soupe* because soups and stews were served so frequently.

For the typical French diner, certain staple foods became rare and expensive or unavailable altogether. Potatoes, coffee, chocolate, and cooking oil were difficult to find, but the rarest commodities and those subject to rationing were bread, meat, and sugar. Butcher shops and pastry shops were ordered closed two days per week, and in 1917 the government banned soft white bread, brioche (soft rolls made with egg and milk), and croissants from being sold at bakeries, just as it had during the Flour Wars of the eighteenth century. The bread that could be purchased was of poor quality, grayish and dry, and in 1917 restaurants were required to limit patrons to no more than 200 grams of bread per meal (Castelot 1972, 336). Because of the drop in French wheat production and the French colonial presence in Indochina (a territory covering what is now Vietnam, Laos, and Cambodia) where rice was plentiful, some colonial lobbyists suggested that the French might use rice flour to make bread. But French resistance to non-French ingredients (even if the Indochinese territory was considered French land) and the slow recovery of French wheat harvests as the war ended prevented rice flour from conquering France. In fact, the attempt to introduce rice flour resulted in a patriotic embrace of bread made from wheat. Restrictions on wheat flour led to some innovations, however, including a fad for baked meringues made of whipped egg whites and sugar.

Between the two wars, development of urban areas and the expansion of the railroad led to an exodus of rural inhabitants to the cities, leaving fewer and fewer farmers to work the soil. As a result, larger farms usurped smaller properties, and these landowners began to industrialize agriculture, creating a separation between local crops and local consumers. Monoculture of single crops on large pieces of land led to shortages when major crops (wheat, for example) suffered bad years. In the French colonies, colonial managers had practiced monoculture of cash crops since the nineteenth century, to produce products for export to mainland France. In West Africa, colonial agriculture was dedicated largely to peanuts, for example. Until World War II, peanut exports constituted nearly half of the total value of exports from the entire territory of French West Africa (Coquery-Vidrovitch and Goerg 1992, 122). Nearly all of these crops were transported to France for processing, leaving little economic development in the colonial territories. After bananas became a popular food in France, manufacturers created chocolate-banana breakfast drinks like Bananavic, Superbanane, and Banania (still sold in France) using images of black men and women in their advertising beginning in 1915.

In World War II (1939–1944), the concern that France was losing its rural character and its ability to provide for itself agriculturally prompted Maréchal Philippe Pétain, head of the collaborationist Vichy government, to advocate for a "return to the land" by young French people who wished to become farmers. A new law offered subsidies to former rural residents who wanted to return to the countryside and start a farm, and it facilitated the division of large parcels of land into smaller, manageable farms. Fewer than a thousand people took advantage of the program in the 1940s, but it remained in place until the 1960s and eventually changed the shape of the fertile farmlands of northeastern France. Under German occupation, restrictions and rationing returned and shortages abounded alongside a robust black market for food. Even products that remained on the shelves had a "war form," such as Camembert that contained a maximum of 30 percent milkfat under the occupation compared to 45 percent before the war (Boisard 2003, 165). The list of rationed items grew longer over the course of the war: bread, pasta, and sugar were first in 1939, followed by butter, cheese, meat, coffee, and eggs in 1940. By 1941 chocolate, fish, potatoes, milk, wine, and fresh vegetables were rationed as well. Of course, wealthy people found ways to circumvent the restrictions, and those who lived in the country and produced their own food often fared better than the urban residents of Paris.

After World War II ended, France experienced a period of economic success known as the *trente glorieuses*, or "thirty glorious [years]," between 1944 and 1974, years of massive economic growth fueled by American financial backing and a great influx of tourists from Europe and the United States. Travel by automobile became possible for more and more people, and restaurant guides like the now famous Michelin Guide sprang up to help travelers find their way. The Michelin Guide, first published in 1900 for the World's Fair of that year, originally offered names and addresses of gas stations and garages for travelers in need of car repair as well as advertising for Michelin tires. In the 1920s the guide focused more and more on hotels and restaurants, and in 1931 it began to publish restaurant reviews using the star system that is known worldwide today. The reviewers first examined restaurants outside of Paris, assuming that the travelers using the guides were Parisians looking for gastronomic delights in the country. The guide began to review restaurants in Paris in 1933. The *Larousse gastronomique*, a hefty encyclopedia of French food that continues to serve as an essential reference work, appeared in 1938, first authored by chef Prosper Montagné. Automobile travel allowed regional cuisine in cities like Lyon and Bordeaux to flourish as restaurants there were discovered by outsiders. The great majority of professional chefs were men, but female chefs and restaurant owners were well known in Lyon's bistros (restaurants that feature traditional cooking) known as "bouchons lyonnais." Eugénie Brazier, known as Mother Brazier, ran two restaurants in Lyon and earned three stars from The Michelin Guide in 1933. She had been trained by another female chef, Françoise Fillioux, who opened her restaurant in 1890, and la Mère Brazier would eventually train the world-renowned, three-star Michelin chef Paul Bocuse, who dominated French gastronomic cuisine from the 1960s until his death in 2018.

Nouvelle Cuisine to the Present

French restaurant cuisine benefited from the economic expansion of the postwar era, and the style of cooking shifted as restaurants became more and more popular, particularly in urban settings. Regional cuisines retained their more rustic character of game meats, cassoulet, roast duck, and braised dishes. But the Parisian temples of gastronomy shifted from heavily decorated dishes with elaborate garnishes and thick sauces to "nouvelle cuisine" in the 1970s, using fresher ingredients and simpler cooking techniques. Chefs chose to steam vegetables rather than boil them, eliminated strong marinades and rich sauces, and embraced lighter cooking with fish and vegetables. Restaurant critics Henri Gault and Christian Millau published their "Ten Commandments of Nouvelle Cuisine" in 1973, encouraging chefs to resist complication and embrace what would later be called "spa cuisine" in the hands of Michel Guérard, a chef whose spa-restaurant in southwestern France became so famous that he graced the front cover of *Time* magazine in 1976. French chefs have shaped gastronomic (restaurant) cuisine since its origins in eighteenth-century France, and French techniques are recognized as the standard for professional chefs even today. For this reason, many ingredients and culinary instructions are expressed in French words but without translation: chefs continue to sauté meat, julienne vegetables, and use a mirepoix, for example.

Of course, restaurant cuisine did not mirror home cooking in France of the modern era. Outside of Paris, French diners ate soups and stews at most meals, generally ate game meat more often than butcher's meat, and consumed lots of bread. As transportation of goods became easier and more of the French owned cars, supermarkets began to appear in cities, offering better access to fresh fruit and vegetables and packaged cheeses, for example. In the twenty-first century, the French eat less bread and potatoes than prior to 1950, and more fresh fruit and vegetables. Bread was once an astonishingly large part of the French diet, but consumption dropped dramatically after the World War II, from more than 100 kilograms per person per year in 1950 to 84 kilograms in 1965 and to 44 kilograms in 1989 (Bertrand 1992, 2). Beef consumption has declined, and government statistics show an increase in pork and poultry. Influenced by American culture, the French now consume more fast food and prepared food than ever before. McDonald's opened its first restaurant in France in 1979, and France is the company's second largest market worldwide. The Belgian-French Quick hamburger chain also maintains a healthy business serving hamburgers and fries, including burgers that follow Muslim dietary guidelines for meat preparation at 22 halal-only Quick restaurants.

Faced with perceived threats to their treasured cuisine from fast food and cultural changes, the French maintain a commitment to the family meal and traditions of the table. The "gastronomic meal of the French" was honored by UNESCO in 2010 as part of its Representative List of the Intangible Cultural Heritage of Humanity. The effort to label the French meal as one of the "wonders of the world" shows the pride that the French have in their culinary traditions and their worry that their traditions will be lost. French leaders hoped that the honor would preserve and promote French gastronomic traditions and bring economic advantages through tourism and new markets for French cuisine. They originally campaigned for UNESCO to recognize French gastronomy as a whole, but they eventually narrowed their petition to the precisely defined French meal with its required elements: an aperitif, or before-dinner drink; at least four courses, including a first course, a main course of meat or fish with vegetables, cheese, and dessert; finished with a digestif, or after-dinner drink. French president Nicolas Sarkozy provoked controversy in 2008 when he introduced the original petition: to make French cuisine part of the UNESCO heritage by saying that France had the best gastronomy in the world and that it deserved to be recognized. Numerous European countries objected, declaring that their cuisine equaled France's, and UNESCO officials found Sarkozy's remarks elitist and counter to the spirit of the UNESCO ideology of recognizing but not ranking cultural practices. The major issue with the initial French petition was that it associated French food almost exclusively with haute cuisine, the elite realm of Michelin-starred chefs. The successful petition to recognize French gastronomy focused on the practice of eating in the French way: a celebratory meal at a table with family and friends, using traditional recipes and local ingredients. This view of French cuisine represented the people of France and their connection to the land, a belief that the French embraced as far back as the Middle Ages. The French meal was the first food-related entry on UNESCO's list of elements that represent the cultural heritage of the world.

Further Reading

Bertrand, Michèle. 1992. "20 ans de consommation alimentaire 1969–1989." *Insee Données*, no. 188 (April): 1–4.

Blanchard, Pascal, Sandrine Lemaire, Nicolas Bancel, and Dominic Thomas, eds. 2013. *Colonial Culture in France since the Revolution*. Translated by Alexis Pernsteiner. Bloomington: Indiana University Press.

Boisard, Pierre. 2003. *Camembert: A National Myth*. Berkeley: University of California Press.

Bouton, Cynthia A. 1993. *The Flour War: Gender, Class, and Community in Late Ancien Régime French Society*. University Park: Pennsylvania State University Press.

Campbell, Christy. 2004. *Phylloxera: How Wine Was Saved for the World*. London: HarperCollins.

Castelot, André. 1972. *L'histoire à table: Si la cuisine m'était contée*. Paris: Éditions Perrin.

Coquery-Vidrovitch, Catherine, and Odile Goerg. 1992. *L'Afrique occidentale au temps des Français: Colonisateurs et colonisés, 1860–1960*. Paris: La Découverte.

Dalby, Andrew. 2014. *Food in the Ancient World from A to Z*. London; New York: Routledge.

Davis, Jennifer J. *Defining Culinary Authority: The Transformation of Cooking in France, 1650–1830*. Baton Rouge: Louisiana State University Press, 2013.

Flandrin, Jean-Louis, Massimo Montanari, and Albert Sonnenfeld, eds. 2013. *Food: A Culinary History*. New York: Columbia University Press.

Hautcoeur, Pierre-Cyrille. 2005. "Was the Great War a Watershed? The Economics of World War I in France." In *The Economics of World War I*, edited by Stephen Broadberry and Mark Harrison, 169–205. Cambridge: Cambridge University Press.

Katz, Solomon H., and William W. Weaver. 2003. *Encyclopedia of Food and Culture*. New York: Scribner.

Spang, Rebecca L. 2001. *The Invention of the Restaurant: Paris and Modern Gastronomic Culture*. Cambridge, MA: Harvard University Press.

Tilly, Louise A. 1971. "The Food Riot as a Form of Political Conflict in France." *Journal of Interdisciplinary History* 2 (1): 23–57.

CHAPTER TWO

Influential Ingredients

France as a territory benefits from multiple zones that produce a wide range of products, such as elements of the Mediterranean diet—olives, olive oil, herbs, and anchovies—in the southeast; vast grain fields in the northeast for bread and flour; hard cheeses like Comté in the mountains of the center and south; butter, cheese, and apples (for apple brandy, among other products) from Normandy and Brittany in the northwest, fresh vegetables and fruit in the garden-like center of the country; and truffles, foie gras, and goose from the southwest. French cuisine has also been influenced by imports from former colonies that still produce tropical fruits, cacao, and coffee. In France, daily eating is based on fresh ingredients from local open-air markets as much as possible, although supermarkets are becoming more popular in larger cities. But most French towns offer an open-air market on two days per week, and the average French citizen shops for food every day or every other day. This chapter will discuss the major ingredients that form the backbone of French cooking and eating.

Grains

France is first and foremost a country of bread, and French bread is primarily made from wheat. Soft white breads with a crusty exterior are now the norm across France, but bakeries also feature *pain complet*, or wholegrain loaves. Soft wheat bread is a fairly recent custom. The move from emmer wheat and spelt to soft wheat took place in the Middle Ages, although rye and oats were still used for bread. Before the Revolution, bakeries offered bread made from numerous grains. In the provinces, loaves of bread might be made of rye flour, barley, or millet, and in times of extreme famine these flours might be mixed with dried beans or other plants. In areas where bread was unavailable due to lack of access to mills or ovens, families substituted a porridge of boiled grains or made flat cakes of buckwheat. In rural areas far from Paris, the custom of eating loaves of soft wheat bread, common practice in Paris for centuries, did not become universal until the nineteenth century, and in some sections of the country, not until after the 1850s.

Buckwheat became a common food as early as the fourteenth century, particularly in northern France where buckwheat galettes (savory crepes) are still common. In Brittany, buckwheat flour is an essential ingredient in traditional galettes eaten as a main dish. White flour crepes are served for dessert with sweet fillings. In the southwest regions of Languedoc and Gascony, chestnut trees provided an abundant harvest, and chestnuts became the basis for porridges and flat cakes. Chestnut flour was mixed with other flours to make a sort of dense bread, although chestnuts were considered food for the poor by many, particularly by urban populations. Chestnut trees became scarce in France in the nineteenth century after disease killed off many trees and rural farmers turned to other crops.

Rice has a relatively small role in French cooking except as an ingredient in desserts. Recipes for *angoulée* (or *riz en goulée*, rice cooked in broth or almond milk) appeared as of 1393 in the *Ménagier de Paris* cookbook, and the dish was likely well known in Paris by 1300 (Hess 1998, 38). *Angoulée* fell out of favor quickly, but pilau (rice simmered in flavored broth and then covered and cooked until almost dry) emerged as a signature Provençal dish in southwestern France in cookbooks of the early nineteenth century, although it was probably part of family meals long before the recipe was printed in cookbooks (Hess 1998, 58–64). Until the 1840s only Carolina rice from the United States and Piedmont rice from Italy were found in France. During the colonial occupation of Indochina (now Vietnam, Laos, and Cambodia), government officials attempted to create a market for rice imported from the colonies to France. Today much of France's rice comes from India, and it is more common in the regions of Alsace-Lorraine, near the German border; Burgundy, in the east; and Midi, the south-central region. Cold rice salads occasionally are served as side dishes in the warmer months, and rice pudding flavored with cinnamon and nutmeg is a favorite dessert, but otherwise rice is uncommon at the French table.

Bread

Bread has been dear to the French people since the Middle Ages. Prior to the eighteenth century, most individuals bought a small amount of grain to be milled for their personal use by the village miller. Patrons paid a fee for the privilege, in cash or in flour. Millers gained an important advance when they shifted from this "contract milling" for individuals to speculative milling of large quantities of grain into flour, to be sold commercially. In effect, millers became flour merchants, and in the 1740s flour overtook wheat as the primary commodity bought and sold in the public market (Kaplan 1984, 273, 599). Bread customs in Paris, since it was the largest city in France, were quite different from those of the small towns and rural areas of the rest of the country.

Paris had two major advantages: access to milled flour, and an abundance of bakers and bread shops in the marketplace. The wheat-producing provinces to the north and east of Paris sent most of their grain crops to provision the capital city, leaving little for local use, and the transportation network to distribute grain to other parts of the country was not yet established. In addition, the remnants of feudalism persisted in the rural areas far from Paris, meaning that powerful nobles maintained ownership of the local mills. Baking bread required milling grain, and peasants were obliged to pay a tax or proportion of their grain for the use of the mill, an imposition they resented even when they could afford it. With many fewer bread shops in the countryside and smaller budgets for purchasing bread, poorer families chose to prepare their bread at home and, if flour was hard to come by, to process their grain into flat cakes or porridges.

In eighteenth-century Paris bread came in a number of forms: the heavy, dense 6-, 8-, and 12-pound loaves of dark bread (*pain bis*), medium-dark bread (*bis-blanc*) in the same sizes, and small loaves of fine white bread (*pain mollet*) made from soft wheat. These soft breads were particularly favored by wealthy Parisians. The Parisian bread market, held two days per week, sold only the large breads but at a better price than the bread shops; the shops were permitted to be open every day and sold bread at a higher price but of better quality. Fewer and fewer urban families baked their bread at home, preferring to purchase it in the market. This social change created a point of conflict: bakers were required by law to provide sufficient bread for the market but they had little incentive to make cheaper dark bread for the poor, from which they made little profit, when there were many wealthy customers who paid handsomely for more expensive white breads. As they had since the Middle Ages, roving bread inspectors were empowered to check bread in markets and shops for weight and quality; these elected officials could seize offending bread and fine the shop owner in case of violation. Bread merchants were prohibited from taking unsold bread back to their shops at the close of the market day; this was to ensure that discounted bread would be available for the poor later in the day, provided that supplies held up. Bakers in Paris occasionally refused to bake enough dark bread (*pain bis*) to meet demand, leading to police attempting to force them to do so.

> ## French Bread
>
> The word for "bread baker" in French (*boulanger*) comes from the word *boule*, for "round bread." All bread prior to the eighteenth century in France was round, often baked in huge loaves meant to last for months. In the twelfth century breads paid as a tithe to the Abbey of Cluny weighed 7.5–15 kilograms each (Mouthon 1997, 211).

As a result of the Parisian vogue for *pains de fantaisie* (soft white breads in different shapes), the shape of bread in France changed from the round *boule* that had been nearly the exclusive form since the Middle Ages to the elongated shapes we recognize today as French bread. Its magic ingredient came from beer: beer makers in Paris (as well as Flanders and Picardie, other provinces of France) produced yeast derived from their fermentation process and sold it to bakers. Bread makers created lighter, airier breads with brewer's yeast than with the sourdough starter used in traditional breads. Bakers in France had used yeast in bread since the seventeenth century, but doctors believed that yeast (and beer, for that matter) had unhealthy effects on the body. An act of Parliament in 1670 made yeast permissible again but only if it came from Paris and was mixed with the traditional natural starter. Long, thin bread shapes offered a greater ratio of desired crunchy crust in contrast to the soft interior crumb. Darker breads had a more substantial texture and a heartier crust and were generally baked in large loaves that would last for several days.

Currently, the French eat bread every day and at nearly every meal. The most common bread shape is the baguette, but *boulangeries* sell different sizes and weights of elongated bread with different names (*ficelle*, *bâtard*, etc.) as well as round breads and whole-grain varieties. Sandwich bread is sold in grocery stores, but the French consumer vastly prefers fresh bread from the local baker, and government regulations keep quality high and price reasonable.

Fish

Historical records indicate that the French have enjoyed freshwater fish from the many rivers that crisscross France since Gallic times. A poem written in 371 CE by Ausonius, prefect of Gaul and native of Bordeaux, praised the many fish found in the Moselle River. Ausonius named chub, trout, perch, and river salmon as fish good for the table, but he called shad "food for the vulgar" (White 1919, 231). At port cities near the oceans, saltwater fish was available early in France's history. Fish was one of the most expensive proteins in France due to the cost of transportation and a short shelf life, but it held a cultural importance for Catholic France.

Salt cod and dried herring were popular commodities in areas of the country without ocean ports or river access, particularly for the Catholic observance of lean days on Fridays and during Lent, when meat was forbidden. The fish market in Paris had existed since King Louis IX ordered it opened in 1263, but it provided fish principally for the royal table. Part of a central market for commodities that required merchants from Paris and surrounding cities to sell their wares on specific days exclusively in this designated area, the early market was limited to grain and fish until the fifteenth century. As French citizens abandoned the church after the Revolution, they also abandoned the cultural tradition of Lenten (lean) days, and the demand for salt cod and herring (now seen as rustic foods) declined precipitously. Wealthier tables sought out freshwater fish and ocean fish conveyed at great expense from distant ports. Continued desire for fish and other seafood, such as oysters, in great demand by the elite in Paris, led to the construction of a designated fish market in the eighteenth century, eventually situated in the central Les Halles market, where the fish pavilion was completed in 1857.

Tilapia Meunière (White Fish with Lemon-Butter Sauce)

Yield: Serves 4

Ingredients
½ tsp salt
¼ tsp pepper
½ cup flour
4 Tbsp butter
4 fillets of tilapia or other white fish, such as cod or haddock
Juice from one lemon

1. Dredge the fish fillets in the flour mixed with ½ teaspoon salt and ¼ teaspoon pepper. Melt 1 tablespoon of butter over medium heat in a nonstick pan. When the butter stops foaming, add the fish, placing the better-looking side down so that it will make an attractive presentation when served. Sauté until the edges begin to brown, and then turn

> carefully, using two spatulas to avoid breaking the fillets apart. When the fish flakes easily with a fork and is browned on both sides, remove to a plate and keep warm in the oven at 200 degrees.
> 2. Meanwhile, melt 3 tablespoons butter over medium heat in the same pan. When the foaming subsides, turn off the heat and add the juice of one lemon. Swirl the pan to mix the butter and lemon. Pour the lemon-butter sauce over the cooked fish and serve with additional lemon wedges.

The French also enjoy various types of shellfish, which are harvested from the Atlantic Ocean, on the west coast of France, and the Mediterranean Sea, on the southern coast. Atlantic fishing brings in herring, mackerel, scallops, oysters, and cod. Mediterranean ports feature spiny lobster, langoustines, sardines, and anchovies, as well as *rascasse*, a fish well suited for bouillabaisse, the fish stew famous in Marseilles. The former Caribbean colonies and now territories of France—such as Guadeloupe and Martinique—and Tunisia, a former protectorate of France, export much of their fresh fish to foreign buyers and continue to eat salt cod as it was introduced to them by colonizers.

Snails (escargots) have been a delicacy for the French since the Middle Ages. The early cookbook *Ménagier de Paris* suggested cooking them in water or oil. Snails were served at the court of Henri IV in the Renaissance, but in later centuries they were thought to be food for lesser tables, particularly disdained in Paris. In the provinces, snails were eaten regularly and with great pleasure. The recipe for snails *à la bourguignonne* (in the Burgundy style)—snails served in the shell with butter, garlic, and parsley—appears to date to the eighteenth century, and this preparation is still associated with Burgundy (Hyman 1986, 44). Snails cooked in garlic and butter are now a regular feature of restaurant menus throughout the country, including bistros in Paris.

Meat

The French source for meat was game in the ancient and medieval eras, particularly for nobles, who hunted for food and for sport. But hunting grounds on noble lands were also open to the people in the Middle Ages and gave peasants access to partridges, quail, and other game birds, as well as wild boar. Peasant families in rural areas raised and slaughtered one pig per year for their personal consumption, but butcher's meat (cuts of meat from cows, sheep, or calves [veal]) generally did not form a large part of the rural diet. On the contrary, rural inhabitants supplemented their diets with game birds, venison, and wild pigs hunted in forests and on common lands. Types of meat mattered to the fashionable Parisians and those who aspired to be fashionable. Long considered a meat of the lower rural classes, pork became an acceptable urban food in certain forms in Paris: smoked or salted pork and ham continued to be associated with lower-class eating, but refined preparations, such as boudin sausages and terrines or pâtés (mousses or terrines of cooked meat), elevated pork to a higher level acceptable on urban tables. Once the central butcher (the Grande Boucherie) was established in Paris, beef became more popular, and pork raised by peasant families could be traded at the market for other meats.

Those who could not afford even the lowest cuts of meat could still draw nourishment from meat broths or bouillon, which was served by charity hospitals and soup kitchens and was the inaugural dish of the Parisian restaurants that were created in the late 1760s. At the end of the eighteenth century, residents of Paris consumed an average of 62 kilograms of butcher's meat per year, while those living in Caen, in Normandy, managed with less than half of that, only 20 to 30 kilograms per person (Watts 2006, 8). Printed cookbooks began to show a distinct preference for butcher's meats over game, but these books only represented the eating habits of the higher classes, who could afford such commodities. Residents of regions of France outside of Paris consumed meat differently from residents of Paris in part because these regions sent much of their supply of livestock to Paris; in particular, Normandy supplied beef, and Languedoc, in the southwest, supplied pork. The creation of the central livestock market in the eighteenth century helped more provincial farmers bring their meat to the profitable market in Paris. By 1873 up to 1.9 million animals were presented for sale there from all parts of France, more than double the number only 50 years before (Husson 1875, 187–89). The most popular meat at markets in the late nineteenth century was mutton and lamb, with veal and beef a close second. French meat eaters also bought imported meat from Germany, Hungary, Italy, and the French colony of Algeria.

In the twentieth century, the French turned almost exclusively to butcher's meats, although the amount of game meat consumed is difficult to measure since hunters find and process this meat on their own. A French government report of 1992 showed that the most popular meat on French tables was beef, with sausages and cured meats second, followed by veal and lamb (Bertrand 1992, 2). Poultry represents an even larger percentage of meat consumption than beef does, and the French now primarily eat chicken and some rabbit, although the demand for rabbit has dropped by about half since the 1960s. For special occasions, French cooks prefer whole chickens or other fowl, and they appreciate different breeds of chicken for different recipes. They eat very little turkey but consume duck as part of the well-known cassoulet (a bean dish from the southwest) and as a dish for a special occasion. Foie gras (fatty goose or duck liver) cooked in brandy is a celebratory dish at Christmas. Goose liver also finds its way into pâtés of chopped meat and spices, also prepared from pork, rabbit, and duck. The *poulet de Bresse*, with its signature blue feet, has a special label called an AOC (*Appellation d'Origine Contrôlée*) backed by regulations on the feed and treatment of these birds. This designation makes Bresse chicken sought after and quite expensive. In a study from 2006, meat represented the largest expense in household budgets (21 percent of the total), followed by bread and grains and then milk products.

France has a tradition of eating horse meat that dates to the nineteenth century. In 1869 specialized butchers for horse meat produced only 500 kilos, but under the Prussian siege of 1870, when no other meat could be brought into Paris, butchers slaughtered millions of kilos of horse meat, and demand remained high just after the war, with 1.5 million kilos produced in 1873 (Husson 1875, 260). After the siege ended and France experienced a rise in the prices of butcher's meats, eating horse became more habitual, and demand grew. Similarly, when the mad cow crisis reached Europe in 1996, and beef was banned or considered dangerous to eat, French consumers ate less beef and significantly more horse and poultry. France still has a few equine butchers, but consumption of horse meat has steeply declined recently. In statistics for 2017, demand for horse meat by consumers had dropped 70 percent since 2000. In the 1990s French diners ate about 1 kilogram of horse meat per person per year, compared to 0.2 kilos in 2017 (Agreste 2018, 163).

Butchery

The practice of butchery before the eighteenth century in France was not limited to cutting animal carcasses into sellable portions of raw meat as it is now; it included slaughtering live animals, selling meat, and selling the by-products of animal processing: hides for tanning, intestines for food and stringed instruments, suet for cooking, and tallow for candles, among others. As such, the butchers controlled the supply of a number of lucrative commodities and were essential to a number of related trades.

Eggs

Eggs are prominent in the French diet at the evening meal, when the French prefer a lighter meal consisting of an omelet or eggs poached in wine or even *pain perdu* (French toast) of leftover bread soaked in egg and fried. It is also common to find fried eggs in galettes (main-dish crepes) and as a topping on pizza. Eggs provide a cheaper protein source when meat prices rise, and they are more accessible to modest households than meat, fish, or shellfish are. Desserts such as custards and meringues include eggs, and hard-cooked eggs find their way into composed salads. Unlike many Western countries, the French do not generally eat eggs for breakfast, preferring a simple meal of toast with jam and coffee or juice.

Dairy Products

The French do not drink much fluid milk, believing that it is a drink for children, but they consume milk regularly in the form of yogurt, butter, and cheeses. Butter is the stereotypical ingredient in French cuisine, but it

---

Omelette aux Fines Herbes
(Omelet with Fresh Herbs)

Yield: Serves 1

Ingredients
2 eggs
1 tsp butter
2 Tbsp of your choice of fresh herbs (chives, tarragon, chervil, parsley, dill), cleaned and stems removed, chopped or torn

1. Whisk eggs with 2 tablespoons of water until well blended.
2. Melt butter in a 10-inch nonstick skillet or omelet pan. Sauté fresh herbs briefly (1–2 minutes) just until fragrant; set aside. Pour eggs into pan and use a spatula to lift the edge of the egg mixture as it cooks, to let the uncooked egg run underneath.
3. When the eggs are cooked underneath but still wet on top, place the herbs on the left side of the eggs. Fold the omelet in half to cover the herbs. Tip the omelet out onto a warm plate so that the underside is now on top. Smooth the omelet with the spatula into a neat oval shape.

Serve with toasted baguette.

was not widely consumed across France until the Renaissance, in part because the church imposed numerous "lean days" on which meat and animal fats were not allowed in meals. After the fifteenth century, as cookbooks indicate, butter was permitted on "lean days" during Lent. La Varenne's *Le cuisinier françois* (*The French Cook*) in 1651 was the first cookbook to publish a recipe for sauces thickened with a roux of flour and butter. Much of rural France did not have a habit for consuming butter until after World War I (Hémardinquer 1970, 261–62). Butters from Normandy are considered the best due to the region's historical cultivation of milk cows. In the present day, butter is so important that some carry an AOC label that indicates they are among the finest products in France and comply with the country's strict regulations on ingredients and flavor. Examples of AOC butters include Isigny, from Normandy, with a unique flavor and colored by the grass the cows eat while grazing, and Beurre de Bresse, from eastern France, one of the most recent AOC butters (Khosrova 2016, 131–32). French butters generally have a higher butterfat percentage (84 percent or higher) than American table butter.

Cheese

The AOC designation, created to regulate and celebrate French wine, is very important for cheese, and cheese is supremely important to the French. The French have been making and eating cheese since the time of the Roman Empire, when Pliny, in *Natural History* (first century CE), praised the soft cheeses from present-day Nîmes, in the South of France. Roquefort cheese, classified as a blue cheese even though it is veined with blue-green mold, has its origins in the eleventh century, when a strain of mold found only in the natural caves near the town of Roquefort produced a pungent cheese like no other. This product earned the first AOC label for cheese in 1925, and in order to carry the label "Roquefort," the cheese must be made in the town and aged in the original caves nearby. The mold that produces the signature blue-green veins is called *Penicillium roqueforti*.

Soft, washed-rind cheeses, like Muenster, and bloomy-rind cheeses, like Brie or Epoisses, date to the Middle Ages and were sometimes called "monastery" cheeses because the monks in abbeys across France perfected the art of cheese making. With milk from their captive flocks of animals and cool cellars for aging, the monasteries were ideal for creating these new types of cheese. Mountain cheeses with a harder-pressed curd, like Comté and Gruyère, also have a long history; they date to the thirteenth century, when cheesemakers in the mountains preserved fresh milk for long storage by making it into giant wheels of cheese (sometimes weighing more than 100 pounds) that could last for years. More modern cheeses tend to be industrialized cheeses made in factories, and there is a divide between artisanal cheese makers, who try to preserve tradition but whose practices do not align with modern food safety protocols, and industrial producers, who dominate the international market.

Camembert cheese changed from an artisanal cheese with origins in the early eighteenth century to an industrial cheese made with pasteurized milk at the end of the nineteenth century, when Louis Pasteur's institute published guidelines for pasteurizing milk for cheese. Manufacturers began to use machines to cut the curd for the cheese rather than ladling it by hand, as they had done traditionally. Now 90 percent of Camembert produced in France is industrial, pasteurized cheese. Artisanal producers prefer raw milk for their cheeses, since the heat from pasteurization changes the flavor of the finished cheese. Raw-milk cheeses are rarely the cause of foodborne illnesses, but they are viewed with suspicion outside of France. In the United States, for example, raw-milk cheese from France cannot be sold unless it is aged for a minimum of 60 days. France is by far the most diverse country when it comes to cheese: one study counted 1,500 recognized types of cheese and 45 name-protected cheeses (to date), the most of any country (Papademas and Bintsis 2017).

The French use cheese in cooked dishes like quiche and *croque-monsieurs* (a grilled ham and cheese sandwich with a creamy sauce), but traditionally a cheese platter of various kinds of cheeses follows the meal. The platter offers a selection of cheeses from mild (like Brie or goat cheese) to strong (like Epoisses or Roquefort), and from different milks (like sheep's or cow's milk). Diners take a small amount of each cheese they would like to try and eat the morsels individually, savoring the flavors and textures. Most of the time, the cheese is eaten by itself, rather than with bread, although sometimes an accompaniment of fig jam or quince paste enhances the flavor of the cheese. In fine-dining restaurants or elegant family meals, the cheese course can replace dessert. Cheese is never served as an appetizer.

Herbs and Spices

Medieval French food was heavily spiced with flavors borrowed from the Arab world, including clove, pepper, cinnamon, nutmeg, ginger, saffron, anise, and grains of paradise (Melegueta pepper). Pepper had been the dominant flavor of ancient cuisine, but it fell out of favor in the Middle Ages and came to be seen as ordinary and common. Pepper rose to

Persillade

Yield: About ½ cup

Ingredients
3 cloves garlic
½ tsp salt
½ cup fresh parsley leaves

1. Finely mince 3 cloves of garlic on a cutting board. Add ½ teaspoon salt. With a heavy knife, chop and mash the garlic with the salt until it forms a paste.
2. Finely chop ½ cup of parsley leaves. Chop and mash the parsley into the garlic-salt mixture until evenly mixed.

Use as a garnish for soup or on cooked fish.

---

prominence again in the Renaissance and through the eighteenth century. In the seventeenth century, in particular, cooks turned away from heavy spices and adopted the use of aromatic ingredients like onions, shallots, garlic, and parsley that are still a feature of French cooking today.

Pistou (French Pesto)

Yield: About 1 cup

Ingredients
1 cup fresh basil leaves
2 cloves garlic
Salt
2 Tbsp olive oil

In a food processor, process 1 cup of fresh basil leaves, 2 cloves of garlic, and a pinch of salt until finely minced and grainy. With the processor running, add 2 tablespoons of olive oil, and process until the mixture forms a loose texture, like a thick sauce. You can also make the sauce in a mortar and pestle. Mash the basil, garlic, and salt until almost smooth, and then drizzle in the oil as you stir.

Add to hot vegetable soup as a garnish before serving.

Influential Ingredients

The *persillade*, a blend of mashed garlic and parsley, can be used to flavor soups and fish dishes, and the French have their own version of the Italian pesto, called *pistou*, used to flavor a traditional vegetable soup from Provence, in the South of France.

Again, the nineteenth century brought influences from abroad, particularly the colonies in Asia. Colonizers sampled the cuisine of Indochina and brought some of these dishes home with them, including curries and pilafs with spices. The efforts of the colonial lobby to promote foods from the colonized (in particular after the Colonial Exposition of 1931) resulted in the publication in women's magazines of the 1930s of recipes using curry, cumin, and other spices. In the French overseas territories of Guadeloupe and Martinique, immigrants from India brought warm spices that influenced the cuisine of the Caribbean islands, where *colombo de cabri* (goat curry) is a signature dish.

The herb-and-spice profile of present-day French cuisine is marked by regional differences. In the north and east, traditional flavorings include onion and black pepper; the southwest, near Spain, uses warm spices like cumin and nutmeg; while the southern coast, influenced by adjacent Italy, freely uses garlic, thyme, and oregano. The herb mixture called *herbes de*

Tian à la Famille Louyot (Similar to Ratatouille)

Yield: Serves 6 as a side dish, 4 as a main dish

Ingredients
1–2 eggplants
2 bell peppers (red or yellow)
2 medium onions
3 medium zucchini
3 medium tomatoes
3 medium potatoes (Yukon Gold or other)
3–4 cloves garlic
1 tsp salt
½ tsp black pepper
4 Tbsp olive oil
2 tsp *herbes de Provence*

1. Preheat oven to 375 degrees. Cut 1 large eggplant or 2 small eggplants, 2 red or yellow bell peppers, 2 medium onions, 3 medium zucchini, 3 medium tomatoes, and 3 medium Yukon Gold potatoes into 1-inch pieces. Place in a large, lidded baking dish or Dutch oven.

2. Add 3–4 whole cloves garlic, 1 teaspoon salt, ½ teaspoon black pepper, 4 tablespoons olive oil, and 2 teaspoons *herbes de Provence* (or substitute ½ teaspoon each of marjoram, thyme, and rosemary).
3. Stir ingredients and place dish in oven, covered, for 20–30 minutes, until the vegetables begin to render their juices.
4. Remove lid, stir, and return to oven uncovered for 30 minutes or until the potatoes are soft (check with a paring knife).

Serve with crusty bread and extra olive oil for drizzling on each serving of tian. Serve warm, at room temperature, or cold the next day.

Provence comes from the southern region of Provence. It is a blend of marjoram, thyme, oregano, basil, and lavender, which is grown in massive fields in that region; *herbes de Provence* are used as a flavoring for ratatouille and grilled fish.

Mustard and Vinegar

Vinegar and vinegar-based sauces, like mustard, were so important that they were sold by traveling street merchants as early as the thirteenth century. The fourteenth-century French cookbooks *Le Viandier* and *Ménagier de Paris* each contain recipes for preparing mustard and recipes that use mustard as an ingredient. Nicolas de Larmessin, a French engraver, drew an image of a vinegar seller and his cart in Paris in 1700, but it is the city of Dijon that was and remains most famous for its sharp, vinegary mustard. Shoppers in the early modern era purchased a bottle of vinegar or *verjus* (sour grape juice used for sauces) or a pot of mustard from the vinegar sellers, or they visited a pharmacy to purchase mustard tablets that they mixed with vinegar to produce the condiment. French consumers historically preferred prepared mustard to mustard powder, and mustard in France comes in various forms, such as milder Bordeaux-style, grainy country style with the mustard seeds still intact, and fiery Dijon style. As early as the eighteenth century, French companies produced mustards flavored with violet and vanilla and more enduring flavors like tarragon and shallot. The well-known mustard company Grey Poupon (now owned by Kraft) was established in Dijon in 1853 and won prizes at the Paris Exposition in 1889 for its famed mustard. Other important Parisian producers, like Maille and Bornibus, challenge the idea that mustard from Dijon is

> ## Vinaigrette for a Green Salad
>
> *Yield:* Serves 4–6
>
> *Ingredients*
> 3 Tbsp olive oil
> 1 Tbsp vinegar
> 1 tsp Dijon mustard
> Salt
> 1 Tbsp fresh herbs (optional)
> 8 cups washed salad greens
>
> 1. In a clean salad bowl, mix together 3 tablespoons olive oil, 1 tablespoon vinegar, 1 teaspoon Dijon mustard, and a pinch of salt until the mixture is thick and emulsified. Taste the dressing and add more oil, vinegar, or mustard until you get the flavor you want. Add a tablespoon of chopped fresh herbs like tarragon or parsley, if you like.
> 2. Add the washed salad greens (about 8 cups) to the bowl. Toss with the dressing just before serving so that the leaves of the greens do not wilt.

the best. The French serve mustard as a condiment with pâté and cornichons, as a spread for sandwiches, as an ingredient in sauces (especially for rabbit), and as an emulsifier in classic vinaigrette (from the French word *vinaigre*, "vinegar") on green salads.

Truffles and Morel Mushrooms

Truffles are a rare fungus found among the roots of certain trees, primarily oak. Truffle hunters first used trained pigs with a keen sense of smell to find the precious mushrooms, but the pigs had a tendency to eat the truffles once found. Hunters turned to dogs as their assistants, and today most hunters prefer to use well-trained dogs. Truffles are part of elite dining and do not figure into day-to-day eating in France, but they are important as a status symbol. No one has yet succeeded in cultivating truffles of good quality; they must be found in the wild and are seasonal (December to March), contributing to their rarity and their sky-high prices. When available, black truffles can cost $1,200 per pound, or about $80 per ounce. In nineteenth-century gastronomy, when the early great chefs were creating the now-renowned classic French cuisine, truffles first gained a following.

In the 1920s the signature dish of Marie Brazier, one of the most famous female chefs in Lyon, was *poulet en demi-deuil*, or chicken in half-mourning, so called because she layered slices of truffle under the skin of the chicken before roasting, making the chicken appear as though it were dressed in black. Most recipes and references for French truffles call for the black variety, of which those from the Périgord region are the most famous. The Périgord region in the southwest is known for truffles and foie gras, a natural pairing.

Morel mushrooms are another delicacy in France, the second most expensive mushroom after truffles. France is the top consumer of morel mushrooms in the world, but acquiring wild mushrooms is very labor-intensive, rendering morels so hard to come by that France imports most of its cultivated morels from China. A new initiative by young French farmers to grow morel mushrooms on farms in France has seen some success. Morel mushrooms must be cooked; they are toxic if eaten raw. The French enjoy morels in a cream sauce as a side dish, in an omelet, or as part of a braised veal or poultry stew. The mushrooms have a spongelike, honeycomb gill structure and soak up the sauce of any dish that includes them.

Sugar

France historically has used less sugar than its European neighbors, and its cuisine is markedly less sweet than some. French cookbooks of the Middle Ages rarely mention sugar, and sweet ingredients like honey, dates, figs, or prunes do not appear regularly on the French table until the eighteenth century. Pastry and other sweet desserts also arrived late to France. At celebratory banquets and feasts before the eighteenth century, the close of the meal would consist of fresh fruit or fruit preserves. The dessert course developed from a final *yssue de table* ("exit from the table") of spiced nuts and dried fruit in the Middle Ages to fresh fruit in the Renaissance and seventeenth century to displays of pasty constructed to look like castles or other ornaments in the eighteenth century.

France's limited use of sugar is due in part to its colonial history and the economic advantage of selling sugar rather than consuming it. In 1775 sugar from French territories Saint-Domingue (now Haiti), Martinique, and Guadeloupe represented half of the exports from these islands to mainland France. Between 1760 and 1791, the growth of the sugar trade in Saint-Domingue enabled France to maintain its supremacy in the world sugar market and was one of the keys to the French colonial system (Tomich 2016, 55). After the Haitian Revolution in 1794, France lost its principal sugar supplier, and French West Indian sugar from the other territories was excluded from the European market. Great Britain, another colonial power in the West Indies, protected its colonies by prohibiting sugar from occupied French colonies to enter the British market. French authorities nearly abandoned sugarcane production in its overseas colonies, particularly when a hurricane in 1813 destroyed much of the crop in Martinique. In order to compete with sugarcane producers, France turned to raising sugar beets on its home soil.

In the rest of the world, beet sugar was a very small part of the market for sugar, but in France it represented major competition for French colonial sugar makers. In essence, France was competing with itself. Beet sugar became a major industry in France with massive government subsidies, but it nearly disappeared after laws enacted in 1814 ended government protection, allowing for an influx of cheap foreign and colonial sugar. A sugar war between domestic and colonial producers ensued in the 1820s and 1830s: tariffs reduced the amount of foreign sugar coming into France and raised the price of colonial sugar, while beet sugar was exempt from duties. By 1837 domestic refineries produced 50,000 metric tons of beet sugar, one-third of French domestic consumption. Eventually, sugar beets became an unprofitable commodity for France, as protections ended and more and more cheap foreign sugar came into the country, but France still produces sugar beets in the northern regions for use in the industrial sugar industry and for the production of alcohol. The French overseas territories produce an amount of sugarcane equal to the domestic sugar beet farms, and beginning in the late 2010s, France has experienced a rise in the export of domestic sugar, since the country's sugar beet crops are thriving.

Over the course of the eighteenth century, sugar became more available and less the exclusive indulgence of the wealthy. Individual cakes and pastries came to be served as the final course at banquets, and eventually pastry shops and chocolate shops opened during the nineteenth century to serve all those who wished to buy a sweet treat. Perhaps because the bread shops or *boulangeries* existed well before sweet desserts did, pastry shops or *pâtisseries* are separate from bread bakeries in France. When speaking of a "bakery" in French, it is necessary to distinguish between the baked products. Even now, the French prefer to buy pastries and cakes from a *pâtisserie* rather than make them at home, since pastry shops are so widespread and since sweet desserts are a special treat in the French diet rather than an everyday indulgence. Current statistics show that French households are less and less likely to make cakes and pastries at home in favor of buying them, based on the decline in sales for granulated sugar and the rise in sales of prepared pastries. Compared to the rest of Europe,

French consumers have been known to buy more jams and honeys but less chocolate than the average European Union country (Besson 2006). In 2016, France was the largest consumer in Europe of jams, jellies, and marmalades, accounting for 36 percent of total European consumption (Mordor Intelligence 2020).

Chocolate

Cacao beans for making chocolate first arrived in Europe from the Americas with the Spanish explorers, and the French first consumed chocolate as a liquid. Hot chocolate had a following with the court nobles in the seventeenth century and soon became a fad even though medical opinion was divided on whether the substance was good or bad for health. The first published recipe to use chocolate was in François Massialot's *Le cuisinier royal et bourgeois* in 1691, for wigeon (a kind of duck) in chocolate sauce. Cultivation of chocolate and coffee became a major industry in the French colonies in Africa in the late nineteenth century and before the colonies gained independence.

Chocolate in bar form became popular in the nineteenth century. Paris was an important center for chocolate in the 1870s, producing 7 million kilos of chocolate, of which 2.8 million kilos stayed in Paris and the rest was exported to other parts of France and foreign countries. This prepared chocolate was used for hot chocolate; eaten as drops or bars; or used in desserts and pastries (Husson 1875). Bar chocolate continues to be one of the most popular dessert purchases by French households, although gummy candies have grown by a larger percentage than chocolate candy in recent years. Nutella (chocolate-hazelnut spread) continues to be extremely popular in France, especially on bread as an after-school snack for children. Sales of chocolate-hazelnut spread more than doubled in France between 1990 and 2004 (Besson 2006).

Vegetables

When France suffered wheat shortages in the eighteenth century, a number of scientists suggested that the solution could be the potato, a newly cultivated crop from the New World. Rural peasants in some parts of France ate potatoes before then but only as a last resort, as potatoes were considered food for animals. Europeans unfamiliar with the potato feared the vegetable was poisonous, but a campaign undertaken by Antoine Parmentier convinced some to embrace it. Responding to a call from the government for a solution to grain shortages, Parmentier and another scientist named Faiguet devised a recipe for bread made from potatoes mixed with flour. Faiguet presented his research to the French Academy of Science in 1761 to limited success, and Parmentier followed in 1778 with a recipe that was half flour and half potato, admitting that bread made only with potatoes was inedible. Parmentier continued to research bread science at the *Ecole gratuite de boulangerie* (free school of bread making), founded in 1782 and dedicated to using science to improve French bread. In the end, the potato could not save France from its bread crisis, but Parmentier continued to promote the nutritional value of the root vegetable. Only in the nineteenth century did the potato rise to the status of haute cuisine, and dishes made with potato purée still carry the label *parmentière*, after their eighteenth-century promoter. Potatoes are now a major part of the French diet, prepared in a gratin (baked with cream and grated cheese) or fried, and France produced over six million tons of potatoes in 2018 (Agreste 2018, 139). French fries, however, originated in Belgium.

Other root vegetables commonly used in French cuisine include carrots, turnips, celery root, and parsnips. Carrots are second to potatoes in domestic production, followed by onions, sweet corn, and green beans. The French eat leafy greens, such as endive and chicory, in salad, and they cook with heartier greens, like cabbage and leeks. Sauerkraut made from fermented cabbage is an important element of the Alsatian specialty *choucroute garnie* (sauerkraut with sausages). Braised endives are a well-loved, home-cooked side dish in France, and small green beans known as haricots verts can be sautéed or blanched and served cold in salads like the *salade Niçoise* found in the southern city of Nice. With their system of open markets giving them access to farm-fresh produce, many French eat seasonally, reveling in asparagus (white and green) and peas in spring and artichokes in summer, for example. Nonetheless, although the French are generally healthy eaters, vegetables (except for potatoes) do not represent a large segment of the French diet.

Fruit

In the Renaissance, French courts finally embraced raw fruits and vegetables, leading the way for the vogue for fruits from other countries. In the Middle Ages, medical treatises counseled against eating raw fruit for its effect on the body's humors: fruit was considered "cold" and "humid," and it was thought that too much fruit could bring on an imbalance, leading to illness. The inherent "cold" quality of fruit, particularly fruit that grew on the ground, like melons and strawberries, could be mitigated if it were paired with a "hot" food like salted ham. For this reason, the court took up the practice of eating melons with ham or even wine, a practice that continues today. Fruit that grew in the air, like pears and apples, was considered less dangerous. The French still favor tree fruit, possibly because these kinds of fruits grow well in the French climate. Louis XIV installed an orange grove at Versailles in the seventeenth century as a show of his power over nature, but the trees did not produce many oranges in the cool northern air of Paris, and they had to be replaced regularly. The orange trees remain at Versailles, as a decoration.

Normandy and Brittany in the north of France are well known not only for cheese, butter, and cream but also for their large production of apples and pears, used for eating and for cider. Apples are first in volume of production among all fruit except for tomatoes, with peaches and nectarines a distant second. In the southeast, near the Alps and the Rhone valley, farmers grow apples as well as apricots, peaches, nectarines, cherries, and olives. One particularity of France is its production and consumption of plums (called prunes in their dried form). Prunes pair well with chicken in a well-known braised dish that marries sweet and savory, and prunes preserved in sugar syrup are a famous candy known as *pruneaux d'Agen*, from the town of Agen in southwest France. In the late spring, the French seek out wild strawberries, known as *fraises des bois* or "strawberries from the woods" at farmers markets, tiny strawberries with a delicate, perfumed flavor. The French care a great deal about freshness and seasonality in fruit and vegetables; they look for local produce at the market and are familiar with different varieties of the produce they use. One exception to eating local fruit is the tropical fruit imported from French overseas territories like Martinique and Guadeloupe. These island nations provide most of the bananas and pineapples consumed on mainland France as well as other "tropical" fruits used in fruit salads and desserts.

Further Reading

Agreste. 2018. "Equidés." *GraphAgri*. Ministère de l'Agriculture et de l'Alimentation. https://agreste.agriculture.gouv.fr/agreste-web/disaron/GraFraChap12.8/detail/.

Agreste. 2019. "Produits Agroalimentaires." *GraphAgri 2019*, Ministère de l'Agriculture et de l'Alimentation. https://agreste.agriculture.gouv.fr/agreste-web/disaron/GraFraChap12.3/detail/.

Bertrand, Michèle. 1992. "20 ans de consommation alimentaire 1969–1989." *Insee Données*, no. 188 (April): 1–4.

Besson, D. 2006. "Quinze Ans d'achats de Produits Sucrés: Moins de Sucre, Davantage de Produits Transformés." *Insee Première*, no. 1088. http://www.epsilon.insee.fr/jspui/bitstream/1/174/1/ip1088.pdf.

Boisard, Pierre. 2003. *Camembert: A National Myth*. Berkeley: University of California Press.

Bouton, Cynthia A. 1993. *The Flour War: Gender, Class, and Community in Late Ancien Régime French Society*. University Park: Pennsylvania State University Press.

Davidson, Alan, and Tom Jaine. 2014. *The Oxford Companion to Food*. Oxford: Oxford University Press.

Hémardinquer, Jean-Jacques. 1970. "Les graisses de cuisine en France: Essais de cartes." In *Pour une Histoire de l'alimentation*, edited by Jean-Jacques Hémardinquer, 254–71. Paris: Armand Colin.

Hess, Karen. 1998. *The Carolina Rice Kitchen: The African Connection*. Columbia: University of South Carolina Press.

Husson, Armand. 1875. *Les consommations de Paris*. Paris: Hachette.

Hyman, Philip. 1986. "L'art d'accommoder les escargots." *L'Histoire* 85:41–44.

Kaplan, Steven L. 1984. *Provisioning Paris Merchants and Millers in the Grain and Flour Trade during the Eighteenth Century*. Ithaca, NY: Cornell University Press.

Katz, Solomon H., and William W. Weaver. 2003. *Encyclopedia of Food and Culture*. New York: Scribner.

Khosrova, Elaine. 2016. *Butter: A Rich History*. Chapel Hill, NC: Algonquin.

Kindstedt, Paul S. 2013. *Cheese and Culture: A History of Cheese and Its Place in Western Civilization*. White River Junction, VT: Chelsea Green.

Mordor Intelligence. 2020. "Europe Food Spread Market, Growth, Trends and Forecast." https://www.mordorintelligence.com/industry-reports/europe-food-spreads-market-industry.

Mouthon, Fabrice. 1997. "Le pain en Bordelais médiéval, XIIIe–XVIe s." *Archéologie du Midi Médiéval* 15 (1): 205–13.

Papademas, Photis, and Thomas Bintsis. 2017. *Global Cheesemaking Technology: Cheese Quality and Characteristics*. Hoboken, NJ: John Wiley & Sons. Ebook.

Tomich, Dale W. 2016. *Slavery in the Circuit of Sugar: Martinique and the World-Economy, 1830–1848*. Albany: State University of New York Press.

Watts, Sydney. 2006. *Meat Matters: Butchers, Politics, and Market Culture in Eighteenth-Century Paris*. Rochester, NY: University of Rochester Press.

White, Hugh G. E., trans. 1919. "Mosella." In *Ausonius*, 1: 231–63. Cambridge, MA: Harvard University Press.

Wilkins, John, F., D. Harvey, and Mike Dobson. 2003. *Food in Antiquity*. Exeter: University of Exeter Press.

CHAPTER THREE

Appetizers and Side Dishes

Before the standard organization of the French meal into a series of courses that included an *entrée*, main course, cheese, and dessert course took hold in the nineteenth century, the form of a meal depended very much on the economic status of the diner. Rural peasants and the urban poor ate a single dish of soup or vegetable stew accompanied by bread, but middle-class and wealthy households in the age of banquet cuisine from the fourteenth through the eighteenth centuries indulged in multiple courses. Individually plated courses are a modern invention; they were not adopted widely until the nineteenth century. Before the change to single plates, the French style of service—appropriately named *service à la française*—organized banquet service into courses, but all of the dishes for each course arrived at the table at once. A dinner for 12 people might offer two soups, four kinds of roasted meat, and six side dishes after the roast course. Each course consisted of only one kind of food: at the roast course, only roasted meat was served, but the service might include poultry, beef, veal, and game. Diners selected freely from the platters near them. For the wealthy, side dishes belonged to their own course called the *entremets*, or "between courses," since meat or fish was always considered the most important part of the meal. Lighter dishes called *entrées* arrived before and after the meat, and fruit or preserves often closed the meal, but side dishes before the nineteenth century were not served on the side of anything. They belonged to their own category.

Entremets (Dishes on the Side)

As a general category, the *entremets* (in-betweens) could consist of almost anything, sweet or savory, hot or cold, simple or elaborate. For elite tables, the side dishes represented a show of wealth by the host of the banquet and the talent of the chef to present an amazing variety of small dishes.

The *entremets* marked the interval between the opening course of soup to the main course of meat. The ingredients and preparation for these side dishes varied according to the status of the household and the event as well as to the number of guests served at each service. *Entremets* could be as simple as a dish of flavored cream or boiled grains and as complex as a swan baked in pastry and decorated with feathers to resemble a live swan, probably more decorative than edible. A festive banquet at a wealthy home might offer 9 or 10 kinds of *entremets*, but a middle-class menu only one or two. In the fourteenth-century bourgeois cookbook *Le Ménagier de Paris* (around 1393), the list of *entremets* included cooked snails, cold jellied fish, a sort of rice pudding called *riz engoulé*, and stuffed chickens. At the Renaissance court of Henri II and Henri III, under the influence of Italian-born Cathérine de Médicis (wife of Henri II and mother of Henri III), imported fresh vegetables like asparagus and artichokes became fashionable side dishes. These prized commodities arrived at the table in separate serving platters, simply cooked with oil and salt rather than simmered in a stew as had been the custom in the Middle Ages. Courses that preceded the roast meat course were not yet labeled *entrées* (French for "openings") as they would be later, but generally consisted of "lighter" meats like poultry or fish, savory pastries, or vegetable stews.

François La Varenne included a menagerie of possibilities for *entremets* in his cookbook *Le cuisinier français* (1651). Many of them contained meat, but La Varenne offered vegetable and egg dishes as well. Antoine Furetière's *Dictionnaire universel* (1690) specified that an *entremets* was a *ragoût* (meat in sauce), and La Varenne accordingly offered 10 different *ragoûts*, including a *ragoût* of truffles. Since the *entremets* course was meant to demonstrate creativity and variety, La Varenne also included two pâtés, seven meat jellies made with gelatin from animal bones, four kinds of fritters, four ways to prepare foie gras (fatty goose liver), six egg dishes, and six kinds of vegetables: among them, cauliflower, artichokes, asparagus, and mushrooms. The French have enjoyed foie gras, a particularly French specialty, for nearly 400 years. Only two uncooked salads made the list: one of sliced lemons with sugar and one with pomegranate. The chef L.S.R. (Le sieur Robert) in his 1674 cookbook *L'art de bien traiter* (The art of good cooking), reprinted in 1693, criticized La Varenne for his hodgepodge of dishes that mixed meats and spices in a way that L.S.R. found outdated. His streamlined menus placed sauced dishes in the *entrée* category and made *entremets* simpler: slices of ham, cooked mushrooms or asparagus, a savory jelly, a few select *ragoûts*, and veal or poultry stews. Dishes in the meat course had small garnishes of root vegetables or roasted oranges but nothing as substantial as a true side dish.

Appetizers and Side Dishes

Entrées (First Courses)

In French an *entrée* is a first course, not a main dish, as in English. First-course *entrées* in French cuisine are often a dish of meat in sauce, as they were in the seventeenth century when the term began to be used in cookbooks. As sauced or "made dishes," the *entrées* stood out from the roast course of boiled or roasted meats, but in this period there was not much differentiation between *entremets* and *entrées* except for their place in the meal (before or after the roast course). In addition to his list of *entremets* in *ragoût*, for *entrées* La Varenne suggested duck, pigeon, and lamb in *ragoût*, as well as beef and pork tongue and nearly every other meat available, in *ragoût*. For each *ragoût*, the cook sautéed meat, simmered it in bouillon with salt and spices, and occasionally garnished it with truffles or root vegetables. The *entrées* in L.S.R.'s cookbook usually include meat or fish on lean days; he supplied recipes for veal, lamb, and chicken in *ragoût* as well as large pies filled with whole birds and marinated veal liver or lamb tongue, sliced and fried. Cookbooks from the seventeenth century show that cooks had begun to move vegetables out of the opening course of the meal and into the *entremets* or side dishes, and fresh vegetables were more in demand at court. Louis XIV and his courtiers at Versailles adored fresh green peas and clamored for them as soon as their season arrived, in the spring. Cooked mushrooms, with and without sauce, appear in every list of *entremets* in seventeenth-century cookbooks. By the eighteenth century, the list of cooked vegetables for *entremets* had expanded to include numerous preparations for artichokes, peas, beans, and haricots verts (slender green beans).

Printed cookbooks generally represent only elite dining with the budget to match. Middle-class households likely adapted these menus to their own capacities, reducing the number of *entrées* or *entremets* served or substituting more affordable ingredients. Instead of expensive poultry, they might use pork, beef, or mutton for the *ragoûts*, or use root vegetables or cabbage in place of asparagus and peas. During Lent or on lean days imposed by the Catholic Church, chefs made meat-heavy menus vegetarian by substituting cooked vegetables for meat and olive oil for butter. The concept of a light dish to open up appetites for the larger courses to come began to take shape in the eighteenth century. These kinds of dishes were called *relevés* ("raised up"), meant to lift up the appetite before or after a main course or the roast course. The French term *hors d'oeuvre* (literally "outside the work") began to apply to food in the late seventeenth century, but it did not at first mean a small bite served before the meal as it does now. Instead, *hors d'oeuvres* were secondary dishes presented at different points of the meal. By the eighteenth century *hors d'oeuvres* occupied the place between the first course of soup and the second course of *entrées*, consisting of fairly substantial but small dishes such as pâté, veal in butter sauce, or fish in cream sauce (Marin 1739). In the nineteenth century, at least in middle-class cuisine, "hors d'oeuvres" became finger food, such as raw radishes with butter, olives, or the recognizably French cornichons (tiny sour pickles). More important meals might offer an hors d'oeuvre of sardines, anchovies, or raw oysters.

Early French cookbooks and classic French cooking place a similar emphasis on using all parts of the animal. Offal (comprising less-desired cuts of meat, including organ meats) appears on menus as a first course even today in traditional restaurants. Early cookbooks suggest foie gras and veal liver as well as kidneys and sweetbreads (thymus gland, usually of veal) and even pigs' tails in sauce. Current menus, just like those from the seventeenth and eighteenth centuries, include frog legs and snails, and less often pigs' feet and beef tongue. *Boudin noir*, or blood sausage, is traditionally prepared using blood saved from the slaughter of a pig, in an effort to avoid waste. Recipes for blood sausage have been in print since the Middle Ages, and many European countries enjoy different versions of these sausages. Blood sausages contain relatively little meat but are a mixture of pork fat, pig's blood, onions and other seasonings, and sometimes thickeners such as grain or bread crumbs. In the French Caribbean, boudin sausages flavored with hot pepper and Creole spices are a traditional snack with a before-dinner drink. Slices of *boudin blanc* can be served cold or hot on their own as a first course or might be baked in pastry or sautéed with apples. Made without blood, *boudin blanc* (white sausage) from the Champagne region uses pork or chicken combined with milk for a pale color and subtle flavor. Another specialty of Champagne, andouillette sausages are not for the squeamish: they consist of pork

---

Rooster's Crest

One ingredient that has disappeared from menus is cockscomb, or rooster's crest, part of numerous *ragoûts* and small dishes through the nineteenth century. La Varenne gave only one recipe for cockscombs, but Menon, in the 1755 *Soupers de la cour* (Court suppers) included ten. Celebrated chef Marie-Antoine Carême, in the nineteenth century, used cockscombs to decorate finished dishes such as aspics (meat juices in gelatin). It would be very surprising to see rooster's crests on a menu today, even though the rooster is a symbol of French pride.

Appetizers and Side Dishes

stomach and intestines stuffed into a casing made from pork intestines. Nevertheless, they remain an acclaimed delicacy in France.

Eggs are commonly served as a first course in France; popular dishes include hard-boiled eggs with mayonnaise or eggs poached in red wine. In the seventeenth and eighteenth centuries, omelets were considered a first course or *entremets*, filled with sugar, cream, or even oysters but rarely with cheese. Omelets have since moved into main dish territory, usually served for a light dinner. In La Varenne's cookbook of 1651, the list of first-course egg dishes are still recognizable even if they no longer belong to the appetizer category today: fried eggs sunny side up (*oeufs miroir*), eggs fried in brown butter, poached eggs with a brown sauce or sorrel sauce, and scrambled eggs with a sprinkle of nutmeg. In the eighteenth century, eggs remained part of the *entremets* or *entrée* course. François Marin, in the 1739 household manual *Dons de Comus*, praised eggs for their versatility and noted that they were an ingredient shared by the poor and the rich, by sick as well as healthy people. His astonishing list of more than 100 ways to prepare eggs included the familiar (fried, scrambled, poached) and the unusual (with oranges, pistachios, cucumbers, or caramel, among others). Omelets merited their own list of 31 options, filled with truffles, herbs or spinach, peas, coffee, ham, asparagus, or oysters. Eggs also appeared in menus across the year since they were permitted on lean days, when the church did not allow the faithful to eat meat.

Vegetables

In the eighteenth century, aside from eggs, *entrées* or first courses for elite tables continued to be meat in sauce. By the nineteenth century, French cuisine had begun to develop bourgeois (middle-class) cooking as a separate category, as more middle-class households could afford to eat like the wealthy or at least imitate some of their practices. New cookbooks addressing bourgeois tables adapted fine-dining recipes with fewer ingredients, and they simplified preparations as well as cut down the number of courses in a meal. But the distinction between *entrée* and main course (or roast) remained. When the system of *service à la russe* (individual plates served to each guest) took over in the mid-nineteenth century, side dishes began to accompany the main dish of usually meat or fish. Side dishes consisted of cooked asparagus, peas, beans in sauce, lentils, or potatoes, after the French at last accepted this vegetable as a worthy ingredient.

Lentils from the town of Le Puy in south-central France have a reputation for high quality and flavor. Cooked with carrots and herbs, they make an earthy side dish for sausages or roast duck. Lentils simmered in liquid or served as a purée appeared in cookbooks as early as the seventeenth century and are still a popular winter dish today. Stuffed tomatoes also counted as a first course in the nineteenth century as they do today, after the tomato earned its place in the cuisine of the Old World, having first been condemned as poisonous and then simply rejected as unfamiliar. Other particularly French vegetables from this period that remain popular in the present day include celeriac (a white root vegetable, usually puréed) and braised Belgian endive. The French have a particular fondness for white asparagus, a harbinger of spring, grown in sandy soil in Gascony in southwest France. White asparagus grows entirely underground, and farmers take great care to keep plants covered with soil so that no green color will develop. Prized white asparagus spears come to the table steamed or sautéed with a lemony hollandaise sauce or a bracing vinaigrette.

Antoine Parmentier introduced potatoes to the French in the eighteenth century, but potato dishes did not become commonplace on French tables for nearly a century. Finally, in the nineteenth century, an explosion of potato side dishes with evocative names began to appear on menus. Mashed potatoes alone are *purée*; whipped with cream and lots of cheese until they are like a fondue, they are called *aligot*, a specialty of the mountainous center region of France called the Massif Central; thickened with egg whites and piped into a rosette they become Duchesse potatoes. Scalloped potatoes baked with butter and cream are known as *gratin dauphinois*, and when made with chicken broth and herbs they are potatoes *boulangères* (in the style of the baker's wife).

Sliced potatoes layered in a circle and cooked in plenty of butter are named Anna potatoes, and of course fried potato sticks are called French fries in English and *frites* in France. There are names for different shapes and sizes of *frites* from *pont Neuf* (thicker) to *allumette* (matchstick), and *frites* are most often served with steak, steamed mussels, or roast chicken. Rice and pasta are far less popular as side starches in French cuisine, where the potato dominates.

In the Antilles, yams and sweet potatoes are common as side dishes since these starchy vegetables grow abundantly there. In Guadeloupe and Martinique, cooked cassava and plantains accompany stews and roasted meats, as do salads of marinated vegetables such as hearts of palm and avocado. Yams and gourds (similar to pumpkins) are cooked and puréed, and other vegetables like plantains and chayote (*christophine* in Antillean French) are prepared as gratins, baked and browned in the oven with milk or cheese. Similar to a small squash, chayote, a vegetable native to the Antilles, is also served in salads, steamed, or puréed.

Appetizers and Side Dishes

> ## Pommes Boulangères (Scalloped Potatoes with Chicken Broth)
>
> *Yield:* Serves 4
>
> *Ingredients*
> 4 large russet potatoes or 6 medium white potatoes
> 1 Tbsp olive oil
> 2 medium onions, halved and thinly sliced
> 4 cloves garlic, sliced
> 3 cups chicken broth
> 2 bay leaves
> ½ tsp dried thyme
> ½ tsp dried rosemary
> Salt, pepper
>
> 1. Heat the oven to 400 degrees. Peel the potatoes and cut into thin slices with a knife or mandolin, or using a food processor. Layer the potatoes in a large baking dish in an even layer.
> 2. Heat olive oil in a large frying pan over medium heat. Cook the onions until soft, about 5 minutes. Add garlic and cook just until fragrant, about 30 seconds. Add the broth, bay leaves, thyme, rosemary, and salt and pepper to taste. Bring to a boil.
> 3. Pour broth mixture over the potatoes and stir gently with a fork to incorporate the onions and herbs with the sliced potatoes.
> 4. Bake until the potatoes are tender (check with the point of a knife) and browned on top, about 60–70 minutes. Remove bay leaves, and serve hot or at room temperature.
>
> Adapted from Jacques Pépin, *Simple and Healthy Cooking* (Emmaus: PA: Rodale Press, 1994), 262.

One of the most well-known vegetable side dishes in France is ratatouille, another modern creation that depends on New World vegetables. The dish of cooked eggplant, zucchini, tomatoes, and peppers with herbs and plenty of olive oil originated in Provence in southern France, with its Italian-inflected cooking. Eggplants and tomatoes were unknown in France until the seventeenth century, and even then, most people considered them ornamental plants since they believed that the fruits of these plants were poisonous. Only in the nineteenth century did the French adopt the custom of eating these vegetables, and the modern recipe for ratatouille dates only to the 1950s. In France, *ratatouille* must be seasoned with an herb mixture called *herbes de Provence*, generally consisting of a blend of oregano, basil, marjoram, thyme, rosemary, and sometimes lavender and named for the region where these herbs are commonly used in cooking. As a side dish, ratatouille can accompany roasted meats, or it can be served on its own as a first course, hot or cold. Many traditional cooks believe that the best ratatouille requires each vegetable to be cooked separately and combined just before serving.

Fish and Shellfish

Oysters symbolized wealth for urbanites in the nineteenth century, as high-ranking members of society consumed them by the dozens at Parisian restaurants. On the coasts, oysters were far more common than inland, but diners still appreciated them fresh from the shell with a little lemon or with an acidic sauce like the classic *ravigote* of vinegar, olive oil, and fresh herbs. Beginning in the seventeenth century, French cultivators established oyster farms along the Atlantic coast for the native Belon, or flat, oyster. A few recipes for cooked oyster dishes, such as oyster stews or stuffed oysters, appeared in seventeenth-century cookbooks such as François Massialot's *Le Cuisinier Royal et Bourgeois* (1691), and Vincent La Chapelle advised cooks to buy oysters only in months containing the letter *R*, a well-known saying even today (La Chapelle 1742, 282). Overfishing in the eighteenth and nineteenth centuries devastated the native French oyster population, and for a time the government instituted a ban on oyster fishing. A Portuguese oyster species replaced the Belon oyster for cultivated shellfish farming, arriving by accident when a ship carrying a load of Portuguese oysters emptied its cargo in a storm (France Nassain n.d.). The Portuguese oysters began to spawn in French waters, but both the Belon and Portuguese species nearly disappeared in the 1970s due to disease, replaced by the Japanese cupped oyster that is the most dominant cultivated oyster species today. Farmers in Brittany have returned the Belon oyster to French waters in limited numbers, and oyster farmers on the Atlantic and Mediterranean coasts cultivate species particular to their regions.

Fish dishes often occupy the first course in French meals as a light introduction to a heavier main course. In the French territories of the Antilles, salt cod fritters have a place in nearly every island cuisine and vary slightly according to name and ingredients. Called *marinades* in Guyana and Martinique, *accras* (or *akras*) *de morue* originated in African cuisine.

Appetizers and Side Dishes

Accras de Morue (Salt-Cod Fritters)

Yield: Serves 6

Ingredients
¾–1 pound of salt cod fillets
1 small onion
1 large clove garlic
½ cup fresh parsley
1 jalapeño pepper, ribs and seeds removed (optional)
Salt, pepper
2 cups all-purpose flour
¾ cup water
1 ½ tsp baking soda
Juice from 1 lime
2 cups vegetable oil for frying

1. The day before you want to make *accras*, soak the salt cod in cold water overnight in a shallow bowl. Change the water 2–3 times.
2. Rinse the salt cod and place it in a deep frying pan with water to cover. Bring the water to a boil, lower heat and cook at a gentle simmer for 10 minutes. Drain the water, let the fish cool to room temperature, and remove all bones and skin. Break the cod into small pieces with your hands or a fork.
3. Mince the onion, garlic, parsley, and jalapeño (if using). Mix these together, and then add them to the cod in a large bowl. Stir gently. Salt and pepper to taste.
4. In a plate or shallow bowl, make a mound of flour with an indentation in the center. Add half of the water slowly and stir together. Slowly add the rest of the water until it resembles thick cream. If it is too thick, add more water. If too thin, add more flour. Stir the flour/water mixture into the cod mixture.
5. Sprinkle baking soda over the cod mixture and then pour half of the lime juice on the cod. The acid mixed with the baking soda will foam and make bubbles that will make the *accras* light and fluffy. If some baking soda remains, add more lime juice. Fold the bubbles into the batter carefully so as not to deflate them.
6. In a deep frying pan or Dutch oven, heat the oil over medium heat. Use two spoons (dip them in water first so the *accra* batter does not stick) to form a 1-inch ball and test the heat of the oil. If the *accra* browns, the temperature is correct. If it burns, turn down the heat, and if it does not brown, turn up the heat. Watch carefully as hot oil can splatter and

burn you. Form the remaining batter into *accras* (1-inch balls) using wet spoons and add them to the oil, 6–8 at a time. When the *accras* are brown on one side, turn them carefully with a wooden spoon or tongs, to cook the other side. Fry the *accras* in batches, taking care not to crowd the pan.
7. Drain the *accras* on paper towels, sprinkle with salt, and serve hot.

Adapted from Prisca Morjon, "Les vrais accras de morue," *Ma Cuisine Créole*, March 29, 2018. https://www.macuisinecreole.fr/single-post/2018/03/29/Les-vrais-accras-de-morue.

Although the island nations of the French Caribbean had (and continue to have) abundant fresh fish, much of the fresh fish was exported, and the residents of the islands consumed dried fish because it lasted longer. Enslaved peoples living in these areas brought their culinary traditions from Africa but had limited access to ingredients like fresh fish unless they were able to catch it themselves. Cod fritters contain salt cod rinsed and reconstituted with water, flour, and spices and then fried in oil until crisp. Salt cod and potatoes are the main ingredients in a well-known first

Brandade de Morue (Salt Cod and Potato Purée)

Yield: Serves 6

Ingredients
1 pound salt cod fillets
1 bay leaf
1 small onion studded with 2 cloves
2 large potatoes
1 ½ cups milk, warmed
6 cloves of garlic, peeled and sliced
Black pepper
¾ cup olive oil, plus extra for greasing the pan and drizzling over finished dish
2 Tbsp fresh parsley

1. Rinse the salt from the cod fillets and place in a bowl of fresh water. Refrigerate overnight, changing the water 2 or 3 times. Rinse again and

Appetizers and Side Dishes

place the fish in a deep pan with water to cover. Add the bay leaf and onion and bring to a simmer. Cook gently for 10 minutes, and then drain and rinse. Discard the bay leaf and onion and remove all bones and skin from the fish. Break up the fish with your fingers and return it to the pan.
2. Peel the potatoes, cut them into 1-inch chunks, and place in a saucepan with water to cover. Bring to a boil and cook until potatoes are very tender, about 30 minutes. Drain.
3. Add the milk and garlic to the reserved fish and bring to a boil. Turn the heat to low, cover, and simmer for 10 minutes, maintaining a gentle simmer. Remove from heat and let cool for 5 minutes. Heat the oven to 400 degrees.
4. Place the cod/milk mixture and the potatoes in a food processor and process for one minute until smooth and well-combined. Add a pinch of black pepper and pulse for 10 seconds. With the processor running, add the olive oil slowly to the fish and process until smooth.
5. Grease a baking dish with a small amount of oil and spread the cod mixture into the dish in an even layer. Bake until hot and lightly browned on top, about 15 minutes. Chop the parsley and sprinkle it on top of the brandade, along with a drizzle of olive oil.

Serve as a first course on its own or with toasted baguette slices as an hors d'oeuvre.

course, in France and in the Caribbean territories, called *brandade de morue*, using cod preserved in salt that will not spoil. More modern Caribbean cooking uses fresh fish, crabs, and other seafood.

Near the Atlantic coast of France, seafood dishes like *coquilles Saint-Jacques* (scallops in a cream sauce served on a scallop shell) and steamed mussels in white wine sauce are common in restaurants, and on the Mediterranean coast, diners enjoy marinated sardines and anchovies. Frogs belong to the fish category as well, and frog legs have been part of the French culinary tradition as an *entremets* since the Middle Ages, although the classic preparation of frog legs cooked in garlic and parsley likely dates to the nineteenth century. As a first course in a bistro or brasserie (a casual restaurant with brewery), frog legs or escargot (snails) are a popular choice. In Lyon, the regional specialty *quenelles de brochet* (pike dumplings) belong to the hearty cuisine of this gastronomic city. Made from puréed white fish and egg whites, they are served covered in lobster sauce and browned in the oven.

Savory Pastries and Pâtés

Savory pastries that contained small birds or other meats appeared frequently as a first course from the Middle Ages to the nineteenth century. Fritters made of vegetables encased in fried dough (called beignets) were also featured regularly on early menus. When Carême revolutionized pastry with his 1833 cookbook, he modernized the first course as well with a French invention called vol-au-vent (literally, "flying in the wind"), a pastry shell filled with creamed mushrooms and chicken. The light-as-air pastry gave a new form to Carême's *entrée*, but the filling reproduced the creamed mushroom and vegetable *entremets* that had been served at wealthy French tables for nearly two centuries. As French cuisine was modernized with the advent of more reliable ovens, new pastries entered the appetizer space, such as *gougères*, cheese puffs made of choux (cream puff) dough associated with the Burgundian cuisine of southwest France.

Influenced by Indian immigrants to the islands, Caribbean-French cuisine includes *samoussas* (samosas), fried triangular pastries served warm as a first course or snack with tea or rum punch. In Réunion, a French overseas department, *samoussas* filled with vegetables, fish, or ground meat are seasoned with warm spices like cumin, ginger, and turmeric. The filling is encased in fine pastry similar to phyllo dough and fried until crisp. The same pastry, called "brick," in French originated in North Africa and is used for a number of warm savory pastries. Called *bourek* in Arabic, the thin flaky pastry is made by mixing wheat flour, salt, and water into a very thin, liquid batter and spreading this batter with a brush onto a hot grill. The delicate sheets of pastry are filled with tuna, ground meat, or vegetables. In Morocco and Algeria, brick pastries are often served as an *entrée*, but sweet fillings in brick pastry make fine desserts.

In the original sense, starting in the Middle Ages, a *pâté* was a baked pie of pastry filled with minced, cooked meat, and the term retained that meaning until the nineteenth century. During the fourteenth century, a new preparation called *pâté en pot* appeared; it was minced meat cooked without a crust in an earthenware pot. Over time the earthenware pot came to be called a terrine, and *pâté en terrine* or simply terrine referred to this preparation. *Pâtés* were served hot, and terrines were served cold. In the nineteenth century, terrines of cooked meat (a sort of cold meatloaf) and *pâtés* with pastry crusts served as first courses. They were made from pork, poultry, or hare on modest tables and goose liver with truffles or duck on wealthier ones.

Appetizers and Side Dishes

Gougères (Cheese Puffs)

Yield: Serves 6 (approximately 24 puffs)

Ingredients
1 cup water
6 Tbsp butter
1 tsp salt
Pinch cayenne pepper
1 ¼ cups all-purpose flour
4 large eggs
1 ½ to 2 cups Gruyère cheese, shredded

1. Preheat oven to 375 degrees. Line baking sheets with parchment paper.
2. In a heavy pot, bring water to a boil. Add butter, salt, and the pinch of cayenne pepper. When butter has melted, lower heat and add flour all at once. Stir constantly until incorporated into a ball.
3. Remove from heat for a few minutes, then add 1 egg to the dough and stir vigorously until absorbed. Repeat with three more eggs, stirring thoroughly after each egg until the liquid is absorbed. After the last egg, stir until dough is smooth and shiny.
4. Stir in shredded cheese (Gruyère is traditional; substitute Cheddar if you like) until incorporated into the dough. Use spoons to portion dough into 1-tablespoon rounds on baking sheet, spaced 1 inch apart. Smooth tops of dough with a wet spoon, if desired.
5. Bake 20 minutes until gougères are golden brown and dry on top. Leave in oven with heat turned off for 5 minutes. Serve immediately.

In the present day, the *pâté en croûte* (pâté wrapped in pastry) still conforms to the early meaning of *pâté*, joined by different kinds of cooked meat confections offered as hors d'oeuvres or first courses. Rillettes made from pork, duck, goose, or rabbit, a sort of coarse spread from pounded cooked meat, can be found in the central regions of France. A soft mousse of duck or goose liver or pork meat or occasionally cooked fish, shaped in a mold and sometimes called a gâteau (cake), makes an elegant first course. Many cold meat pâtés and terrines are garnished with jellied aspic, a shiny meat gelatin that adds sheen and flavor. More simply, a French meal might begin with a slice or two of cooked or smoked ham served on its own or with a slice of melon.

Soups

Soup often serves as a first course for a French meal in the present day, particularly in the colder months. With a long history, soups moved from a main dish (or the only dish) to a first course when the cost of living in France permitted rural populations to access better food and better jobs. Soup as a first course remains a tradition in France, although the tradition changed as more of France became urbanized in the twentieth century. In the eighteenth century, residents in the region of Auvergne, in central France, ate soup every day, sometimes three times per day, and rural residents in the Burgundy region in 1964 ate soup made of vegetables and bread three meals a day. In 1970 a study showed that for lunch, only 4 percent of city residents ate soup as a first course compared to 76 percent of rural farm families. For the evening meal, 80–90 percent of French families ate soup followed by lighter dishes of eggs, cheese, or *tartines* (toast with toppings), whether they lived in rural or urban areas (Claudian and Serville 1970, 180). The turn away from soup at lunch is a hallmark of urban life in France, as city residents take less time for lunch and view soup as too old-fashioned.

For the wealthy, prior to the twentieth century, soup or potage nearly always started the meal, followed by hors d'oeuvres, *entremets*, and *entrées*. Most cookbooks before the nineteenth century began with lengthy chapters on soups (potages). La Varenne in 1651 listed 49 different potages to start the meal on a day when meat was allowed, including a *potage de santé* or "health soup," which contained capon broth and herbs but no vegetables. Nicolas de Bonnefons, in his 1654 manual *Délices de la campagne* (Country delights) suggested that a proper *potage de santé* made from good broth would keep a bourgeois family healthy; if made of cabbage, it should "taste entirely like cabbage" without frivolous additions like chopped meat or breadcrumbs (Bonnefons 1654, 215–16). On church-imposed lean days and during Lent, potage made from meat broth was sometimes replaced by a soup made of almonds.

In the nineteenth century, Carême defended and elevated the soup course in his 1833 cookbook *L'art de la cuisine française* (The art of French cooking), intended for elite tables. His section on soups included five "health soups" and numerous other refined soups, some called *à la royale* or *à la princesse* or named after historical figures who glorified France, in Carême's opinion. These soups featured elegant ingredients to define them as fine cuisine, such as new green peas and asparagus tips. Among the dozens of soups in Carême's cookbook, there were simple cream soups and extravagant preparations like the *potage de profiteroles* featuring pastry

Appetizers and Side Dishes

Soup

Soups, particularly for the middle and lower classes, were very often thickened with bread or bread crusts and sometimes consisted only of water and hard bread. This practice efficiently used up bread, so that nothing was wasted, and provided a hearty meal for those with little money. In French, the term *soupe* refers to a broth thickened with bread, while *potage* comes from the word *potager*, for "vegetable garden," and is therefore made with vegetables. Soup is so closely tied with bread in France that *soupe* in texts prior to the eighteenth century sometimes meant bread. Bread manuals by Antoine Parmentier (1778) and Paul Malouin (1779) gave instructions for *pain à soupe* (soup bread), a loaf with a thick crust good for soaking in broth or water, if it were the only liquid available. Jules Gouffé in 1856 began the soup section in his cookbook with a recipe for Bread Soup, showing that the tradition had not been lost.

puffs with a savory filling. Turtle soup was a delicacy among the wealthy, and an acquired taste, but Carême recognized its importance by including five variations on "French turtle soup" and a recipe for English and American turtle soup for good measure. In another book, Carême expressed his unwavering opinion about the importance of soup as a first course for practical and aesthetic reasons, declaring that a fine soup prepared with skill brings joy to diners and allows them to admire the elegance of the table setting "at the same time that it prepares the active stomach for copious ingestions" (Carême 1833, I.40–41).

Gouffé, in his bourgeois cookbook, proposed more down-to-earth soups, like hearty cabbage soup and soup made from bread boiled in broth to the consistency of porridge. He also distinguished soup (thickened with bread) from potage (with vegetables). Simple, satisfying potages of onion or leeks resemble their modern counterparts, especially the traditional and homey French potato-leek soup.

The terms of French cuisine are important for the soup course: soups are thickened with bread or other starches, and potages have more broth and vegetables. On more elegant tables, a clear soup called a consommé might begin the meal. Perfect consommé, made from meat and vegetables, must be absolutely clear. Before serving, chefs skim the fat, strain out the cooked ingredients, and clarify the broth by using a "raft" of egg whites to trap all remaining fat and impurities so that only clear, shimmering, highly concentrated liquid remains. Because it contains so much collagen from

> ### Potage Poireaux-Pommes de Terre (Potato-Leek Soup)
>
> *Yield:* Serves 4
>
> *Ingredients*
> 3 leeks
> 2 medium Yukon Gold or other potatoes
> 2 Tbsp butter
> 8 cups water
> 2 tsp salt
> ¼ tsp black pepper
> Sour cream or plain yogurt for serving
>
> 1. Clean dirt and grit from leeks, separating leaves at the bottom of the stalk under running water. Trim the leeks, leaving the white part and first inch of the green part; slice thinly. Cut two medium Yukon Gold potatoes into thin slices.
> 2. Heat butter in a large, heavy pan and melt over medium heat. Add leeks and potatoes and cook until leeks are transparent but not browned, about 5–8 minutes.
> 3. Add water, salt, and pepper. Bring to a boil, and then lower heat and cover. Simmer until potatoes are tender, about 20 minutes.
> 4. Cool slightly, then process soup in a blender until smooth, filling the blender only halfway each time. Pour blended soup into a serving bowl and serve. Drizzle sour cream or plain yogurt over each serving if desired.

meat, consommé must be served very hot, because it will gel as it cools. Also belonging to fine cuisine is a creamy soup called a velouté, made from cauliflower or other puréed vegetables with a base of flour and butter and thickened with cream and egg yolks; a bisque is a creamy soup made from seafood such as lobster or crayfish.

Salads

La Varenne in 1651 gave recipes for only two raw fruit salads in his cookbook and mentioned a cooked salad of curly endive or lettuce. Lettuces and greens in the seventeenth century were often cooked and served warm or cold, to alleviate the perceived danger of raw greens. According to the medical beliefs of the early modern period, raw greens were "cold" and

Appetizers and Side Dishes

could bring an imbalance to the body unless they were balanced with "hot" foods like salt and oil. Vinegar was also considered "cold," but it added flavor. Olivier de Serres, in an agricultural guide for wealthy landowners that was published in 1600, gave instructions for growing vegetables and provided a few recipes. His writing adhered to medicinal dietary guidelines for greens but also considered flavor: to serve fennel, for example, he advised hosts to put salt and oil in separate pitchers so that guests could season to taste but also so that the seasonings countered the "cold" greens (Serres 1600, 8:846). Serres also suggested that thrifty gardeners preserve fennel in vinegar to eat *en salade* all year.

Raw or cooked, a green salad in the seventeenth century might include other vegetables and decorations, like cooked beets and edible flowers. In the late seventeenth century, L.S.R. added many more cold vegetable preparations to his cookbook, including a spring herb salad and a baby lettuce salad, as well as cucumbers, beets, and olives. L.S.R. confirmed that vinegar was essential for salads. He instructed his readers to use the best olive oil and a selection of flavored vinegars (raspberry, rose, carnation, and tarragon) for salads and cold vegetables (L.S.R. 1693, 49). Three ingredients—oil, salt, and vinegar—constitute the basic vinaigrette dressing we know today, with the addition of a little mustard for binding. The French most often dress lettuce salads with some form of vinaigrette flavored with fresh herbs or shallots, in contrast to British and American diners, who have a wide selection of salad dressings from oil and vinegar to creamy blue cheese.

The French eat salad after the meat course and before dessert, a tradition that has a long history. When the medical theory of dietetics (balancing the qualities of foods classified as "cold" or "hot" and "moist" or "dry") took precedence over flavor in selecting foods until the seventeenth century, cooks and diners positioned greens and "cold" fruits like melons at the beginning of a meal to give the stomach time to digest them, or paired them with "hotter" foods like meat. But the Parisian elite adopted a new practice in the seventeenth century, serving lettuce salads with the roast course as a refreshing counterpoint, and the practice took hold. In a cookbook on garnishes and salads from 1698, François Massialot offered recipes that reflected the custom of the time of dressing green salads with sugar. In a list of seasonal salads, Massialot classified curly endive "served with sugar" as a winter option; for spring, lamb's lettuce garnished with anchovies, sliced lemons, or violets when the flowers were in bloom; and a long list of lettuces for summer and fall.

Green salad is never a first course in France but always comes after the main course, with the exception of a frisée (curly endive) salad with warmed goat cheese, a favorite of the central and western regions of France where goat cheese is produced. Salads of cooked vegetables and cold meats, on the other hand, are welcome as a first course. The *salade niçoise* named after the coastal city of Nice, its birthplace, consists of tuna, olives, green peppers, anchovies, hard-boiled eggs, and tomatoes but no lettuce. It is generally served as a *salade composée* in which each ingredient is placed separately on the plate rather than tossed together. Niçoise cuisine features products from the South of France such as olives, olive oil, and anchovies, the latter given Nice's proximity to the ocean.

For most cookbooks in the seventeenth and eighteenth centuries, "salad" meant cooked vegetables served cold, usually with a vinegar-based or cream sauce. Cucumbers, green beans, beets, carrots, and cauliflower were the most prominent salad components. Marin in *Dons de Comus* suggested stuffed cabbage and lettuce, fried before serving, stuffed cucumbers, and stewed carrots and turnips, although he also proposed simple salads of curly endive or lettuce to accompany the roast course. For rural families, vegetables like cabbage, squash, and turnips grown in their own gardens and cooked with a little salt pork became the soup or stew that simmered all day and served as lunch and dinner. With herbs, asparagus,

---

Salade aux Pois Chiches (Chickpea Salad)

Yield: Serves 4

Ingredients
2 small shallots, peeled
3 Tbsp olive oil
¼ tsp salt
2 tsp Dijon mustard
1 Tbsp vinegar or lemon juice
2 cans (15 oz. each) chickpeas, drained and rinsed
½ cup fresh parsley, chopped

1. Thinly slice shallots.
2. In a large bowl mix together olive oil, salt, Dijon mustard, and vinegar or lemon juice. Whisk together until emulsified.
3. Add the shallots, chickpeas, and chopped fresh parsley. Stir until the chickpeas are coated with the dressing, and then refrigerate for at least one hour. Stir before serving.

and watercress gathered from the forest lands, they were able to add seasonal variety to their otherwise monotonous meals, and seasonality is still valued by the French. Prized and elegant on royal tables, asparagus and watercress were foraged foods for the rural peasants, free for the taking and cooked with no fanfare. The same vegetables had very different meanings depending on the economic status of the dining table.

In the present day, side dishes and first courses in France still depend on context. At a high-end, Michelin-starred restaurant, a meal might begin with an *entrée* of foie gras; at a brasserie it might be snails with garlic and butter; and at home a family might prepare a vegetable salad or a plate of charcuterie (cold meats like salami and ham). Side dishes could be delicate white asparagus in a restaurant, braised endive in a local bistro, or a gratin of potatoes at a family meal. As with much of French cuisine, first courses and side dishes must follow certain rules. The first course should complement but not reproduce the main dish; at a restaurant, for example, fish before fish is frowned upon. A diner who chooses an *entrée* of fish quenelles (dumplings) followed by a filet of sole would be encouraged to select again. Seasonality remains important to the French table as well. In spring, peas and artichokes fill the open markets and appear on menus; in fall, French diners would not expect spring peas but would enjoy scallops and Belgian endives in season, celebrating the freshest produce of each growing season rather than expecting asparagus all year. Of course, not every French meal follows the pattern of *entrée*, main dish, side dish, and dessert established hundreds of years ago. For a casual meal, the modern French might choose French fries on the side of their hamburger, or a tomato and mozzarella salad, or an order of Vietnamese fried spring rolls, called *nems* in French, after the Vietnamese term. In 2016 a poll of the French public revealed that their favorite *entrées* included the expected terrine of foie gras and warm goat cheese salad but also the more humble baked eggs (*oeufs cocotte*), the Middle Eastern salad of bulgur and parsley called tabbouleh, and a warm tomato tart. For soups, squash velouté made the list as well as traditional onion soup baked with cheese (Chan 2016). With the ongoing influence of international cuisines and the industrialization of food, French *entrées* and side dishes continue to change, but the classics will remain.

Further Reading

Bonnefons, Nicolas de. 1654. *Délices de la campagne*. Paris: Pierre-des-Hayes.
Carême, Marie-Antoine. 1833. *L'art de la cuisine française au XIXe siècle : traité élémentaire et pratique*, Vol. 1. Paris: Chez l'auteur.

Chan, Kaling. 2016. "Les Entrées Préférées des Français." *Cuisine Actuelle*, February 22, 2016. https://www.cuisineactuelle.fr/dossiers-gourmands/tendance-cuisine/les-entrees-preferees-des-francais-283753.

Child, Julia, Louisette Bertholle, and Simone Beck. 2001. *Mastering the Art of French Cooking*. New York: Alfred A. Knopf.

Claudian, Jean, and Yvonne Serville. 1970. "Aspects de l'évolution récente du comportement alimentaire en France: Composition des repas et 'urbanisation.'" In *Pour une Histoire de l'alimentation*, edited by Jean-Jacques Hémardinquer, 174–87. Paris: Armand Colin.

Flandrin, Jean-Louis, Massimo Montanari, and Albert Sonnenfeld, eds. 2013. *Food: A Culinary History*. New York: Columbia University Press.

France Nassain. n.d. "The History of the Oyster." Accessed July 24, 2020. https://www.francenaissain.com/en/the-oyster/the-oyster-and-its-origins/the-history-of-the-oyster.

Gouffé, Jules. 1867. *Le livre de cuisine*. Paris: Hachette.

La Chapelle, Vincent. 1742. *Le cuisinier moderne*. Paris: V. La Chapelle.

La Varenne, François. 1651. *Le cuisinier français*. Paris: David.

L.S.R. [Le sieur Robert]. (1674) 1693. *L'art de bien traiter*. Lyon: Claude Bachelu.

Marin, François. 1739. *Les Dons de Comus*. Paris: Prault.

Massialot, François. 1691. *Le cuisinier royal et bourgeois*. Paris: Charles de Sercy.

Massialot, François. 1698. *Nouvelle instruction pour les confitures, les liqueurs, et les fruits*. Paris: Charles de Sercy.

Mennell, Stephen. 2006. *All Manners of Food: Eating and Taste in England and France from the Middle Ages to the Present*. Urbana: University of Illinois Press.

Menon, François. 1753. *La cuisinière bourgeoise*. Brussels: Foppens.

Serres, Olivier de. 1600. *Le Théâtre d'Agriculture et Mesnage des champs*. Paris: Métayer.

Toussaint-Samat, Maguelonne. 2009. *A History of Food*. West Sussex, UK: Wiley-Blackwell.

Willan, Anne, and Mark Cherniavsky. 2012. *The Cookbook Library: Four Centuries of the Cooks, Writers, and Recipes That Made the Modern Cookbook*. Berkeley: University of California Press.

CHAPTER FOUR

Main Dishes

In France the main dish or *plat principal* generally means meat. Of course, in the Middle Ages through much of the nineteenth century, only wealthy households could afford the best cuts of meat in any quantity. But the French early on gained a reputation for *ragoûts*, or meat in sauce, as an *entrée*. The concept of "main dish" is complicated in French cuisine by the organization of meals from the Middle Ages to the late eighteenth century into a series of small courses served all at once but normally including several entrées and a "roast" course for large cuts of meat. By the end of the eighteenth century, French meals generally followed a three-course system, with a main dish centered on meat or fish. Historically, French cuisine rarely includes vegetarian options as a main dish, apart from a few egg dishes, and the French generally relegate vegetables to side dishes. Aside from the meaty standards, most regions in France have a traditional main dish soup, and sometimes the main dish at a French meal can be as simple as an omelet or sausages with lentils. Home-cooked meals for a family gathering often involve a grand platter of meat in sauce or an impressive roast, but main dishes even for weekday meals reflect the importance of quality ingredients in French cuisine.

Roasted Meats

In the Middle Ages, before the cookbooks that standardized French cuisine were published (in the seventeenth century), platters of boiled or roasted meats occupied the center of a feast. It was believed to be healthier for the body to boil meat before roasting it, since roasting dried the meat and had the potential to cause illness. Most medical authorities considered food not in terms of pleasure but dietetics, the scientific practice of matching the qualities in food to the qualities of the human body, called humors (cold, hot, wet, and dry). In order to stay healthy, diners had to match their food to their personal humors; if they were sick, they were advised to eat food with contrasting humors. For example, beef was believed to be a hot, dry food, off-limits to those with a melancholic (wet and cold) personality. After the publication of a cooking manual called *De honesta voluptate*, by Platina in 1474, cooks and diners in Europe adopted a new strategy: pairing foods with opposing humors in the same dish to make balanced and healthy food. Hot, dry meat was paired with a cold, moist sauce (such as vinegar or mustard) to produce a dish suitable for all diners.

Medieval and Renaissance banquets, even in middle-class homes, offered several main dishes at once. This system was called *service à la française*, or French service, and it offered a multitude of dishes all at once to diners, who would serve themselves as they wished or, in the case of wealthy households, ask to be served by valets or other staff. French service was replaced in the late eighteenth century by *service à la russe*, or Russian service, a composed plate offered to each diner for each course. In French service, the main course or "roast course" consisted of platters of roasted meats, meats in sauce, roasted or boiled fish, and poultry of various kinds. In *Le Ménagier de Paris*, one of the earliest printed cookbooks in France, composed around 1393, suggested menus for roast courses include river and ocean fish, venison pastries, and fresh herring or rabbits, partridges, stuffed pork, and pheasants. Wealthy French tables in the Middle Ages featured fresh pork and game (like wild boar or venison) more often than beef, with fish representing an expensive indulgence that was nevertheless required on lean (Lenten) days and poultry occupying the highest rank among meats in terms of prestige and cost.

On church-imposed lean days in the Middle Ages, meat, eggs, and dairy were not allowed. Days requiring abstinence from meat included all of Lent (the 40 days before Easter); Wednesday, Friday, and Saturday of the week beginning each new season of the year; the vigil day before feast days; and every Friday. Since those following the church's dietary rules relied on fish, in the fourteenth century the Parisian parliament created a special office, called "the seafood office," dedicated to overseeing the capital's fish supply (Denjean and Feller 2013, 26). Herring was the most consumed fish in medieval Europe; salted or smoked herring was easy to preserve and could be shipped long distances, but herring was also popular as a fresh fish (Laurioux 2013, 82). In the Renaissance and seventeenth-century, wealthy tables used freshwater or ocean fish as a first course, and shellfish, particularly crayfish, served as a garnish for other meats served in the main course. In the eighteenth century, particularly after the French Revolution, the consumption of fresh fish soared after the establishment of more robust rail links connecting the port cities to interior France. In addition, the upheaval of the French Revolution diminished the power of the Catholic Church in French society. As a result, fewer French citizens observed Lenten practices, and the demand for salted fish declined. The total consumption of freshwater fish increased from 587 kilograms per year in 1789 to 2 million kilograms in 1873, about 1.1 kilograms per person per year (Husson 1875, 328). Ocean fish consumption increased from 2.4 million kilograms in 1789 to 23 million kilograms in 1873, or 12.5 kilograms per person (Husson 1875, 320).

Rural families and those with less money ate mutton or salt pork when they ate meat at all, since it was too expensive to be a daily indulgence. Until the seventeenth century, *la viande* ("meat") in French was a general term for the centerpiece of a meal (sometimes called *la graine*), and did not specifically refer to animal flesh, because these meals were not always centered on meat. To make meat last longer, it was preserved in salt; families often slaughtered the "family pig" in the fall and salted the meat to make hams and bacon that would last all winter if used sparingly. Peasants with access to hunting grounds ate game as well and occasionally caught river fish, but the feudal system closed off this food source to the poor after the Middle Ages. The method of preserving meats by smoking them became important in the French Caribbean territories when crews on long sea voyages between ports needed food that would last the journey. Smoked fish and game, called *boucané* from the word *boucan* for the grill stand, traveled well and provided needed protein. *Poulet boucané* (marinated, smoked chicken) remains a popular main dish in Guadeloupe and Martinique, using the same technique likely developed in the seventeenth

Rules for Eating Meat

In ninth-century France Catholic monasteries adopted new, stricter rules about eating, following the rules of Saint Benedict, a reformer from the sixth century. No butcher's meat was permitted at all except for the sick, who were thought to need it for strength. Poultry was permitted on eight days of the year, during Easter and Christmas. Meals could include animal fat except on Fridays and certain "abstinence" days, including Lent. On lean days, small quantities of fish were allowed, but supplies were scarce. And a new ruling allowed diners to eat beaver tail but not beaver meat on lean days since the beaver's tail is always in water and was therefore considered fish (Ariès 2016, 219).

Poule au Pot (French Chicken in a Pot)

Yield: Serves 4

Ingredients
2 leeks, trimmed
4 whole carrots, washed and peeled
1 whole chicken (3–4 pounds)
Salt, pepper
2 bay leaves
1 onion, studded with 4 whole cloves
2 small turnips, peeled and cut in quarters

1. Trim off most of the green parts of the leeks and the root ends. Rinse well, especially between the leaves. Cut off the ends of the carrots, but leave whole.
2. Place the chicken in a large stew pot. Sprinkle with 1 teaspoon salt and ½ teaspoon pepper, and add the bay leaf. Add just enough water to cover. Bring to a boil and add the onion and vegetables. Cover and simmer over low heat until the meat reaches 160 degrees in the thigh, or until the meat begins to separate from the bones. Skim the foam occasionally while cooking.
3. Remove the chicken and vegetables from the pot and place on a large platter. Cover with foil to keep warm. Degrease the broth with a large spoon. Taste the broth and add salt if needed.

Serve the broth as a first course and the chicken and vegetables as a main course.

Adapted from "Poule au pot à l'ancienne," Marmiton, accessed April 10, 2020, https://www.marmiton.org/recettes/recette_poule-au-pot-a-l-ancienne_21529.aspx.

century. Modern recipes call for marinating chicken in lime juice, garlic, and chives and then slowly smoking the meat over wood coals for hours. In Guadeloupe, *poulet boucané* can be found at roadside stands near the beach.

The turkey did not have a large place in early French cuisine, but mentions of the New World bird appear in sixteenth-century texts like *Gargantua* by François Rabelais (1534). In the sixteenth century, turkey cost eight times as much as chicken; it became popular because of the high status given to poultry by the elite and because its large size made an impressive show at banquets (Quellier 2013, 198). Wealthy diners at extravagant

Main Dishes

banquets also regularly feasted on swans, cranes, storks, herons, and peacocks. Extravagant birds like these disappeared from lists of household expenses in the late seventeenth century as tastes changed (Girard 1977, 507). In the meantime, the middle class grew, and more households had access to meat. By the seventeenth century, cookbooks show a preference for beef, veal, and mutton but less of an interest in game, fish, and vegetables. Of course, cookbooks can only tell us about the food habits of the middle and upper classes, since only wealthier people employed cooks in need of cookbooks and the lower classes could not afford the kinds of ingredients featured in these books. Modern-day French families still serve roasts for Sunday lunch, for example, when there is more time to cook and enjoy a long meal. Poultry (usually chicken) still tops the list in popularity, with leg of lamb a close second.

The Importance of Sauce

Records and excavations of rural (poorer) homes in the Middle Ages reveal that most had metal utensils, iron skillets, and copper pots and kettles for cooking, which were used to fry, fricassee, and braise meats. Only good-quality meat was roasted (often boiled before roasting), and grills and spits for roasting were found almost exclusively in well-to-do homes (Piponnier 2000, 341). Grills were also used for toasting bread, an important ingredient in thickening sauces, another element of elite cuisine. Cooked meat was seasoned with light sauces made of crushed spices mixed with white wine or vinegar and thickened with toasted bread or crushed almonds. Only in the seventeenth century did French cooks turn to thickening sauces with a roux of cooked flour and butter. In 1651 François La Varenne's cookbook *Le cuisinier français* featured the first published recipe for a sauce with a flour-butter roux, called a *liaison*. La Varenne included a small number of sauces for a large number of roasted meats, all with a base of some combination of vinegar, verjuice (unfermented grape juice), and citrus. Stone mortars for pounding spices (another expensive commodity) and making sauces appeared in well-equipped kitchens, and even modest homes likely owned a wooden mortar and pestle to make seasonings with vinegar and herbs (Piponnier 2000, 342). Seventeenth-century cookbooks as a rule included recipes for a coulis, or master sauce of reduced meat juices and other aromatics that was used as the basis for other sauces and for sauced meat dishes. Sauce making in France took off from there. François Marin's *Dons de Comus* cookbook in 1739 gave 50 recipes for sauces; the 1742 sequel, *Suite des dons de Comus*, featured 95 new sauce recipes.

The seventeenth-century innovations in cooking, including the art of sauce, brought new trends in main dishes as well. La Varenne's cookbook spells out preparations for various kinds of poultry (duck, goose, pigeon, quail, partridge), hare, wild boar, veal, and lamb. The accompaniments are sometimes surprising to the modern reader (turkey with raspberries, for one, or lamb marinated with lemon and orange), but *Le cuisinier français* represents the transition from medieval cooking that often paired sweet or spicy sauces with meat to a more refined style of cuisine that sought to match flavors rather than contrast them. Some of La Varenne's dishes are recognizable as "classic" French cooking, even today. His beef *en daube* (beef cooked in wine) resembles the well-known beef Burgundy, and many of the cooking terms and sauce names are still used, such as fricassee and Robert sauce (with onions and mustard).

For main dishes in this era, meats were roasted and served in sauce or braised in sauce as a ragout, a quintessentially French dish. The French were so enamored by sauced dishes that they gained a reputation for them, and some countries (notably Great Britain) accused the French of covering poor-quality food under a blanket of sauce. La Varenne also introduced the innovation of stuffing meats before roasting, and of stuffing poultry with shellfish, as in the modern oyster stuffing eaten with turkey (Wheaton 2015, 117). In the late seventeenth century, rival cooks began to criticize La Varenne's style of "meat in sauce" as too old-fashioned and disorganized. L.S.R.'s cookbook offered what he called a new, more refined model of cooking that deviated from La Varenne's "mountain of roasted meats" and "abundance of ragouts" in favor of carefully selected meats in a beautiful presentation (L.S.R. 1693).

As French cuisine moved into the eighteenth-century Age of Enlightenment, it became more "reasoned," with fewer combinations of meats and more straightforward alignment of flavors, such as fish with seafood garnishes and meat with meat stock. Marin's *Dons de Comus* (1739) features dishes that have a French esthetic in ingredients or in style: beef tongue in sauce, fillet of beef with cornichons, veal brains in marinade, braised leg of mutton, roast suckling pig, and duck in orange sauce. Marin also gives instructions for preparing game meats, a section that disappears from cookbooks in the nineteenth century. His cookbook pays special attention to fish, with a section on ocean fish and one on freshwater fish in various sauces and styles.

Sauces for main dishes, beginning in the seventeenth century, were composed of several elements: a master or mother sauce, aromatics and flavorings, and meat juices from the roasted or braised meat. L.S.R. (or Le sieur Robert, "Sir Robert") in *L'art de bien traiter* (first published in 1674 and reprinted in 1693) referred to a *coulis universel* that was an early version of the sauce Espagnole, later to become the "mother sauce" for all French brown sauces. Eighteenth-century cookbook authors copied earlier sauce recipes for established meat sauces like "green sauce" with herbs or "cameline sauce" with cinnamon, or they gave general instructions for making sauced dishes by starting with a coulis and adding a thickener and flavorings. If French cuisine today is known for its sauce, one person deserves most of the credit: chef and cookbook author Marie-Antoine Carême. In *Le cuisinier parisien* (The Parisian cook, 1828) and *L'art de la cuisine française au XIXe siècle* (The art of French cuisine in the nineteenth century, 1833) Carême simplified sauces into a trio of mother sauces: Espagnole (browned roux with concentrated veal stock), velouté (blond roux with poultry stock), and béchamel (blond roux with milk). To create the lengthy list of other named sauces in Carême's books, he combined these mother sauces with flavorings to make a secondary sauce, such as adding egg yolks to velouté to make sauce Allemande (German sauce). In the twentieth century, Auguste Escoffier, another monumental chef and author of *Le guide culinaire* (1903), introduced tomato sauce as the fourth foundational sauce in French cuisine. He refined Carême's recipe for Espagnole sauce by adding tomato purée, but Espagnole remained at the top of the pyramid of mother sauces.

French Beef

Meat has an important symbolic resonance in France (as it does elsewhere) as a sign of power and wealth. In the late seventeenth century, cookbooks document a change to quick-cooking meats (likely adopted from English practice) in the terms they use: *ros de bif* (roast beef) in François Massialot's *Cuisinier royal* of 1698, "beff steks" [sic] in Vincent La Chapelle's *Cuisinier moderne* in 1735, and "biftecks" (steaks) by the early nineteenth century in a number of cookbooks. The change from boiling to roasting or grilling meat also indicates that more French had access to higher-quality cuts of beef that were suitable for quick cooking and tender enough to eat without long cooking. During the revolutionary era (eighteenth century) the public demanded regulation of butchers and meat sellers, and the government imposed fixed prices on certain meats so that all people, no matter their income, had access to some kinds of meat. The prime cuts (steaks, roasts) remained out of reach for the poor, but organ meats and lesser cuts carried a legally mandated lower price, and different cuts of meat held "social and political marks of distinction" (Watts 2006, 25).

But boiled beef has an important place in French cuisine in the form of pot-au-feu. Pot-au-feu, or beef boiled with vegetables, is considered by some the national dish of France. It combines red meat with earthy root vegetables and offers a full meal in one pot: soup from the broth, meat for protein, and vegetables for nutrients. Traditionally, pot-au-feu is divided into the bouillon used for soup, and the *bouilli*, or boiled beef, as the main dish served with vegetables. The *Larousse gastronomique* suggests carrots, turnips, parsnips, onion, leeks, and celery. Jules Gouffé opens the first chapter of *Le livre de cuisine* (The book of cuisine, 1867) with pot-au-feu, instructing the reader to use several cuts of beef to obtain both a rich broth and succulent boiled meat. Carême gave pot-au-feu in *Art de la cuisine* the ultimate praise by dedicating his entire first chapter to the dish, and *boeuf à la mode* (braised beef) was the first recipe in the domestic cooking journal *Cuisinière cordon bleu*, in 1895.

Braised beef with wine has a prominent place in cookbooks and on French tables, and even in French literature. La Varenne's *Le cuisinier français* (1651) contains a recipe for *boeuf à la mode* of larded beef cooked in bouillon with herbs and "all kinds of spices," approaching the medieval style. He also includes the more modern *pièce de boeuf à la daube,* cooked in bouillon and wine. Marcel Proust, in his twentieth-century novel *In Search of Lost Time*, evokes the beauty of the family cook's *daube de boeuf à la gelée* with its "crystals of aspic identical to transparent blocks of quartz" (Proust [1918] 1962, 458), a more elite version of the dish. In a survey of French restaurant patrons in 2017, beef was the most popular main dish (Vastine 2017).

Stews and Braises

Pot-au-feu with beef is well known all over France, but there are similar regional dishes. The *potée lorraine* from eastern France has a similar profile, a dish of long-simmered pork shoulder and white beans with vegetables and herbs, and the *potée au choux* adds cooked cabbage. As much as *pot-au-feu* is a beloved classic dish, it fell out of favor for elite cuisine in the twentieth century, when better cuts of beef became more accessible for all diners. Particularly in restaurants, diners preferred steak and quick-cooked meats, and pot-au-feu was replaced in popularity by steak-frites, grilled hanger steak with French fries, a bistro mainstay. A cut of grilled beef tenderloin large enough to serve two diners carries the name Chateaubriand, possibly in homage to nineteenth-century author François-René de Chateaubriand. Other, more unusual meats play a role in French cuisine as a legacy of the hierarchy of meat that dates to the Middle Ages: classic French cookbooks and restaurants serving bistro cuisine might feature quail, rabbit, *civet* of hare (stewed hare), and braised tripe (cow stomach). In home cooking, French families may serve these meats for a special occasion but more often choose beef, pork, lamb, or poultry, just as their ancestors did many centuries before.

Another long-cooked dish with simple ingredients, coq au vin (chicken cooked in wine) combines two products with heavy symbolism in France: the rooster, symbol of Gallic pride, and red wine. The two elements are linked in Latin, the language of Roman Gaul, since *gallus* in Latin means both rooster and Gaul. Coq au vin comes from Burgundy, a region known for its fine red wines, but other regions have developed their own versions with white wine. This dish also reflects the seventeenth-century tradition of meat in sauce, and it has a peasant pedigree as well, since early versions of coq au vin made a delicious dinner out of an old bird and local wine. The traditional recipe calls for chicken (or rooster) to be marinated overnight in a bottle or two of red wine with aromatics like garlic and herbs, and then slowly braised in the marinade with bits of salt pork, small onions, and button mushrooms. *Boeuf bourguignon*, or beef with Burgundy wine, is prepared much the same way and might be served as the main course for a Sunday lunch with the extended family.

Many of these recipes came of age in the nineteenth century, when sauces reached their high point. A light stew of lamb and spring vegetables carries the name *navarin d'agneau*; like *ragoût*, *navarin* is another word for stew, but this term was derived from the word *navet*, for "turnip," a primary ingredient in the dish. *Blanquette de veau*, veal in a cream sauce with mushrooms and pearl onions, originated as a way to reuse cooked veal, but Gouffé, in *Le livre de cuisine* (1867) offered a recipe for *blanquette* made from raw veal. *Blanquette de veau* is one of the few French main dishes served with rice.

Another minor legume, lentils have top billing in a dish of salt pork with lentils (*petit salé aux lentilles*), the closest one might come to vegetarian cuisine in classic French cooking. In the region of Puy-en-Velay in southern France, the famous green lentils accompany duck sausage for a hearty main course. Rabbit served in mustard sauce still appears on French tables, recalling the old preference for game meats, and *hachis parmentier* (ground beef topped with mashed potatoes) is named for Antoine Parmentier, a chemist who lobbied for potatoes to be accepted on French tables. In the eighteenth century, potatoes were uncommon in Europe and believed to be poisonous. Parmentier believed that cooked potatoes made into bread might be the answer to feeding the poor; his bread experiment failed, but his legacy endures in dishes named for him that feature potatoes.

> ## Hachis Parmentier (French Shepherd's Pie)
>
> *Yield:* Serves 4
>
> *Ingredients*
> 1 Tbsp butter
> 1 large onion, chopped
> 2 garlic cloves, minced
> 1 pound ground beef
> 1 Tbsp flour
> Salt, pepper
> ½ tsp dried oregano
> ½ tsp dried thyme
> 1 large tomato, diced
> ¼ cup water
> 1 egg, lightly beaten
> 2 cups leftover mashed potatoes (room temperature)
> 1 cup grated Parmesan cheese
>
> 1. Heat the butter over medium heat until melted. Add the chopped onion and cook until translucent, about 5 minutes. Add the garlic and cook until fragrant, about 30 seconds. Add the ground beef and cook until no longer pink. Add the flour and cook for one minute, stirring often. Stir in 1 teaspoon of salt, ½ teaspoon pepper, and the dried herbs.
> 2. Add the diced tomato and ¼ cup of water. Cook and stir until most of the liquid is evaporated. Off heat, stir in beaten egg. Place meat mixture in an 8 x 8-inch baking dish.
> 3. Heat oven to 350 degrees. Stir ¼ cup of the Parmesan into the mashed potatoes. Sprinkle ¼ cup of parmesan over the meat mixture, and then spread the potatoes on the meat mixture in an even layer. Smooth with a spoon wet with a little water. Sprinkle the remaining parmesan cheese over the potatoes.
> 4. Bake until golden brown on top, about 20 minutes. Serve hot.
>
> Adapted from "Hachis parmentier," Marmiton, accessed April 10, 2020, https://www.marmiton.org/recettes/recette_hachis-parmentier_17639.aspx.

Far from mainland France and nineteenth-century French kitchens, another stewed meat dish, called *colombo de cabri*, is known as the national dish of Guadeloupe. Traditionally made with goat (*cabri*), the dish is a curry made with a signature spice mix called *colombo*. It is the result of the culinary influence brought by immigrants from India after slavery ended, who imported spices like turmeric, cumin, and coriander. *Colombo* represents the essence of the hybrid identity of the Caribbean islands since it combines native ingredients (goat, vegetables) with warm spices from another culinary tradition, adopted and adapted into Creole cooking. A similar dish made with chicken and spices is sometimes called *colombo* or *poulet antillais* (Caribbean chicken). The *blaff de poisson* (poached fish) from Guadeloupe has a Creole name (*blaff* means "broth" in Creole) and takes advantage of the abundant local fish on the island. It features delicate flavors of fish marinated in lime juice, onion, and herbs and then cooked gently in an herb-infused broth. *Blaff de poisson* and *colombo de cabri* are often accompanied by rice, cooked yams, and breadfruit.

Main Dish Soups

The French also hold fast to another long-standing tradition as a main dish: soup. Early cookbooks devote entire sections to potage (thin soups) and *soupe* (soups thickened with bread) of all kinds, usually as part of a first course. For nonelite cuisine, soup was more often a main course or the only meal of the day. Main dish soups efficiently stretched a small amount of meat to feed many people and could be kept hot in a cauldron over a fire or on a stove all day long. Among the poor, vegetable soups were made from produce grown in the family garden and flavored with a bit of bacon or pork fat.

Marthe Daudet's 1913 cookbook, *Les bons plats de France*, divided France into four regions, each represented by a soup: pot-au-feu, onion soup, potato-leek soup, and cabbage soup. Of these, only pot-au-feu and cabbage soup can be considered main dishes, but similar creations occupy center stage on the French table, depending on the region. The *garbure*, a thick soup of bread and cooked cabbage, originated in Béarn in southwestern France in the Pyrenees Mountains, bordered by the Basque provinces near the Spanish border. In his 1739 cookbook, Marin included a hearty cabbage soup called *galbure*, but the dish appears to have existed

Soup for Dinner

The tradition of soup as a main dish for dinner continues: a study of French habits in the 1960s showed that nearly 90 percent of families, both urban and rural, ate soup as their evening meal, often supplemented by a plate of eggs or some cheese (Claudian and Serville 1970, p. 180).

well before Marin's cookbook as a stew of greens and pork fat. In the Gascon dialect from the neighboring region of Gascony, *garburo* meant a soup of cabbage and goose confit (goose preserved in fat), and the term *garbure* emerged in eighteenth-century works like the *Dictionnaire portatif de cuisine* (Portable dictionary of cooking) in 1767 (2:222). Truly a peasant dish, in the present day *garbure* remains a filling but simple soup of cabbage and salt pork, made authentic in the Béarn region by the addition of their specialty *lard rance* (rancid lard), an acquired taste.

In Marseille on the Mediterranean coast, fresh fish is abundant, and the well-loved fish soup bouillabaisse has many defenders. The key elements in bouillabaisse are several varieties of local fish, some firm and some flaky; shellfish like mussels or clams; a savory broth with tomatoes, spices, and saffron; and a sauce called a *rouille* (garlic mayonnaise with red peppers) served as a garnish. The term dates to the nineteenth century, but a fisherman's stew of leftover fish from the day's catch certainly existed before cookbook authors put the recipe in print. Jean-François Revel, a French food historian, claims that bouillabaisse in Marseille is renowned because the fish found in the Gulf of Lion are particularly savory and firm and that the glory of the soup is not in its "banal" recipe but is directly linked to the ingredients and their provenance (Revel 2007, 33). He insists that "true bouillabaisse" can only be found "in the circumstances where it was born, after the fish comes in, on the coast, and it becomes tasteless as soon as one attempts to recreate it far from its origins" (Revel 2007, 34). Those who stake a claim to "true bouillabaisse" insist on using rockfish and *rascasse* (scorpion fish) in the stew, fish that are difficult to find elsewhere. Because of its powerful flavors and long list of ingredients, bouillabaisse has become less and less common on French tables, but it maintains a strong presence as the signature dish of Marseille.

Bouillabaisse reigns as the best-known fish stew in France, but many coastal regions offer a stew of fish or seafood in a seasoned broth, all with specific local ingredients. The *bourride marseillaise* is a bouillabaisse with only three fish: monkfish, bar, and whiting, with *aïoli* (garlic mayonnaise) stirred into the bouillon. *Cotriade* might be considered northern bouillabaisse, a fish stew made in Brittany from local fish with garlic, potatoes, and onions. On the Atlantic coast, Breton fishermen since the eighteenth century have made this fish stew out of the lesser types of fish left at the end of the day, such as mackerel and mullet. On the present-day French table, whole, cooked fish remains a dish for special occasions, served much less frequently than beef or poultry is. In restaurants, a classic dish of sole *en meunière*, fillet of sole served with a lemon and butter sauce, represents the elegance of French cuisine with a delicate fish in a subtle

Main Dishes

sauce, as do *coquilles Saint-Jacques*, scallops served in a cream sauce topped with toasted bread crumbs. Near the coast of Brittany and Normandy (and elsewhere with a good fish market), *moules-frites*, or mussels with French fries, are a hands-on main dish, requiring the diner to pluck the mussels from their shells and dip them in a white wine and garlic broth. The French fries are a necessary accompaniment, inseparable from the mussels as much as *steak-frites* always pairs steak with French fries.

In the French Caribbean, soups and stews are also part of the island culinary tradition. Every island cuisine (and nearly every cook) has a different recipe for callaloo, a stew of greens and vegetables based on the leafy green vegetable native to the place where the dish is prepared. Often made from amaranth or taro leaves in Trinidad and Tobago and Guyana, the same name graces stews made from other hearty greens. In Guadeloupe callaloo with crab is served at Easter, and callaloo with crawfish is a special occasion dish. Another hearty soup called *bébélé* in Guadeloupe includes tripe (cow stomach) and plantains. Like many dishes in Caribbean cuisine, callaloo and *bébélé* originated in slave cuisine. Africans were brought to the islands during the Triangle Trade, a trade route between Europe, Africa, and the Americas. It brought European goods, like ammunition, to Africa in exchange for enslaved people who were taken to America and the Caribbean as forced laborers and traded for products from slave plantations there, such as cotton and sugar, which were then shipped to Europe. The Triangle Trade was heavily implicated in the slave trade in the seventeenth and eighteenth centuries. Enslaved people brought from West Africa to the French Caribbean islands adapted the recipes they knew from their home countries to new ingredients found in the Caribbean, to create Creole or hybrid dishes. Often these dishes used humble ingredients, such as lesser cuts of meat and wild greens, the only foods available to slaves. Combined with spices and local vegetables, the recipes took on the character of their adopted home. These dishes carry new significance as part of island cuisine, since modern-day cooks embrace their complicated heritage and carry these dishes forward.

Regional Classics

Other regional specialties have a rabid following, and "authentic" recipes, such as cassoulet, have their staunch defenders. Very simply put, cassoulet is a casserole of beans, sausages, and pork, duck, or goose meat, a specialty of southwestern France near the border with Spain. But cassoulet is far from simple: even in cassoulet country, there are three styles of cassoulet, each with their own partisans. In the town of Castelnaudry, halfway between Toulouse and Carcassonne, where residents claim the oldest recipe for the dish, cassoulet contains goose, pork sausages, and pork shoulder; in Carcassonne it may include leg of lamb or partridge; and in Toulouse it is made with duck. Cassoulet gets its name from the *cassole*, or clay pot—created by potters in a village near Castelnaudry—in which it was cooked when the dish had its origins in the fourteenth century. Similar dishes in Taillevent's fourteenth-century cookbook, *Le Viandier*, called for meat, sauce, and broad beans or fava beans.

Like the pot-au-feu, cassoulet served many with few ingredients and was a humble dish. In the sixteenth century, Spanish explorers brought new vegetables to Europe from the Americas, including the haricot and flageolet beans that became an essential part of modern cassoulet. French cooks who want to preserve the authenticity of cassoulet insist on a particular type of white bean for cassoulet: the haricot lingot. Cassoulet from Castelnaudry took its modern form in the eighteenth century. In the present day, there are as many cassoulet recipes as there are chefs. Restaurant versions of cassoulet use more expensive ingredients or a more decorative

Cassoulet

Yield: Serves 4

Ingredients
2 cups dried white beans
½ pound of ham with rind
1 pound of bone-in pork ribs or ham hocks
1 onion, chopped
1 large carrot, chopped
Salt, pepper
2 legs of duck confit, or 2 chicken thighs and 2 chicken legs
4 pork sausages (sweet, not hot)
1 pound of pork shoulder cut into 1-inch pieces, or 1 pound boneless country ribs
4 garlic cloves, peeled

1. Soak the beans overnight in cold water.
2. The next day, drain the water. Put the beans in a saucepan with 6 cups of water and bring to a boil. Cook for five minutes, then drain and reserve.

3. Boil 6 cups of water along with the ham, bone-in pork or ham hock, onion, carrots, ½ teaspoon salt, and ¼ teaspoon pepper. Cook broth for one hour, then strain out the solids, reserving the broth and the ham. Save the ham and rind. Add the beans to the broth and cook for one hour or until soft.
4. In a large skillet, sauté the duck confit until crisp and the fat has rendered. Or brown the chicken thighs and legs skin side down for 5 minutes until well browned. Flip and cook on the other side for 5 minutes. Set aside and remove skin from chicken pieces.
5. Drain all but 1 tablespoon of fat from the pan. Brown the sausages in the fat for 5–7 minutes until well-browned. Set aside and repeat with the pork shoulder or ribs. Set aside browned pork.
6. Drain the beans and reserve the broth. Add the garlic to the beans.
7. In a large, oven-safe dish, layer the ham on the bottom, followed by one-third of the beans, and the pork and chicken. Add the rest of the beans, and tuck the sausages into the second layer of beans, leaving part of the sausages sticking out. Pour the reserved broth into the pot until it just covers the beans. Sprinkle with pepper.
8. Bake at 350 degrees for 2 hours. During this time, when a browned crust forms on the top of the beans, stir it in as the beans cook. Legend has it that the best cooks stir in the crust 7 times. If the beans seem too dry, stir in another tablespoon or two of broth.

Serve hot from the casserole dish.

Adapted from "La Recette du Cassoulet de Castelnaudary," Grande Confrérie du Cassoulet de Castelnaudary, accessed April 9, 2020, https://www.confrerieducassoulet.com/la-recette.html.

presentation, such as a toasted bread crumb crust, but at its heart cassoulet is a hearty, peasant dish.

In Alsace, neighbor to Germany on France's eastern border, a platter of sauerkraut with sausages and many cuts of pork called *choucroute garnie* often appears as a main dish. Sauerkraut braised with parsley, thyme, peppercorns, and bay leaves serves as a bed for cooked sausages, smoked ham, and pork loin, often accompanied by potatoes for a German-inflected feast. In Strasbourg, the selection of sausages may include blood sausage (made from pig's blood), and cooks sometimes add pork belly to the mix of meats. *Choucroute garnie* can be found in bistros and some restaurants, but like cassoulet and pot-au-feu, it is most often served at home.

Choucroute Garnie
(Alsatian Sauerkraut with Sausages)

Yield: Serves 6

Ingredients
2 16-oz. packages prepared sauerkraut
1 bay leaf
1 tsp dried thyme
5–6 whole peppercorns
1 onion studded with 2 whole cloves
1 pound kielbasa or smoked sausage, cut into 1-inch pieces
1 pound smoked ham
Vegetable oil
6 fresh pork sausages
1 pound boneless pork chops

1. Heat sauerkraut on low heat in a large saucepan or Dutch oven with bay leaf, thyme, peppercorns, and onion until simmering. Add the kielbasa or smoked sausage and ham; cover and simmer.
2. Meanwhile, heat 1 teaspoon vegetable oil over medium-high heat in a skillet. Cook the fresh sausages until brown on all sides. Set aside. Brown the pork chops, about 3 minutes on each side. Return the sausages to the skillet and add ¼ cup water. Lower the heat to medium, cover and simmer until meats are cooked through.
3. When ready to serve, remove the cloves, bay leaf, and peppercorns. Place the warmed sauerkraut on a large platter and slice the ham and pork chops. Arrange the sausages, ham, and other meats decoratively around the sauerkraut. Serve with Dijon mustard and cornichons (small dill pickles).

More recently, couscous has gained a following in France due to an influx of immigrants from North Africa. The term *couscous* refers to tiny, pasta-like grains of semolina that are steamed until fluffy, but as a main dish couscous consists of a stew of vegetables or meats with warm spices, such as cumin and cinnamon, served on a bed of couscous grains. A pyramid-shaped cooking vessel called a *tagine* helps keep the cooked ingredients moist as they braise, and it also lends its name to the finished meat or vegetable stew.

Main Dishes

Eggs and Vegetarian Dishes

For a meal that requires less time in the kitchen and fewer ingredients, the French turn to egg dishes as a main course. Most famous among them is quiche, a tart made of egg custard with vegetables or other fillings. Quiche Lorraine with bits of pork *lardons* (uncured pork belly), perhaps the most well-known type of quiche, comes from the Lorraine region in eastern France. The traditional recipe uses only eggs, cream, and lardons, with perhaps a bit of nutmeg, but other versions include cheese or onions, and quiches might contain spinach, mushrooms, or other vegetables as well. Other popular main-dish egg creations include omelets, eggs poached in red wine or broth, scrambled eggs with morel mushrooms or truffles, or simply fried eggs called eggs *sur le plat* (on the platter).

Quiche Lorraine

Yield: Serves 4

Ingredients
1 prepared pie crust
1 cup cooked ham or bacon, cut into cubes or crumbled
5 eggs
⅓ cup whole milk or heavy cream
Salt, pepper
1 Tbsp butter, melted

1. Heat the oven to 375 degrees and put a metal baking sheet in the oven to preheat. The heated cookie sheet will help cook the bottom pie crust.
2. Line a 9-inch pie plate with prepared pie crust (homemade or store-bought). Crimp the edges into a fluted pattern or with a fork.
3. In the bottom of the pie plate, sprinkle cooked ham or bacon. Distribute evenly over the pie crust.
4. In a mixing bowl, whisk together eggs and milk or heavy cream. Add ¼ teaspoon salt and ¼ teaspoon black pepper. Whisk until foamy.
5. Carefully pour the egg mixture over the cheese and ham in the pie plate. Drizzle melted butter over the top of the egg mixture.
6. Place on the cookie sheet in the oven at 375 degrees for 20 minutes, and then reduce the heat to 350 and continue to cook for 10–15 minutes more, until the top is browned and the center of the quiche is set.
7. Cool for 10 minutes before cutting into wedges to serve.

Vegetarian dishes exist in French cooking but are not widespread, especially in traditional cuisine. Since fish has always belonged to a special category in France (and perhaps because fish was allowed during Lent, when meat was forbidden), some French consider fish dishes to be vegetarian. Apart from vegetarian soups, some French families enjoy vegetarian lasagna or baked stuffed tomatoes (*tomates farcies*) as a main dish without meat. In southeastern France near the Swiss border, particularly in winter, locals consume *raclette*, named for both the type of cheese and the main dish. Similar to fondue, *raclette* consists of melted cheese served over boiled potatoes and cured meats and is entirely appropriate in the mountainous region of Savoy.

In restaurants and at home in France, main dishes with meat remain dominant. French diners continue to opt for roast leg of lamb or braised *boeuf bourguignon* as the center of an important family meal, or they choose steak or duck breast (*magret de canard*) when dining out. The idea of enjoying a long-cooked dish full of delicious flavors appeals to many French diners but is not the reality for most. When dining at home, Sunday lunch remains the occasion for a signature dish like pot-au-feu, *blanquette de veau*, or perhaps chicken braised with prunes, but for weeknight meals many families might choose a frozen entrée or a bowl of soup with bread. The most popular main dish in France for a Sunday lunch might very well be the simplest: a roast chicken purchased from a rotisserie stand at the open market. Above all, main dishes in France reflect the general principle of French cuisine: tradition matters, but quality ingredients prepared well do not have to be extravagant to be the centerpiece of a great meal.

Further Reading

Ariès, Paul. 2016. *Une histoire politique de l'alimentation*. Paris: Max Milo.

Carême, Marie-Antoine. 1833. *L'art de la cuisine française au XIXe siècle: traité élémentaire et pratique,* Vol. 1. Paris: Chez l'auteur.

Claudian, Jean, and Yvonne Serville. 1970. "Aspects de l'évolution récente du comportement alimentaire en France: Composition des repas et 'urbanisation.'" In *Pour une Histoire de l'alimentation*, edited by Jean-Jacques Hémardinquer, 174–87. Paris: Armand Colin.

Dalby, Andrew. 2014. *Food in the Ancient World from A to Z*. London; New York: Routledge.

David, Elizabeth. 1999. *French Provincial Cooking*. New York: Penguin.

Denjean, Claude, and Laurent Feller. 2013. *Expertise et valeur des choses au Moyen Âge I: Le besoin d'expertise*. Madrid: Casa de Velazquez.

Dictionnaire portatif de cuisine. 1767. Paris: Vincent.

Girard, Alain. 1977. "Le triomphe de la 'La cuisinière bourgeoise': Livres culinaires, cuisine et société en France aux XVIIe et XVIIIe siècles." *Revue d'histoire moderne et contemporaine* 24 (4): 497–523.

Husson, Armand. 1875. *Les consommations de Paris*. Paris: Hachette.

King, Shirley. 1979. *Dining with Marcel Proust: A Practical Guide to French Cuisine of the Belle Epoque with 85 Illustrations*. London: Thames & Hudson.

Laurioux, Bruno. 2013. *Manger Au Moyen Age: Pratiques et Discours Alimentaires en Europe aux Xive et Xve Siècles*. Paris: Hachette.

L.S.R. 1693. "Préface." *L'art de bien traiter*. Lyon: Bachelu.

Pinkard, Susan. 2010. *A Revolution in Taste: The Rise of French Cuisine, 1650–1800*. Cambridge: Cambridge University Press.

Piponnier, Françoise. 2000. "From Hearth to Table: Late Medieval Cooking Equipment." In *Food: A Culinary History*, edited by Jean-Louis Flandrin, Massimo Montanari, and Albert Sonnenfeld, 339–48. New York: Columbia University Press.

Proust, Marcel. (1918) 1962. *A l'ombre des jeunes filles en fleurs* in *A la recherche du temps perdu*. Edited by P. Clarac and A. Ferre. Paris: Gallimard.

Quellier, Florent. 2013. *La Table des Français: Une Histoire Culturelle, 15e–Début 19e Siècle*. Rennes: Presses universitaires de Rennes.

Revel, Jean-François. 2007. *Un Festin en Paroles: Histoire Littéraire de la Sensibilité Gastronomique de L'antiquité à Nos Jours*. Paris: Tallandier.

Saveur Cooks Authentic French. 1999. San Francisco: Chronicle Books.

Tebben, Maryann. 2014. *Sauces: A Global History*. London: Reaktion.

Vastine, Clémence. 2017. "Les plats les plus commandés par les Parisiens au restaurant sont . . ." *Le Figaro Madame*, September 28, 2017. https://madame.lefigaro.fr/cuisine/commande-restaurant-les-parisiens-preferent-le-tartare-de-saumon-et-la-piece-de-boeuf-280917-134467.

Watts, Sydney. 2006. *Meat Matters: Butchers, Politics, and Market Culture in Eighteenth-Century Paris*. Buffalo, NY: University of Rochester Press.

Wheaton, Barbara K. 2015. *Savoring the Past: The French Kitchen and Table from 1300 to 1789*. New York: Touchstone Books.

CHAPTER FIVE

Desserts

In French cities and towns, there are many places to buy something sweet. Patisseries, or pastry shops, offer an array of éclairs, fruit tarts, macarons, and chocolate croissants, among other treats. Tea salons are a quiet refuge to enjoy an elegant pastry and a cup of tea. Crepe vendors and gelato stands sell sweet snacks to go. These items, all delicious, only truly become desserts when they end a meal. In France dessert belongs with a meal, and it carries a certain formality, perhaps because the dessert course originated at royal tables. In spite of their tradition as pastry experts, the French are not dessert fanatics, but they do recognize the importance of something sweet to end a good meal.

Early Desserts

Before the eighteenth-century, dessert was unknown in France. The term *dessert* did not yet exist, and only the wealthiest people had access to sugar. Dishes that included sugar or other sweet ingredients like fruit preserves and honeyed nuts were prepared in wealthy households by a separate kitchen, called the *office*. Cookbooks from the sixteenth to the eighteenth centuries in France contain few dishes that we might recognize as desserts, such as artichokes preserved in sugar syrup, in a garden manual by Olivia de Serres called *Le Théâtre d'agriculture* (Theater of agriculture) (1600). François Massialot, in his *Nouvelle instruction pour les confitures* (New techniques for preserves, 1692), confirms with his title that these dishes are new in France. His book gives hands-on practical advice for making jams, sweet beverages, candy, and salads with preserved fruit. Massialot defines *dessert* in his cookbook as "various kinds of almonds, cookies, marzipan, and meringues" and fresh fruit (1698, 27), and he includes an early recipe for crème brûlée, custard browned on top with a hot iron.

> ## Meringues
>
> *Yield:* Serves 4
>
> *Ingredients*
> 4 egg whites, carefully separated from yolks*
> 1 ¼ cups granulated sugar
> Food coloring (optional)
>
> 1. Preheat oven to 250 degrees. Let egg whites come to room temperature.
> 2. Whip egg whites with an electric mixer until foamy. Add sugar in three steps, whipping thoroughly after each addition, until the egg whites are at "soft peak" (hold their shape when you lift the beater). Carefully fold in a drop or two of food coloring, if using.
> 3. Using a pastry bag, pipe the egg mixture onto a baking sheet lined with parchment paper in 1-inch circles. Alternatively, spoon the mixture into 1-inch rounds. Bake for 30–45 minutes until meringues look dry but are not browned. Cool on a wire rack until completely cool.
>
> *The egg whites will not create a meringue if there is any trace of egg yolk.

Those who ate fruit or sweet dishes served at the end of the meal in the seventeenth century did so because they believed that it helped with digestion and because of the pleasure of a rare taste of sugary food. The term *dessert* began to be used in informal language in France in the seventeenth century to refer to the sweet course served after the roast course (*Dictionnaire* 1694). At court, in formal speech the word *fruit* was still used for this closing service, mainly because most dishes in the final course consisted of whole fruit or fruit preserves. Most seventeenth-century manuals also suggested that dessert platters be decorated with *enjolivements*, or embellishments, such as colored paper decorations or flowers, to indicate that these dishes had a decorative function. Dessert was an out of the ordinary treat, and its presentation on banquet tables underlined its special value.

At the eighteenth-century courts, sugar and sweet foods were used by the nobility to showcase their wealth, since sugar was still very expensive and fairly rare for the common person. Specialized cookbooks for confectionery (sugar cooking) began to appear in the eighteenth century. François Menon published a cookbook called *La Science du maître d'hôtel confiseur* (The science of the steward-confectioner) in 1750, in which he

Desserts

identified 13 stages of cooking sugar between the boiling point and caramelization. Menon's book introduces one of the first recipes for airy chocolate mousse as well. An author named Emy wrote *L'art de bien faire des glaces* (The art of making ices) in 1768, and Joseph Gilliers published *Le cannaméliste français* (The French candymaker) in 1751, but his book lists recipes for sweets alongside those for salads and pickled vegetables. By the eighteenth century, the word *dessert* in dictionary entries was limited to dishes served at the end of the meal, including fruit, cheese, jams, and pastries. France consumed less sugar (less than two pounds per year per person) in the eighteenth century than other countries in Europe did, even though France was the world's leading sugar producer via the island of Saint-Domingue (now Haiti) by the time of the French Revolution. After the French Revolution, French speakers rejected the aristocratic word *fruit* for the sweet course in favor of the bourgeois term *dessert* (Flandrin 2007, 103).

At eighteenth-century banquets, wealthy hosts demonstrated their affluence by displaying sugar sculptures, decorative pieces shaped like Greek statues or architectural forms that were not meant to be eaten. By placing these constructions entirely made of sugar paste at the center of dessert displays, rich patrons declared to their guests that they were wealthy enough to purchase sugar solely for decoration. Called *pièces montées* ("raised pieces"), large decorative displays made of pastry and icing resembled castles or monuments but were not meant to be eaten. Beauty and visual artistry were important elements of the dessert course, both for the edible pieces and the purely decorative elements.

Plain fruit remained an important part of dessert courses even in the eighteenth century, made elegant with decorations and arranged on pedestals or on small plates stacked into pyramids or towers (Wheaton 1996,

Sugar Sculptures

The fragile sugar sculptures at high-society banquets in the eighteenth century were beautiful but cumbersome. They broke easily and attracted insects and mice in storage. But the sugar sculptures were so popular at the time that household stewards eventually found a reusable and more durable alternative. The porcelain industry at the Manufacture Royale at Vincennes (later revived as Sèvres porcelain) responded to the need by creating a new biscuit porcelain in pure white in the early 1750s. This porcelain was used to create figures that perfectly matched sugar sculptures but that could be stored and reused (Day 1999, 60).

188). The term *historié* for a dessert service would refer to plates of fruit or pastries that were decorated with small ornaments. A banquet table would not be complete without a tower of fruit and small pastries on porcelain or pewter plates. This tradition remains at French weddings in the form of the *croquembouche*, a tower of small cream puffs decorated with spun sugar and sugar flowers.

In the early nineteenth century, the dessert course in elite settings still had visual aspects and still used *pièces montées* made of confectionary paste: a mixture of flour, sugar, and egg whites. The nonedible elements were relegated to the ornamental *assiettes montées* ("raised plates") in William Jarrin's *The Italian Confectioner* (1820), a book about French desserts written in English by an Italian immigrant to France. These decorations occupied the center of the table and consisted of sculpted figures made from plaster or paste and tinted with natural or chemical colors. Frozen desserts made of iced fruit or cream were also highly fashionable in the eighteenth century in wealthy homes, since it was difficult to obtain ice to use for freezing. The fact that they were rare made these desserts especially desirable. Frozen treats were molded in pewter or lead containers and colored with food colorings made from vegetables. Decorative frozen desserts remained popular until the late nineteenth century. In *Le livre de pâtisserie* (The book of pastry; 1873), Jules Gouffé includes a charlotte russe (a molded cake) with a frozen filling and a Nesselrode pudding (frozen custard shaped in a mold) with chestnut sorbet. In the twentieth century, fine tables preferred elaborate pastries to frozen confections.

When the Revolution changed French dining habits and chased many of the noble households out of their stately manors, the tradition of decorative dessert displays faded. Without the extravagant budgets of the pre-revolutionary era, pastry chefs resorted to more practical presentations of desserts, and decorations, if used at all, were styled from pasteboard or paper (Tebben 2015, 16). But when Marie-Antoine Carême revived elite dining in the nineteenth century, he also resurrected *pièces montées*. His book *Le pâtissier royal parisien* (The Parisian royal pastry chef; 1815) gave instructions for making Doric, Ionic, and Corinthian columns out of gum paste and sugar, as well as designs for Roman and Greek helmets, fountains, and ruins. These images were part of the iconography of the early nineteenth century in France after Napoleon I took power by force and named himself emperor. The Roman and Greek symbols, particularly military emblems, were in style as a return to classical icons and a rejection of the monarchy's excess (Adams 2007, 187).

The tradition of decorative pastry continues in the present day in France. Aside from the exquisitely beautiful pastries found in patisseries

Desserts 85

all over France, the competition for the Meilleur Ouvrier de France (Best worker in France) rewards entrants who have exceptional skills in a selected field, from woodworking to cooking. Chefs work for years to hone their skills before the contest, hoping to earn the coveted title and the right to wear the blue-white-red collar that marks them as MOF winners. The MOF competition is held only every four years and requires that a chef be nominated and survive several preliminary rounds. They also must dedicate several months before the competition to practice. In pastry, nominated chefs must demonstrate that they have mastered all of the required skills of pastry making. In the final competition, each pastry chef must present a showpiece made entirely of melted, blown, and spun sugar prepared prior to the competition and not meant to be consumed. In addition, chefs create a *pièce montée* illustrating that year's theme and fabricated from delicate sugar elements such as flowers, butterflies, ribbons, and human or animal figures. Finally, entrants prepare a batch of lollipops, an array of dipped and decorated chocolates, and a selection of mini pastries, all of which will be tasted and rated by the judges. Since the competition began in 1924, fewer than 200 chefs have won the MOF award, and in 2018 only 5 entrants out of 15 were awarded the honor.

Beyond the Banquet

Simple desserts meant for pleasurable eating also appear in Carême's works, such as the *pommes au riz* (rice pudding formed into apple or other fruit shapes) in *Le cuisinier parisien* (The Parisian cook; 1828). His final cookbook, *L'art de la cuisine française au dix-neuvième siècle* (The art of French cooking in the nineteenth century; 1833) gives recipes for jellies, creams, fritters, and puddings, demonstrating that bourgeois cuisine had become more important and that the dessert course was no longer exclusively part of banquets or elite dining. Cookbooks from the nineteenth century show that *dessert* finally means sweet dishes and only sweet dishes. The *Grand livre des pâtissiers et des confiseurs* (Great book of pastry makers and confectioners, 1833) by Urbain Dubois only includes recipes for sweet pastries and desserts. Even decorative desserts were meant to be eaten: some of the nineteenth-century dessert creations resembled vegetables, such as carrots, radishes, and mushrooms made of almond paste. Other items on dessert tables were shaped like nondessert foods, such as "sausages," made from the casings used for meat sausages and quince paste, or "ham," made with red and white almond paste. Gouffé's book featured a beehive meringue cake with pistachio bees, and a *jambon de carême* (Lenten ham), a chocolate-cream filled cake shaped like a decorated ham (a "ham" that does not violate Lenten rules of abstinence from meat) (1873, 219–22).

Eventually, as sugar became cheaper and more available, pastry chefs created large architectural forms that could be cut apart and eaten; then they moved on to creating miniature versions that they served on individual plates. Some dessert displays used large cakes or meringues on a pedestal as a centerpiece; these creations were technically edible but presented a challenge for elegant service. Instead, pastry chefs offered small versions of the decorative dessert, and these were meant to be served to guests. The *Grand livre des pâtissiers* contains many desserts we recognize today, including savarins—ring-shaped sponge cakes often baked in decorative pans—and the charlotte, made of ladyfingers or cake slices fitted into a mold and filled with custard or mousse.

A similar molded cake made from ladyfingers from the seventeenth century (called *biscuits de Savoie* in cookbooks of that era) bears the name *gâteau de Savoie* or Savoy cake. The same name applied to a cake baked in a decorative mold that was often used in *pièces montées* in the nineteenth century. In Victor Hugo's *Notre Dame de Paris* (*The Hunchback of Notre Dame*), he called a church in Paris "the most beautiful Savoy cake that has ever been made out of stone" ([1832] 1959, 160).

Mille-feuilles, whose name means "1,000 layers," also were known in the nineteenth century, but the early version of these desserts used marzipan or genoise (sponge cake) layers spread with pastry cream instead of thin puff pastry, as is now the norm. Dubois instructed pastry chefs to make enormous savarins, charlottes, and mille-feuilles for decorative purposes and to surround the centerpiece with miniature versions of the same pastry for service. This change marks another shift toward inclusion of the lower classes with regard to dessert, since mille-feuilles and savarins were sold in pastry shops and accessible to the general public beginning in the nineteenth century. Dessert was no longer the exclusive realm of the elite and no longer reserved for special occasions; it could be a daily treat for middle-class households and an occasional indulgence for almost everyone.

Nineteenth-century cookbooks introduced the Saint-Honoré cake, a multilayer dessert with a base of puff pastry topped with Chiboust cream (pastry cream thickened with egg whites, named for a nineteenth-century pastry chef) and with caramel-covered cream puffs that were garnished with vanilla-scented whipped cream called Chantilly, the name of a château outside of Paris. The dessert showcases the history of French dessert in its named ingredients (Chiboust and Chantilly), and the dish itself is named for the patron saint of French bakers. The cake is said to have been

Desserts

Charlotte aux Framboises (Raspberry Charlotte)

Yield: Serves 6

Ingredients
1 ½ cups water
2 Tbsp raspberry jam (preferably seedless)
¼ cup granulated sugar
1 package ladyfingers
1 cup whole milk Greek yogurt
1 Tbsp heavy cream or sour cream
2 cups fresh or frozen raspberries

1. In a small saucepan, mix 1 ½ cups water, raspberry jam, and sugar. Heat on low heat until the sugar dissolves and the jam melts. Remove the syrup from heat.
2. Prepare a tall bowl, baking dish, or soufflé pan (the pan should be the same height as the ladyfingers). Wipe the inside of the bowl lightly with a little water. Place a layer of plastic wrap in the bowl with an overhang of 4–5 inches.
3. Dip the ladyfingers lightly in the raspberry syrup and arrange them neatly on the bottom and vertically around the sides of the bowl.
4. Mix the yogurt and heavy cream or sour cream. Add one layer of raspberries to the bottom of the bowl. Spread a thin layer of the yogurt-cream mixture on the berries. Add two more layers of raspberries and yogurt-cream. Top with remaining ladyfingers dipped in raspberry syrup. Pour remaining syrup over cake.
5. Cover the cake with the overhanging plastic wrap. Add more plastic wrap if needed. Cover with a plate and refrigerate overnight.
6. When ready to serve, open the plastic wrap on the top of the cake. Unmold the charlotte onto a platter. Remove plastic wrap and serve with whipped cream if desired.

Adapted from "Charlotte simplissime aux framboises," Marmiton, accessed April 23, 2020, https://www.marmiton.org/recettes/recette_charlotte-simplissime-aux-framboises_20372.aspx.

invented by Chiboust (no first name given) in his pastry shop on the aptly named Saint-Honoré street in Paris in 1846, in an area occupied by numerous bakeries and restaurants. In the same area in the eighteenth century, pastry chef Nicolas Stohrer had created a new wave of interest in a well-known cake, the baba (a butter cake). His innovation of adding a perfumed sugar syrup with wine elevated the basic cake to something special. The exiled Polish king Stanislas Leszczynski, for whom Stohrer created the recipe, was so entranced by it that he named it after his favorite literary character: Ali Baba, from *A Thousand and One Nights*. Later recipes began to include rum, and the dessert is now known as the baba au rhum. Open since 1730, the Stohrer pastry shop still exists on the rue Montorgueil in Paris; it is the city's oldest patisserie.

In Gouffé's cookbook, he writes that *éclair* is a new name for a pastry previously called *pain à la duchesse* ("duchess bread"), an elongated cream puff filled with custard and iced with chocolate or coffee glaze. French dictionaries date the first use of *éclair* for an elongated pastry to 1864; the name *éclair* means "lightning" in French, and the most widely accepted etymology of the term suggests that the pastry earned its name because it is eaten quickly, like a flash of lightning. The Fauchon pastry shop in Paris is the undisputed king of modern éclairs, offering jewel-like pastries with colorful icing and sophisticated flavors (such as a savory éclair with foie gras and truffles and an éclair with the image of the Mona Lisa) alongside the very traditional chocolate and coffee éclairs.

All sorts of desserts in France have cream puff or *chou* dough as a base. Éclairs and *choux farcis* (filled cream puffs) are the most common, but other *chou*-based desserts include profiteroles (cream puffs filled with whipped cream or ice cream and sometimes topped with chocolate sauce) and *religieuses* (pastries consisting of a large cream puff topped by a smaller one, both filled with chocolate or coffee pastry cream and topped with ganache). The Saint-Honoré cake uses filled cream puffs as a top layer, and the Paris-Brest cake is a large cream puff split in half and filled with pastry cream, almonds, and praline. The cake resembles a wheel or a bike tire, since it commemorates the Paris-Brest bike race begun in 1891, before the advent of the Tour de France. The Paris-Brest cake is a twentieth-century innovation, created in 1910 by Louis Durand, pastry chef at Maisons-Laffitte in Paris.

Éclair Week

For "ÉCLAIR Week," occurring every September since 2012, Fauchon pastry chefs try out radical new flavors and even sweet-savory combinations, all in limited editions. In past years, the menu has featured éclairs with lemon meringue, raspberry and avocado, and crab Saint-Honoré.

Profiteroles (Cream Puffs with Chocolate Sauce)

Yield: Serves 6

Ingredients
1 cup water
6 Tbsp butter
½ tsp salt
1 ¼ cups all-purpose flour
4 large eggs
6 oz. dark chocolate, chopped
½ cup heavy cream
2 cups whipped cream or 1 pint ice cream (any flavor)

1. Preheat oven to 375 degrees. Line baking sheets with parchment paper.
2. In a heavy pot, bring water to a boil. Add butter and salt. When butter has melted, lower heat and add flour all at once. Stir constantly until incorporated into a ball.
3. Remove from heat for a few minutes, then add 1 egg to the dough and stir vigorously until absorbed. Repeat with three more eggs, stirring thoroughly after each egg until the liquid is absorbed. After the last egg, stir until dough is smooth and shiny.
4. Use spoons to portion dough into 1 tablespoon rounds on baking sheet, spaced 1 inch apart. Smooth tops of dough with a wet spoon, if desired.
5. Bake 20 minutes until puffs are golden brown and dry on top. Leave in oven with heat turned off for 5 minutes. Poke a small hole in the bottom of each puff with chopstick or toothpick. Let cool.
6. Melt the chocolate in a large bowl in the microwave on 50% power for 2 minutes, stirring after every 30 seconds. Stir until completely melted. Slowly add the heavy cream and whisk until smooth. Place the bowl over a pot of simmering water to keep it warm.
7. When the puffs are cool, slice each one in half and fill with whipped cream or a small scoop of ice cream. Place 4 puffs on each of 6 plates and drizzle with chocolate sauce.

Pastries with a Pedigree

Names and invented stories that link desserts to French history make the desserts relevant to French cuisine, an effort that is especially important because desserts are fairly recent in French culinary history and are not nutritionally important. Because Paris had a larger population and more concentrated wealth than other cities in France, it was the source of many French food trends. Importantly for dessert, it had a larger number of middle-class workers who could afford to indulge in an extra course at a restaurant or a special treat from a pastry shop. Before the nineteenth century, most French did not make desserts at home but purchased them from patisseries. Paris served as a place of innovation for desserts since it had more restaurants and pastry shops and since fashionable restaurants tried to stand out with new creations, sometimes named for a celebrity or an important historical event. Since dessert was never an essential part of a meal, creative names and new forms created a market for the sweet course. Although French pastry chefs are skilled at innovations in pastry and cake making, they are fairly conservative with flavors. Since the nineteenth century, most traditional desserts have featured common fruit flavors (strawberry, raspberry) and vanilla, chocolate, and coffee creams. Of course, high-end restaurant desserts and fashionable Parisian pastry shops regularly break the rules.

The macaron cookie of almond flour with a ganache filling, now practically the symbol of French baking, dates to the mid-nineteenth century as well, although almond cookies with a similar rounded shape were known much earlier. Parisian pastry chefs more recently have turned the macaron into a trendy dessert; it is one pastry that does not stick to traditional flavors. Available in a rainbow of colors, macarons come in chocolate, lemon, and pistachio for those who like classic flavors, and in everything from champagne to lavender or tea for those who are more daring. Renowned pastry chef Pierre Hermé created an iconic dessert out in 1997 with the Ispahan, a supersized pink macaron filled with rose-petal-flavored cream and fresh raspberries and litchis. His pastry shop in Paris has become a destination for the Ispahan dessert and for his chocolate creations. The French "opera cake" is an elegant dessert made of thin layers of almond sponge cake called *joconde*; it is flavored with coffee, filled with chocolate ganache and coffee cream, and topped with shiny chocolate glaze. Created in 1955 by Cyriaque Gavillon, another famed Parisian pastry chef who worked at the Ritz Hotel before opening his own shop, the opera cake gets its name because it resembles the stage of the Opéra Garnier, in Paris.

Tarte Tatin, upside-down apple tart, is one of the few classic desserts with origins outside of Paris. In 1898 Caroline and Stéphanie Tatin, chef-owners of a restaurant in central France, either made an apple tart without a crust or accidentally turned an apple tart upside-down after baking it, creating a layer of caramelized apples on a pastry crust. The dessert first became a signature item in their restaurant before it gained fame after a Parisian food writer named Curnonsky spread the word about the sisters'

Desserts

restaurant and their delicious dessert. In all likelihood, the *tarte Tatin* existed in French country cooking as the *tarte renversée* long before the Tatin sisters made it famous (Wells 1985). French apple tart, an open-faced tart on a flaky crust with sliced apples decoratively arranged in a circle, likely has existed as long as pastry has in France. A simple recipe of apples and a little sugar in a buttery crust, the apple tart remains one of the most popular and enduring French desserts.

Some French desserts have invented histories that are difficult if not impossible to verify: notably for desserts like peach Melba and crêpes suzette. Peach Melba combines fresh peaches poached in sugar syrup with raspberry purée and vanilla ice cream. It is said to have been invented in 1894 by Auguste Escoffier, one of the most famous chefs of French cuisine, when he was head chef at the Savoy Hotel in London. As the story goes, Escoffier named the new dessert for opera star Nellie Melba, who was a guest at the hotel during her run in the main role of Richard Wagner's *Lohengrin*, in which a swan appears. Escoffier witnessed a performance by Melba and was said to have been so inspired by her unparalleled talent that he created a dessert in her honor when she dined at the restaurant. The original creation of peaches and vanilla ice cream appeared at the table nestled inside a swan carved from ice and covered with spun sugar, a dramatic dessert worthy of the most famous opera star of the era (Toussaint-Samat 2004, 87).

Later, Escoffier amended the recipe to include raspberry purée as an adaptation of another French dessert called *Pêche Cardinal*, named for the red robes worn by cardinals in the Roman Catholic Church. In his 1903 cookbook, Escoffier claims that he improved Pêche Cardinal by adding vanilla ice cream and that he named the new dessert after Nellie Melba because he knew that she loved Pêche Cardinal, but this happened only after he became chef at the Ritz Carlton Hotel in London (1903, 133). Many of the origin stories of French desserts are based on memory, and most dishes (desserts or otherwise) are re-creations or adaptations of earlier recipes, making specific histories challenging to establish. Whatever the true origin, Escoffier insisted on one point: no Chantilly cream (vanilla whipped cream) must ever tarnish the elegant peach Melba. He decried variations on his dessert that he interpreted as abominations, but none was so sacrilegious as the addition of whipped cream.

The origin of crêpes suzette, dessert crepes with an orange sauce, has also been attributed to Escoffier. Escoffier's recipe in *Guide culinaire* (1903) calls for tangerine juice and curaçao (an orange liqueur) as a sauce for crepes folded in quarters and warmed in butter and sugar. This recipe is also supposedly named for an artist, Suzanne Reichenberg, who was a celebrated actress at the Comédie Française. But a notice in the *International Herald Tribune* of April 1893 for the Parisian restaurant Maire advertised crêpes suzette and peach Melba as specialties of the chef. The recipe underwent a transformation when it landed in the United States. In its most well-known version, crêpes suzette calls for crepes to be warmed in a sauce made from orange liqueur and then flambéed or set aflame. This dramatic service style belongs to the American recipe, since French recipes do not call for flames. The "flambéed" version of crêpes suzette was perhaps invented by a French chef named Henri Charpentier, who claimed to have accidentally ignited the cognac in the sauce at a dinner for the Prince of Wales. Charpentier spent most of his career working in U.S. restaurants. The American version of Escoffier's *Guide culinaire,* called the *Escoffier Cookbook* (1969) calls the dish "Suzette Pancakes" and includes the instructions to flambé the crepes and serve the dessert while the flames are still active (1969, 755). American crêpes suzette are generally flavored with oranges and cognac or rum, but French chefs prefer tangerine and curaçao. It is, of course, very likely that a French chef well before Escoffier thought to flavor warm crepes with an orange or tangerine sauce. Both crêpes suzette and peach Melba had a popular following in the 1970s but are seen now as "old-fashioned" desserts that have fallen out of favor.

Classic Desserts with French Style

Fruit tarts made with pastry cream and beautifully ripe berries, peaches, or even kiwis decorate the cases of pastry shops all over France and are offered as individual or full-size tarts. Made with just a few ingredients, fruit tarts nevertheless reflect the care of the baker in the artfully arranged fruit glazed with apricot jam on a smooth custard base. The classic lemon tart or *tarte au citron* often appears on the list of favorite French desserts for its simple but satisfying combination of crumbly crust and bracing lemon curd filling. Lemon tarts with meringue add a layer of lightly browned sweetened egg whites, much like the American lemon meringue pie. The French art of cooking carries through to dessert in the precision required for even basic tart shells. There are three basic crusts for sweet recipes in French desserts, each with a specific name and technique. *Pâte sucrée* (sugared dough) contains only flour, butter, salt, sugar, and water to make a flaky base for apple tarts. *Pâte sablée* (sandy dough) has more butter and sugar to make it sweeter and more crumbly; it is used for fresh fruit tarts. *Pâte feuilletée* (flaky dough) has equal quantities of butter and flour with a little water and salt, and it is notoriously difficult to make and use. The layers of butter rolled into the dough create thin, flaky layers perfect for mille-feuilles and delicate pastries.

One of the eternal desserts of France that never goes out of style, cherry clafouti is a specialty of Limousin, in south-central France, where black cherries grow in abundance. It has been described as flan with cherries because of its egg-rich, custardy batter; it resembles a thick pancake dotted with cherries and dusted with powdered sugar. Residents of Limousin are highly protective of their signature cake, claiming that it originated there in the mid-nineteenth century, but there are references to clafouti in literature as far back as François Rabelais (in the sixteenth century) and Jean de la Fontaine (in the seventeenth century). Clafoutis is traditionally made with sweet cherries or pitted prunes. In Yazmina Reza's 2006 play *The God of Carnage*, two French families get into an argument about

---

Crème Brûlée

Yield: Serves 4

Ingredients
4 egg yolks
3 Tbsp granulated sugar, plus 4 tsp for topping
1 ¾ cups whole milk
¼ tsp vanilla extract (optional)

1. Heat oven to 325 degrees. Whisk the egg yolks and 3 tablespoons sugar until sugar is dissolved. Pour in the milk and whisk gently until combined. If you like, stir in a ¼ teaspoon of vanilla extract.
2. Divide the mixture equally into 4 small oven-safe bowls or ramekins (1/2 to 1-cup size). Place the bowls in a metal roasting pan and place in the oven. While the bowls are in the oven, pour water into the pan until it reaches halfway up the bowls.
3. Bake until the custard is just set, 45–60 minutes. Shake the pan gently to make sure the custard is solid but still jiggles a little in the center.
4. Remove the custards from the roasting pan and dry with a towel. Sprinkle the remaining sugar evenly over each custard, covering the surface evenly.
5. Heat the broiler. Place the custards on a baking sheet and caramelize the sugar under the broiler until brown and bubbly, 1–3 minutes. Watch carefully so that you do not burn the sugar.

Adapted from "Crème brûlée facile," *Elle à table*, accessed April 23, 2020, https://www.elle.fr/Elle-a-Table/Recettes-de-cuisine/Creme-brulee-facile-2894406.

(among other things) whether a clafouti is a cake or a tart, and whether pears and apples belong in the dish or cherries alone.

Crème brûlée (literally "burnt cream") is challenging to do well at home, with its top layer of sugar melted with a blowtorch. The sugar layer was not part of the original seventeenth-century recipe since granulated sugar was not widely available and since sugar was far too expensive to be used as a topping. The sprinkle of caramelized sugar that defines this dessert today, and which likely makes it the most popular dessert in French restaurants, probably first appeared in the nineteenth century. Crème brulée also lends itself well to adaptations, such as the addition of lavender or other flavors.

Crème caramel and other baked custards share the same basic elements as crème brûlée but contain more egg yolks and are baked longer. These individual custards are then unmolded onto a plate for serving. Crème caramel ingeniously contains its own sauce; the caramel forms from sugar and butter in the bottom of the baking dish on top of which the custard bakes. When unmolded, the thin caramel sauce flows over the baked

---

Riz au Lait (Rice Pudding)

Yield: Serves 4

Ingredients
4 cups whole milk
6 Tbsp granulated sugar
1 vanilla bean or ½ tsp vanilla extract
⅔ cup short-grain or Arborio rice
Zest of one citrus fruit (orange or lemon suggested), cut into one long strip
Fruit jam or fresh fruit (optional)

1. Heat milk, sugar, and vanilla bean or vanilla extract over low heat until sugar has dissolved. Remove vanilla bean, if using.
2. Bring to a simmer, and then slowly stir in rice. Add citrus zest to pot. Simmer on low heat until the rice is tender but not too soft, 30–40 minutes, stirring occasionally. Remove zest.
3. Let cool on stovetop, and then transfer to a bowl and refrigerate until completely cool. The rice will absorb more milk as it cools.

Serve in individual bowls garnished with spoonsful of jam or fresh cut fruit. Blueberries or strawberries are especially good. Serve with butter cookies, if you like.

custard as an accent to the eggy, vanilla flavor. Savory dishes with rice are fairly rare in French cuisine, but rice pudding as a dessert is a comforting and common ending to meals. Short-grain rice slowly simmered in milk and sugar turns soft and slightly sticky, and the liquid makes a sort of custard. Rice pudding is served in individual dishes or pressed into a buttered baking dish to make a sort of cake. In Guadeloupe, coconut custard (*flan-koko*) is a favored dessert, using fresh coconut and coconut milk.

On the opposite end of eggy custards and milky rice are the light, ethereal airy desserts that carry undeniably French names. Mousses, especially chocolate mousse, are first described in seventeenth-century cookbooks, but modern versions are unquestionably lighter in texture since they are prepared with electric mixers. Chocolate mousse gets its airy texture from beaten egg whites, the key to meringues, into which melted chocolate must be folded carefully so as not to deflate the fluffy whites. Soufflés depend on the same principle of perfectly whipped egg whites that hold their puffy texture if the other ingredients are delicately mixed in. The French word *souffler* means "to blow" or "to whisper," a suggestion of the light texture intended in these desserts. Dessert soufflés are often flavored with chocolate or coffee, and some have ice cream at the center. Soufflés are less common on dessert menus than they once were, perhaps because they must be made to order and served as soon as they come out of the oven, before they deflate.

Oeufs à la neige (floating islands, or literally "eggs in the snow") begin with sweetened whipped egg whites that are formed into egg shapes and poached in vanilla-flavored milk until just firm. The "eggs" are served on a layer of custard sauce called crème anglaise, or English cream, and sometimes accented with caramel. A similar dessert using sweetened egg whites carries the unusual name *omelette norvégienne* ("Norwegian omelet"), perhaps because its finished oval shape somewhat resembles an omelet and because its ice cream filling suggests cold northern climates. The *omelette norvégienne* resembles baked Alaska, with a layer of sponge cake surrounding an egg-shaped layer of ice cream, both covered entirely with sweetened egg whites. The cake is frozen until just before serving, when the meringue layer is browned in the oven or under the broiler to color it just slightly. When decorated with spun sugar, the *omelette norvégienne* makes a showstopping final course.

More recent desserts, like snacks and other popular foods, have adopted American recipes and even English names. The "crumble" of cooked fruits topped by a sweet and crumbly baked topping can be found on restaurant menus and in cookbooks for the home baker. Favorite flavors include pear, chocolate, strawberry rhubarb, and apple. A "cake" in French refers specifically to a loaf cake; there are dessert versions but many savory "cakes" exist in French cooking, with ingredients like salmon or cheese. The word "cake" existed in French in the late eighteenth century to refer to a kind of tart but was not commonly used in the dessert sense until the 1960s, when it first appeared in standard French dictionaries. In English, a cake can take many forms, but in French dessert it has a standard shape (rectangular loaf) and traditionally contains dried fruit, since it was originally an imitation of the British fruitcake. In France, dessert "cakes" might be flavored with chocolate, lemon, or plain yogurt.

The American import cheesecake has also become very popular on French tables in the twenty-first century, as have brownies and muffins that are also called by their English names in French. Other desserts that might carry the name "cake" in English have more specific names in French, such as the *fraisier*, a cake with fresh strawberries and strawberry mousse often served at summer parties. The *quatre-quarts* (what we know as pound cake) gets its name ("four-fourths") in French from the ingredient list: the dessert contains four equal "quarters" of flour, butter, sugar, and eggs. Perhaps the most popular dessert for all occasions is the *moelleux* or *fondant au chocolat*, a gooey chocolate cake whose name means "soft" or "melty" chocolate. The name, although untranslatable in English, perfectly describes the appeal of the cake.

French desserts range from the classic and complicated to the very simple. In a fine restaurant, diners will discover desserts drawn from Escoffier's elegant cuisine with decorative elements and perfect pastry. The Saint-Honoré cake and *oeufs à la neige* remain on restaurant menus alongside the ubiquitous crème brûlée. In pastry shops, French families choose a glittering fruit tart or a selection of beautifully decorated pastries, perhaps éclairs or mille-feuilles. At home, ambitious cooks prepare the perfect *moelleux au chocolat* or opera cake, and more traditional bakers offer a *quatre-quarts* or a truly timeless *tarte aux pommes*. But French dessert does not require pastry or even sugar. On a summer evening, a French meal might conclude with *verrines*, the French word for parfait, layers of fruit and cream in a tall dessert dish, or some fresh strawberries macerated in red wine, an elegant and utterly simple dish. In the Caribbean, caramelized bananas or mango sorbet with just a few ingredients end the meal on a sweet note. Other desserts use whole fruit as a central element, such as pears poached in wine or caramelized whole oranges, a reminder that at the beginning French dessert meant fruit and only fruit. Even more simply, a diner might choose a whole apple or pear, carefully peeled and cut into slices, eaten thoughtfully as a refreshing end to a satisfying meal.

Further Reading

Adams, Stephen. 2007. "Sèvres Porcelain and the Articulation of Imperial Identity in Napoleonic France." *Journal of Design History* 20 (3): 183–204.
Carême, Marie-Antoine. (1815) 1834. *Le pâtissier royal parisien*. London: Mason.
Day, Ivan. 1999. "Sculpture for the Eighteenth-Century Garden Dessert." In *Food in the Arts: Proceedings of the Oxford Symposium on Food and Cookery 1998*, edited by Harlan Walker, 57–66. Devon, UK: Prospect Books.
Dictionnaire de l'Académie Française. 1694. Paris: Académie Française.
Escoffier, Auguste. 1903. *Le guide culinaire*. Paris: Flammarion.
Escoffier, Auguste. 1969. *The Escoffier Cookbook*. New York: Crown Publishers. Originally published as *Le guide culinaire* (Paris: Flammarion, 1903).
Flandrin, Jean Louis. 2007. *Arranging the Meal: A History of Table Service in France*. Berkeley: University of California Press.
Gouffé, Jules. 1873. *Le Livre de Pâtisserie*. Paris: Hachette.
Hugo, Victor. (1832) 1959. *Notre Dame de Paris*. Paris: Garnier.
Massialot, François. 1698. *Nouvelle instruction pour les confitures, les liqueurs, et les fruits*. Paris: De Sercy.
Tebben, Maryann. 2015. "Seeing and Tasting: The Evolution of Dessert in French Gastronomy." *Gastronomica* 15 (2): 10–25.
Toussaint-Samat, Maguelonne. 2004. *La très belle et très exquise histoire des gâteaux et des friandises*. Paris: Flammarion.
Wells, Patricia. 1985. "Fare of the Country: As French as Tarte Tatin." *New York Times*, March 24, 1985.
Wheaton, Barbara. 1996. *Savoring the Past*. New York: Touchstone.

CHAPTER SIX

Beverages

France is best known for its fine wines, and its most famous beverage might be the sparkling wine known as champagne. Today, family celebrations would be incomplete without a bottle of carefully selected wine to complement the meal. The French indulge in sweet fruit drinks, coffee, hot chocolate, sodas, and juices, but at the French table, only water or wine (or possibly beer or cider) is served. But before wine became a symbol of fine dining in France, alcoholic drinks were simply a way to make water safer to drink. The French, like their neighbors in Europe and around the world, eventually devised innovative ways to bring clean water to residents of the cities. But fermented drinks were less likely to cause illness and were thus a healthier option than plain water. From the seventeenth to the twentieth centuries, the French turned to water from natural springs and thermal sources not just as a safe way to quench thirst but as a cure for diseases. Over the course of modern history, the French regularly associated beverages with health (or warned that they could be harmful to health), from coffee to hot chocolate to wine and spirits. For pleasure or for health, beverages are a well-regulated part of the French diet.

Wine and Beer

The sixth-century Greek physician Anthimus recorded common beverages he observed among the Franks in northeastern Gaul, including an early form of beer called *cervisa*, honeyed wine called *hydromel*, and a sort of mead made with wormwood (the active ingredient in absinthe) called *aloxinum*. We know from Anthimus and other texts of the period that beer (or beer-like drinks) were more popular than wine in Gaul and its neighboring territories since the tribes in these areas had Celtic and Germanic heritage, both fond of fermented grain drinks like beer. The Romans brought the custom of drinking wine made from grapes to Gaul when they conquered the territory, but certain areas of what would later become

France maintain their allegiance to beer even today. As a drink, beer had a lower status than wine. Wine drinkers were typically part of the elite, while the poorer classes drank beer, cider, or heavily watered-down wine. It was customary in the ancient period and the Middle Ages to mix wine with water to purify it, and to add water to wine to thin it out since early wines were rougher and more acidic than they are today. This custom persisted until nearly the end of the eighteenth century, when finer wines entered the market in greater quantity.

The great French wine regions were established as early as the Middle Ages, and the first French wines were produced in monasteries by monks for their own consumption. At the Corbie monastery in northern France in the ninth century, monks had a daily allotment of at least two goblets of wine (more on feast days), but the lay workers who lived at the monastery received two goblets of beer, not wine, with meals (Hocquet 1985, 677). With carefully tended vineyards and deep knowledge of the best methods for producing wine, the medieval monks started the tradition of excellent wine in France: the Corbie monastery cultivated the pinot noir grape, now one of the most prized varieties, in the fifteenth century, and the popes in Avignon managed a monastery winery known as Châteauneuf du Pape on the Rhone River; it is still one of the most renowned wine producers in France (Dion 1959, 186). Their fine wines gained a following and were later sold to earn revenue for the abbeys, which were meant to be self-sufficient. As the French nation began to form in the early Middle Ages, Christian Franks aligned themselves with wine in rejection of the barbaric Germanic custom for beer, claiming that wine was justified in the Bible but that beer was pagan and common. By the eleventh and twelfth centuries, wine was the primary beverage for most French people, even the poor. In the countryside, of course, fresh water from a spring or river provided the rural poor with an easy (and free) way to quench their thirst.

The northern regions of Brittany and Normandy, known for growing excellent pears and apples, preferred cider to beer or wine and drank it almost exclusively beginning in the twelfth century. Hard cider from apples or pears has a low alcohol content and is lightly bubbly. Cider from Brittany pairs well with the other specialty of the region: buckwheat galettes and crepes. In the Renaissance, those in the cities who found wine too expensive turned to cider, beer, or water boiled with honey, herbs, or vinegar to purify it. Nicolas de Bonnefons offered a recipe for *hidromel* (here meaning water with honey) in his book on gardening, called *Délices de la campagne* (Country delights; 1654) to be made at home by boiling rainwater and honey and storing it in barrels (1654, 77). The rest of France eventually adopted cider, and national consumption of cider doubled between the nineteenth and twentieth centuries, from 5.8 to 14.6 gallons per person per year (Teuteberg and Flandrin 2013, 452).

Wine served an essential purpose as a source of calories in Revolution-era French diets, and it had great cultural importance for the French long before the eighteenth century. Poorer classes used alcoholic beverages as a source of cheap calories; they were safer than water to drink and cheaper than many food items. But wine production was occasionally at odds with grain cultivation, requiring the same sort of intervention seen in the bread and meat trades. Demand for wine in the early part of the century, and the temptation to make money from this increasing demand, prompted the clearing of grain fields in the southwest and north to plant vineyards. The resulting grain shortages led to royal orders from Louis XV forbidding new vineyards between 1731 and 1759. But wine was an extremely profitable agricultural product, and even small vineyard owners could eke out a profit with a few acres of land.

The temptation to produce wine for sale shaped the parceling of land in the Champagne region and the southwest in a profound way, and it changed the landscape of wine as these regions attempted to provide enough wine to Paris. Traditional grape varieties that made higher-quality wines often had low yields; many vineyards in the northern regions turned to high-yield varieties that made great quantities of mediocre wine, of little interest to wine connoisseurs and the international market, who would pay more for better wine and help producers reinvest in their properties. With a glut of subpar wine on the market, prices fell; ultimately, large producers created a monopoly in the nineteenth century by buying small vineyards after small producers could no longer maintain economic

Barley Water

Barley water has recently made a comeback as a healthy drink, but the drink originated in the ancient world. Sixth-century physician Anthimus mentioned barley water (*ptisane*) in his writing, a kind of thin barley soup consumed as a beverage particularly by the sick. Barley water with sugar and ground almonds became a popular drink in the Middle Ages, and later versions of the beverage were called *orgemonde* ("Orgeat" 2014, 577). Eventually the name was shortened to *orgeat* and the recipe evolved, leaving out the barley and adding citrus juice. These drinks, similar to modern lemonade, were sold by street vendors called *limonadiers* in the seventeenth century.

stability. On a more positive note, the Champagne region had been known for its common wines since the sixteenth century; faced with a glut of ordinary wine, producers in this region focused their attention on foamy white wines that would soon become the signature wine of the region, known around the world by the nineteenth century as a symbol of celebration (Brennan 1997, 246).

White wine from the Champagne region had a following at the sixteenth-century French court because these light wines were more expensive (and therefore a status symbol) and were thought to be healthier than heavy red wines. The wines from Ay, a town in the Champagne region, had the best reputation of all, highly praised by the king and his entourage (Dion 1959, 632). A monk in the neighboring Abbey of Hautvilliers whose name was Dom Perignon focused his wine-making efforts on perfecting these fine white wines, following the tradition of monastic wine production, and wine from Champagne further polished its reputation. But these early wines did not yet have their signature sparkle. In the late seventeenth century, a new technique called fining (adding a substance to remove impurities) produced clear, bubbly wines. In the eighteenth century, winemakers discovered that racking (pouring aged wine into a new container) allowed them to remove the sediment left from spent yeast and sugar, making these fine wines even better and more profitable because they earned a higher price (Brennan 1997, 248). Only in the eighteenth century, when consumers began to seek out sparkling wines as a fashionable drink, did modern champagne as we know it take France and the world by storm.

The monk at the Abbey of Hautvilliers, Dom Perignon, would later be called the father of French champagne but only after a publicity campaign in the nineteenth century invented the story that would retroactively create the myth. Dom Grossard, a former Benedictine monk, began a campaign in 1821 to celebrate the accomplishments of the Hautvilliers abbey, including the invention of sparkling wine attributed to Dom Perignon but with no evidence to support his claim. The practice of adding sugar to create a second fermentation and produce bubbles in wine or cider had been used since the late Middle Ages. Nevertheless, at the 1889 Universal Exposition in Paris, the union of Champagne wine producers distributed an illustrated pamphlet telling the story of Dom Perignon and naming him the "father" of sparkling wine (Guy 2003, 28). In the 1880s the wine producers worked to earn sparkling wine from Champagne a special status. By 1900 the name *champagne* designated a natural product of the Champagne region that was made *mousseux* (bubbly) by a second processing phase, distinguishing it from sparkling wine from other regions that used the second fermentation technique. Then as now, the term *champagne* legally designates the wine from this region created with this technique; other sparkling wines are forbidden from using the name "champagne" and must instead use terms like *méthode champenoise* (Champagne method) or *vin mousseux* (sparkling wine).

Geography generally determined good wine in the eighteenth century. The Bordeaux region produced a quarter of all French wine in this period, and wines from Burgundy had long been recognized for their excellent quality. As a "common good" like bread and meat, wine earned protectionist measures from the government, with a greater effect on Paris, where wine brokers held a monopoly on river traffic, effectively closing the Seine to regional producers hoping to sell their wine directly in the city. Winemakers argued for intervention against brokers who manipulated wine prices, limited quantities, and were accused of adulterating wines. Authorities intervened much less dramatically in wine than in grain or meat, and changes came about on the initiative of those in the wine business with benefits mainly to the wealthy.

Beginning in the 1750s, trade journals began to offer advice to wine buyers on purchasing and transporting wine, promoting direct purchases from regional wholesale merchants in Bordeaux and Burgundy, and disparaging Parisian wine brokers accused of fraud. Elite consumers also drove the adoption of glass bottles in the eighteenth century since wine sold in barrels, as it had been until then, was more prone to spoilage if it was not consumed quickly. Taverns and *marchands de vin* (wine bars run by wine merchants) served enough customers to empty a barrel before the wine oxidized, but individual consumers wishing to preserve their fine wines for aging demanded smaller quantities and glass bottles. The move to bottles also helped to keep the gas bubbles in white wines, and this technological change enabled champagne to become the trademarked, brand-name commodity wine it is now.

After the Revolution, authorities seized and sold noble estates, emigrant-owned properties, and church-owned lands, called *biens nationaux*, or national common goods. Much of this property had been used as vineyards, and small producers eagerly purchased these new tracts of land suddenly available for sale. As a result, more wine came on the market, and more consumers had access to it. The urban working class consumed wine in cabarets, one of only a few businesses licensed to sell wine in individual portions, and in the *guinguettes*, dance halls on the outskirts of cities, introducing the lower classes to a better quality of wine. City dwellers drank wine regularly in taverns and *marchands de vin*, but rural populations generally abstained from wine until the revolutionary era made the drink more plentiful and a higher standard of living gave them greater access to this very French tradition.

To preserve and celebrate its wine traditions, French winemakers officially classified the finest wines of Bordeaux in 1855 in preparation for the Universal Exposition in Paris of that year, where Napoleon hoped to show off the best of France. The Bordeaux winemakers ranked the region's wineries from first- to fifth-growth, based on the prices paid for their wines. Wineries with the highest-priced wines were thought to produce the best quality wine: the first-growth (*premier cru*) category included Château Lafite, Margaux, Latour, and Haut-Brion, all still producing astonishingly expensive wine today. In 1935 the French government created the *Appellation* and *Dénomination d'Origine Contrôlée* (AOC and DOC) designations, legislating rules and guaranteeing authenticity and quality of wines with this label to the French and to the world. From the AOC classifications, Burgundy winemakers also established *grand cru* and *premier cru* classifications based on geography rather than producer. Burgundy and Bordeaux wines are without question the best in France, but other regions boast quality wines as well, including the Loire valley for crisp, white wines, Provence for rosé, and Alsace for Riesling, a sweet, white wine.

Wine for Health

Prior to the twentieth century, the term *alcool* in French meant only spirits, not fermented drinks such as wine, beer, or cider. These drinks, even if they contained alcohol, were considered *boissons hygiéniques* ("hygienic drinks") (Marrus 1974, 119). Spirits were thought to be dangerous to health, but fermented drinks were not. The classification of wine as a hygienic drink in France began even earlier, after the Prussian siege of 1870, when the French government hoped to raise morale by encouraging national pride. Officials began a campaign to restrict distilled liquor and increase distribution of wine, declaring it key to the health of every French person and the entire nation (Guy 2002, 39). Wine was the pride of France, but spirits seemed foreign and beer had roots in Germany, France's enemy. Public rejection of hard liquor also came in response to the steep rise in consumption of these beverages and the resulting temperance movement in France. During World War I, reformers called distilled alcohol the "internal enemy" and again sanctioned wine and beer as hygienic (Brennan 1989, 78). Public sentiment aside, the only law passed that restricted alcohol sales was aimed at absinthe, the green liquor derived from wormwood that triggered hallucinations in some drinkers. It was banned in France in 1915 but returned to circulation later in the

Beverages

twentieth century in a new formula, without wormwood or hallucinogenic properties.

The French hold true to this perception of wine even today since most families have wine on hand, but the use of hard alcohol has declined and beer has far less importance than wine. The selection of beverages in current French households follows economic patterns since more educated or wealthier consumers buy more fine wine and nonalcoholic drinks, and those with modest educations and budgets buy more table wine and beer. The French have a cultural education in wine, and they think carefully about selection and storage of wine: if a house or apartment has a "cave" or cellar for storing wines at the proper temperature, the household is likely to spend more money on fine wines, and those without a storage space tend to limit themselves to table wine that does not benefit from aging (Boizot 1999, 148).

Wine remains the largest part of the household beverage budget, followed by bottled water, fruit juices, beer, and soft drinks. French families with children buy more bottled water and fruit juice for their families than households without children, and small children might occasionally be allowed to drink fruit juice with a meal, in violation of the traditional water-or-wine-only rule. Government statistics for 2018 show that the French spend more on bottled water (flat and sparkling) than on other nonwine drinks, with beer and nonalcoholic drinks like fruit juice and sodas roughly equal (Insee 2019).

Mineral Water and Sodas

France is home to all kinds of water: consumers worldwide recognize French brands like Perrier, Evian, and Badoit, and French shoppers find many more labels in grocery stores. Originally sold only at pharmacies, at designated water vendors, and at the source or spring, bottled water has become an increasingly large part of the household budget in France. Water from thermal spas and natural springs contains a high mineral content and was long believed to treat or prevent illness. Regulations for mineral water date to the seventeenth century, when King Henry IV sought to protect certain water sources by royal edict. In 1605 Henry IV appointed the royal physician to lead the effort to document and regulate mineral water sources, establishing the link between water and medicine, a characteristic that would persist in France for several centuries (Raynal 2004, 591). The first legal definition for French mineral water in 1922 proclaimed that the label *mineral water* could only be applied to water with therapeutic properties that was collected from a natural source that had been recognized by the government ministry and that adhered to all pertinent laws and regulations. Bottled water had to carry a label specifying what kind of water it was (spring, mineral, sparkling, or artificially enhanced) and the location of the source, but water companies also used this label to advertise the therapeutic qualities of each brand of water. Vichy water, for example, from the center of France, claimed to relieve liver and stomach issues, kidney stones, and diabetic symptoms.

Following the rules set by the Royal Society of Medicine beginning in 1605 and over the course of two centuries, mineral water could only be sold at the source by approved vendors and at the price set by the Society. Finally, in 1823 a new ruling allowed pharmacies and approved water vendors to sell mineral water free from government inspection and taxes because these kinds of water were considered medicine (Raynal 2004, 592). With authorization to transport these waters from their source, and with the opening of a new marketplace, the water industry expanded rapidly in France, with pharmacists buying their own springs and bottling operations popping up throughout France to sell these hyperlocal products. The reputation for a certain water might only be known to the local area, limiting the demand for each spring's water to the cities and towns close to the source. With modernization and greater demand, many of these smaller productions have disappeared, and the large water companies ship water all over the country.

In the 1930s, when French consumers bought an average of seven liters of bottled water per year, water companies expanded their efforts to create a national market for bottled water with publicity, sponsoring sporting events and hiring celebrities for their advertisements, but the war years intervened. In 1957 a new law allowed water vendors to process the water they sold after taking it from the source, a change from previous rules requiring that water be sold exactly as it emerged from the earth. Water companies developed techniques for removing iron particles that turned the water a rusty color and gave it an unpleasant taste, and for adding gas so that they could customize water with larger or smaller bubbles and heavier and lighter carbonation (Raynal 2004, 595). Some French mineral waters are naturally carbonated, and others are enhanced with extra fizz. The largest water companies, like Evian and Vittel, built huge modern factories to respond to new sanitary conditions for bottled water imposed by the government in 1964, and the increased production pushed these large companies to sell their water in supermarkets as well as pharmacies. Between 1950 and 1970 the major national companies grew exponentially. The Perrier bottle shape and green color, created in 1904, became iconic and stood out among its competitors, and the Perrier group owned more than half of French bottled water production in 1972 (Marty 2008, 89). By 1995 the French were purchasing 10 times as much bottled water as they had in 1950, reaching approximately 108 liters per person per year (Boizot 1999, 143).

Once bottled water became available in cafés, hotels, and restaurants, it was no longer associated with therapeutic treatments, and it became a sought-after commodity, although medical claims were permitted on water bottle labels until 1980. Some bottled water brands are still associated with their medical origins, even if they are successful consumer brands today: Evian and Vichy, for example, still promote the healthy qualities of their products as natural mineral water from the original source. By law, the only health claims allowed on French mineral water are that the water aids digestion, can support and promote healthy liver function, and can be a laxative or diuretic. In order to stand out to shoppers, French bottled water brands emphasize the specific qualities of each product related to health. Brands owned by Danone group (including Evian) claim to be best for babies because they are low in mineral content; Nestlé produces water high in minerals and advertises the health benefits of mineral water; and sparkling water brands have different levels of bicarbonate for digestion (Marty 2008, 95).

The popular French-Algerian soft drink Orangina also has a connection to a pharmacy. In 1936 in Marseille, the Algerian-born French entrepreneur Léon Beton bought the formula for an orange drink from a pharmacist from Spain to make use of juice from his orange grove in French-occupied Algeria. The original formula contained orange juice, carbonated water, sugar syrup, and orange essence. Beton named his product Naranjina, after the Spanish word for "small orange," and it sold well locally, but his son Jean-Claude's ingenious advertising and marketing, featuring a textured round bottle shaped like an orange, created a successful following for the soda in Algeria and eventually in mainland France. In 1952 a group of distributors began to sell the beverage throughout France. The company maintained its home office in Algeria until Algerian independence in 1962, when it moved to Marseille on the southern coast of France (Lippman 2010). Unlike most commercial sodas, Orangina contains natural fruit pulp and must be shaken to be enjoyed properly; Orangina advertising emphasized the unique characteristic of the drink encouraging consumers to "secouez-moi!" (shake me!). In 1998 the company resisted a hostile takeover by the Coca-Cola Company, but it was later purchased by an American group and is now owned by the Japanese conglomerate Suntory.

> ## Local Colas
>
> Coca-Cola and Pepsi are, of course, found everywhere in France (along with diet versions called Coca Light and Pepsi Light), but regional colas scattered across the country can be found in cafés and markets. These local sodas are usually made with natural ingredients and are fairly recent inventions. Among them are Anjou Cola (now called Loire Cola), which appeared in 2010 and uses chamomile grown in the western, Atlantic region of Anjou; Corsica Cola, which belongs to the island of Corsica in the Mediterranean; and Paris Cola, released in 2013 and entirely made in France, bottles included.

Coffee, Hot Chocolate, and Tea

As a beverage, milk was considered to be barbaric by the Romans in Gaul because the neighboring Franks drank it and the Franks were seen as inferior. The Gallo-Romans preferred to use fresh milk to make cheese rather than to drink what they saw as a "raw" ingredient. Centuries later, at the start of the Renaissance, the residents of Brittany stood out from the rest of France because, unlike people in the other regions of the country, they drank milk and buttermilk (Laurioux 2013, 33). Subsequent generations of French people maintain the tradition set by the Gallo-Romans: even today the French consume very little fluid milk. It is considered a drink for children or at best an ingredient in a morning hot chocolate or café au lait.

Coffee, hot chocolate, and tea reached France at roughly the same time, in the seventeenth century, as refreshments for royalty. Spanish explorers brought cacao from the New World to Europe and started a fashion for drinking the exotic beverage. Famous hot chocolate fans include Anne d'Autriche, wife of Louis XIII, and Maria Theresa, Infanta of Spain and first wife to Louis XIV. Cardinal Jules Mazarin, prime minister under Louis XIV, brought expert cooks from Italy to prepare coffee, tea, and chocolate for the court as early as 1642 (Coe and Coe 2000, 155). The first cups of French hot chocolate likely had little or no sugar and were certainly dark and bitter, judging by the descriptions found in aristocrat Madame de Sévigné's letters about the habits of society ladies in and around Louis XIV's court. Sévigné encouraged her daughter to drink chocolate for energy and to aid digestion, but warned that too much chocolate could bring on fevers.

> ## Lait de Poule (Hen's Milk)
>
> *Yield:* Serves 2
>
> *Ingredients*
> 2 egg yolks
> 2 Tbsp sugar
> 2 cups whole milk
>
> 1. Whisk the egg yolks and sugar together in a bowl until combined.
> 2. Heat milk in a small saucepan until just boiling, then remove from heat. Let stand 5 minutes.
> 3. Add the milk slowly to the egg mixture, whisking constantly. When fully combined, pour into mugs and serve. Sprinkle with a little nutmeg if you like.
>
> *Traditionally, the French drink "hen's milk" to feel better when they have a cold or the flu.*
>
> Adapted from Paul Bocuse, *Paul Bocuse in Your Kitchen* (New York: Pantheon, 1982), 342.

Because it came from Spain and the New World, warm climates very different from temperate France, chocolate was believed to have hot and dry qualities that would affect the body, particularly aristocratic French bodies, which were thought to be delicate and sophisticated. Drinking chocolate was served regularly at all public functions at Versailles until 1693, when its use was suppressed under the influence of the moralistic Madame de Maintenon, companion of Louis XIV. During the height of chocolate mania in seventeenth-century France, so many aristocratic women drank chocolate that the Catholic clergy forbade hot chocolate during Lent, inspiring a lengthy debate on whether drinking chocolate was considered solid food (violating the Lenten fasting rules) or a beverage.

In France, chocolate evolved from its Spanish origins into a more refined product. Different types and flavors of chocolate mark the ages: in the seventeenth century, *chocolat baroque* was in vogue, with its complex, dense flavor and strong aromas. By the eighteenth century, French chocolate drinkers sought more elemental flavors. The *chocolat des Lumières* (Enlightenment chocolate) contained more sugar and added vanilla and

> ### Chocolat Chaud (French Hot Chocolate)
>
> *Yield:* Serves 2
>
> *Ingredients*
> 2 cups whole milk
> 8 oz. dark chocolate bar, roughly chopped
> ½ tsp ground cinnamon (optional)
> ½ cup heavy cream
> Unsweetened whipped cream for serving
>
> 1. Heat the milk in a small saucepan over medium-low heat until just starting to simmer.
> 2. Slowly whisk the chopped chocolate into the hot milk, stirring constantly until fully incorporated. Add the cinnamon, if using. Stir in the heavy cream when all of the chocolate is melted.
> 3. Whisk the mixture until frothy, and heat until hot (but not boiling).
> 4. Pour into mugs and garnish with whipped cream.

cinnamon (Camporesi 1992, 185). In his 1825 *Physiologie du goût*, gastronome Brillat-Savarin praises hot chocolate as nutritious, easy to digest with none of the difficulties brought on by coffee, suitable even for weak stomachs, and useful for treating chronic disease ([1825] 1982, 119). The affluent elite lingered over a decadent cup of chocolate late in the morning, but the working class replaced a meal with hot chocolate or café au lait at home or from a street vendor, beginning in the nineteenth century. In the present day, drinking chocolate still has a place both as an everyday morning beverage at home and as a decadent treat.

French children enjoy Nestlé chocolate powder mixed with milk and served in a bowl (used as a large cup) for breakfast or, for an afternoon treat, a bottle of Cacolac, a milky chocolate drink created in Bordeaux in 1954 and sold in cafés and grocery stores. The chocolate shop Angelina in Paris serves "old-style" drinking chocolate in an elegant boutique on the rue de Rivoli, one of the most fashionable streets in the capital. Opened in 1903, Angelina embraces its reputation as "the meeting place for Parisian aristocracy," and its house specialty is dense, rich "African" hot chocolate, a secret blend of chocolates from Niger, Ghana, and the Ivory Coast, served in a pitcher with porcelain cups and an individual pot of whipped cream for garnish ("La Maison Angelina" n.d.).

Coffee in France had a similar start in the seventeenth century, as a foreign beverage with few initial early adopters due to its bitter taste and its high price. Turkish visitors and the Ottoman ambassador brought coffee to the court of Louis XIV at a moment when the French elite had a fascination with Eastern cultures, but it was also known in other parts of France. Coffee likely first entered France through Marseille in the south (an important Mediterranean port and international city) and had a following in Lyon, where world travelers who had experienced coffee in other countries in the East sought it out. Armenian immigrant coffee vendors opened coffee shops in Paris as early as 1672, although the Sicilian café-owner Francesco Procopio is commonly given credit for the first café; since his establishment belonged to an official guild, it was the first legal café (McCabe 2014, 129).

Madame de Sévigné at first criticized coffee as poisonous in her letters, but she later endorsed it, following the lead of the king who embraced it and made it fashionable. Like chocolate, the original form of Turkish coffee was thick and strong-tasting, and the French took time to become accustomed to it, eventually softening the flavor with milk. Once medical authorities suggested that coffee with milk had health benefits, the drink gained a true following. Philippe Sylvestre Dufour composed *Traité nouveau et curieux du café, du thé et du chocolat* (New and curious treatise on coffee, tea, and chocolate) in 1685, proclaiming the advantages of café au lait (coffee with milk) for patients with various illnesses. Coffee blended with milk and sugar fit the taste preferences of the French more easily than bitter, black coffee, and the French embraced café au lait as a fashionable drink and as a source of nutrition. Like chocolate, café au lait had a decadent quality that seemed luxurious to the wealthy and earned criticism from church officials.

By the eighteenth century, most city residents had access to cafés for an individual cup of coffee, and some of the French adopted coffee pots for home use. In the 1760s home inventory records in Paris showed that 40 percent of middle-class homes and 20 percent of lower-class homes owned a coffee pot (Roche 2000, 246). The French made coffee and chocolate a habitual part of their diet by the end of the eighteenth century, and increasing demand for these products led to the development of cacao and coffee plantations in the French colonies in Africa and the Caribbean. Revolutionary-minded citizens and philosophers like Diderot and Rousseau adopted the café as a meeting place, emboldened by the energy they drew from the caffeinated drink and disdainful of the slothful, aristocratic chocolate drinkers.

By the mid-nineteenth century, urban residents replaced their traditional breakfast bowl of soup with a bowl of coffee and milk, and workers often took a bowl of café au lait as a replacement for a meal. The signature coffee drink of the French may be café au lait since the addition of milk may have been the most important factor in making coffee palatable to the general French public. At home, the French overwhelmingly drink coffee as a breakfast beverage, and very often adults take an espresso after lunch. A 2015 survey of French consumers over the age of 18 showed that 52 percent preferred coffee at breakfast, compared to 25 percent who chose tea and 14 percent who drank hot chocolate (Statista 2015). New coffee pod technology has made it easier to drink espresso at home, and this version of coffee has a large following in France. In 1999 Nespresso introduced its coffee pods and coffee maker system in France, and today 500 million coffee pods are sold in France each year.

Tea has a smaller presence in France than coffee does, but tea salons offer an elegant place for a cup of tea and a fancy pastry in the middle of the day. Tea leaves were imported to France by the Dutch as early as 1636, but coffee quickly surpassed tea in popularity, and it remained a beverage exclusively for the wealthy for much of its early history in France. François Massialot, in his 1692 book on after-dinner drinks, sweets, and jams, asserts that coffee is more common than tea because tea is much more expensive. While coffee and chocolate were overtaking French elite society, the French East India Company set out for India and Persia (now Iran) in search of goods for trade, as the Dutch and British had done. The French tea seller Mariage Frères (Mariage Brothers), opened in 1854, remains one of the few French companies associated with tea. Originally only a wholesale business, Mariage Frères now operates tea shops in Paris, Tokyo, and Berlin.

Banania

The history of French colonialism had direct effects on the preference in France for coffee and chocolate over tea, and the introduction of bananas from overseas territories encouraged the creation of another hot breakfast drink: Banania. Made of chocolate, bananas, and cooked grains, the drink created by journalist Pierre Lardet in 1912 was marketed as nutritious food for children. Lardet enjoyed a similar drink on his travels in Nicaragua and believed that he could sell such a product in France; he registered the trademark for Banania in Paris in 1914. Early advertising for Banania emphasized the healthy ingredients in the drink that would nourish children and adults and give long-lasting energy. In addition, the banana drink evoked the foreign lands of France's growing colonial empire and the exotic foods eaten there. The first image featured in Banania advertisements was a Caribbean woman. The famous Senegalese marksman that later adorned the box, in recognition of the Senegalese fighters' service in World War I, became part of the brand's advertising in 1915.

Lardet sent a train full of Banania to the front lines during the war to nourish the soldiers there but also to gain valuable publicity. Grateful soldiers remembered the fortifying beverage when they returned home, and Banania became a drink for children and adults alike. The beverage enjoyed a near-monopoly in France among chocolate breakfast drinks, surviving World War II and restrictions on chocolate and milk, and in the postwar period the colonial imagery disappeared from packaging, replaced by a smiling sun or a child. Finally, in the 1960s, companies like Nesquik and Poulain introduced their own chocolate breakfast mixes, but loyal fans of Banania (a unique product with an unchanged recipe since the beginning) kept buying it. The banana-chocolate drink can still be found on supermarket shelves more than a century after it first appeared in France.

Café Beverages

French cafés serve a large number of different kinds of coffee drinks, but the most traditional are plain espresso and café noisette (espresso with a light foam). Café au lait (called café crème in Paris) is a morning beverage, usually only ordered by French people before noon and definitely not after lunch. Noncoffee drinks include tea, tisanes (herbal teas), freshly squeezed fruit juices, soft drinks, and *limonade*, a lightly flavored French lemon-lime soda. For lemonade, the French ask for *un citron pressé* (literally, a juiced lemon) and mix the lemon juice with a carafe of water and sugar to taste.

Traditional cafés will also offer a number of cold drinks using flavored syrups and *limonade*, called *diabolos*. A *diabolo menthe* has mint-flavored syrup, for example, and classic *diabolo* flavors include currant, lemon, and grenadine (pomegranate). Adding beer to *limonade* makes a *panaché*. A drink called *menthe à l'eau* combines mint syrup with mineral water, and children might ask for cold milk mixed with mint or one of the fruit-flavored syrups. Fruit juices are popular at breakfast or as an aperitif, and the French purchase more orange juice than any other juice, but they consume less fruit juice on average than other European countries do, and much less than the United States does.

Citron Pressé (French Lemonade)

Yield: Serves 2

Ingredients
Juice and peel (yellow part only) from 1 large lemon
1 cup sugar
2 cups water

For the lemon syrup:

1. Cut the lemon peel into thin strips. Place in a saucepan with the water and sugar and bring just to a boil. Stir and simmer for 5 minutes, until all of the sugar is dissolved. Then remove from heat.
2. Pour the syrup into a jar and refrigerate until well chilled.

To make a *citron pressé*:
1. Put one tablespoon of lemon syrup in the bottom of two tall glasses.
2. Add ice and pour half of the lemon juice in each glass. Stir in cold water until you like the taste. Add more lemon syrup or water if needed. Serve.

Diabolo Menthe (Mint-Flavored Sparkling Water)

Yield: Serves 2

Ingredients
2 cups fresh mint leaves, cleaned and torn if large
2 cups water
1 cup sugar
Green food coloring (optional)
Sparkling or still mineral water

For the mint syrup:

1. Place the mint leaves in a heatproof bowl or pan. Boil the water and pour it over the mint leaves. Cover the bowl or pan and let stand at room temperature for 12 hours or refrigerate overnight.
2. Strain the mint from the water and put the water in a clean pan. Heat the mint water slowly over low heat and add the sugar a little at a time, stirring until it is completely dissolved. Add the green food coloring (if using) until the color is as green as you like.
3. Remove from heat, let come to room temperature, then pour into a clean bottle or jar and refrigerate.

Beverages

> To make a *diabolo menthe*:
>
> 1. Put two tablespoons of mint syrup in the bottom of two tall glasses.
> 2. Add ice and fill with sparkling or still water. Stir until the color is even. Serve.

Drinks in Other French-Speaking Countries

The French overseas territories have their own beverage traditions as well, including a lucrative production of rum in Guadeloupe and Martinique. Rum is the basis for *ti punch*, the signature alcoholic drink in the French Caribbean composed of juice from a specific kind of lemon, cane sugar syrup, and local rum. It is an essential part of festive celebrations in French Guyana, Martinique, Haiti, and Guadeloupe, where it is said to have originated to commemorate the abolition of slavery in 1848. As the story goes, the residents of the island celebrated their newfound freedom by appropriating their ex-masters' stocks of sugar cane and rum, products their enslaved labor had produced, and mixing these ingredients in large barrels to serve the gathering. *Ti punch* carries the weight of this historical event, and it celebrates local products.

In Morocco, mint tea is a traditional beverage offered to guests as a sign of hospitality. Moroccan mint tea is an infusion of green tea, fresh mint, boiling water, and sugar. Once brewed, the tea is poured into glasses from a height to oxygenate the drink and make it lightly frothy, enhancing the flavor. Mint tea in Morocco is traditionally prepared by the male head of the household and is served at three different moments during the day. The tea leaves and mint remain in the teapot, resulting in a soft, light flavor in the first glass and a bitter, darker brew in the last.

Every drink has its appointed place in French practice: cocktails, soft drinks, and juices for the aperitif (before-dinner drink) or with an after-school snack; coffee after a meal, on its own; and café au lait for breakfast only. Even if wine is considered the national drink, France has regional preferences. In the regions that produce fine wines, residents tend to purchase *vins d'appellation*, or labeled wines from noted wineries; areas without much wine production choose table wine or local wines. The eastern part of France (close to Germany) enjoys beer more than the rest of France does, and the northern regions produce and consume more cider and cognac. For nonalcoholic drinks, France enjoys an array of beverages based on water and fruit juice. Day or night, for a special occasion or a daily breakfast, there is a corresponding drink in France.

Thé à la Menthe (Moroccan Mint Tea)

Yield: Serves 2

Ingredients
2 cups cold water
2 tablespoons loose green tea, or 2 teabags
2 branches fresh mint (more to taste)
Sugar

1. Boil the water for the tea, and then turn off the heat. After the water has just stopped boiling, pour it over the tea in a teapot. Let steep for one minute.
2. Add the mint branches, and submerge them in the water. Let steep for 2 to 4 minutes. Add sugar to taste.
3. To serve, pour the tea into two heatproof glasses from a height of 6 to 12 inches, in order to mix in the sugar and froth the tea. Pour the tea back into the teapot and pour it again into the glasses, increasing the distance if you can (without spilling the tea). This serving technique takes practice. Return the tea to the teapot, and pour it into the glasses a third time. Serve.

Further Reading

Boizot, Christine. 1999. "La demande de boissons des ménages: Une estimation de la consommation à domicile." *Economie et Statistique* 324 (1): 143–56.

Bonnefons, Nicolas de. 1654. *Délices de la campagne*. Paris: Pierre-des-Hayes.

Brennan, Thomas. 1989. "Towards the Cultural History of Alcohol in France." *Journal of Social History* 23 (1): 71–92.

Brennan, Thomas. 1997. *Burgundy to Champagne: The Wine Trade in Early Modern France*. Baltimore, MD: Johns Hopkins University Press.

Brillat-Savarin, Jean-Anthelme. (1825) 1982. *Physiologie du goût*. Paris: Flammarion.

Camporesi, Piero. 1992. *Le goût du chocolat*. Paris: Grasset.

Coe, Sophie, and Michael Coe. 2000. *The True History of Chocolate*. London: Thames & Hudson.

Dion, Roger. 1959. *Histoire de la vigne et du vin en France: Des origines au XIXe siècle*. Paris: Roger Dion.

Garrigues, Jean. 1991. *Banania: Histoire d'une passion française*. Paris: Editions du May.

Guy, Kolleen M. 2002. "Rituals of Pleasure in the Land of Treasures: Wine Consumption and the Making of French Identity in the late 19th c." In *Food

Nations: Selling Taste in Consumer Societies, edited by Warren James Belasco and Philip Scranton, 34–47. New York: Routledge.
Guy, Kolleen M. 2003. *When Champagne Became French: Wine and the Making of a National Identity*. Baltimore, MD: Johns Hopkins University Press.
Hocquet, Jean-Claude. 1985. "Le pain, le vin et la juste mesure à la table des moines carolingiens." *Annales* 40: 661–86.
Insee. 2019. "Consommation des Ménages en 2018." *Insée Statistiques*, May 29, 2019. https://www.insee.fr/fr/statistiques/4131372?sommaire=4131436.
"La Maison Angelina." n.d. Angelina. Accessed June 21, 2019. https://www.angelina-paris.fr.
Laurioux, Bruno. 2013. *Manger au Moyen Age: Pratiques et discours alimentaires en Europe aux XIVe et XVe siècles*. Paris: Hachette.
Lippmann, Marion. 2010. "Orangina: Une histoire à rebondissements." *20 Minutes*, October 9, 2010. https://www.20minutes.fr/economie/559143-20090910-economie-orangina-une-histoire-agrave-rebondissements.
Marrus, Michael R. 1974. "Social Drinking in the 'Belle Epoque.'" *Journal of Social History* 7 (2): 115–41.
Marty, Nicolas. 2008. "L'eau embouteillée: Histoire de la construction d'un marché." *Entreprises et Histoire* 50: 86–99.
Massialot, François. 1692. *Nouvelle instruction pour les confitures, les liqueurs, et les fruits*. Paris: Saugrain.
McCabe, Ina Baghdiantz. 2014. *A History of Global Consumption: 1500–1800*. London; New York: Routledge.
"Orgeat." 2014. In *The Oxford Companion to Food*, edited by Alan Davidson and Tom Jaine. Oxford: Oxford University Press.
Pépin, Pierre-Yves. 1963. "Le commerce extérieur de la France, analyse et commentaire (1950–1960)." *L'Actualité économique* 38 (4): 586–625.
Raynal, Cécile. 2004. "La vente des eaux minérales par les pharmaciens." *Revue d'Histoire de la Pharmacie* 92 (344): 587–606.
Raynal, Cécile. 2005. "La vente des eaux minérales embouteillées [deuxième partie]." *Revue d'Histoire de la Pharmacie* 93 (345): 45–60.
Roche, Daniel. 2000. *A History of Everyday Things: The Birth of Consumption in France, 1600–1800*. Translated by Brian Pearce. Cambridge: Cambridge University Press.
Sévigné, Madame de. 1972. *Correspondance. Vol. 1: 1646–1675*. Paris: Gallimard.
Statista.com. 2015. "Préférences des français en matière de boissons chaudes au petit-déjeuner en 2015." https://fr.statista.com/statistiques/479234/boisson-chaude-preferee-petit-dejeuner-france.
Teuteberg, Hans Jurgen, and Jean-Louis Flandrin. 2013. "The Transformation of the European Diet." In *Food: A Culinary History*, edited by Jean-Louis Flandrin, Massimo Montanari, and Albert Sonnenfeld, 442–56. New York: Columbia University Press.

CHAPTER SEVEN

Holidays and Special Occasions

With a reputation as the birthplace of gastronomy, it is no surprise that France and the French territories celebrate special occasions with sumptuous food. Many holidays in France, as elsewhere in the world, feature specific dishes reserved for that day. Other holidays provide an excuse for cooking an elaborate meal and enjoying excellent food and wine with family and friends. Although the French strive to eat well every day, holiday meals and celebrations are the moment to create dishes that recall family traditions or showcase the elegant cooking of bygone eras. Many of the French holidays have a connection to Catholic feast days since the Catholic Church had a major influence on French life beginning in the Middle Ages. Holiday foods often have a basis in folklore or religious practice, and they have evolved over time as the French embrace old traditions and invent new ones. Celebrations in France mark a national holiday, such as the *Fête Nationale* on July 14, or a seasonal event, such as the arrival of the new vintage of Beaujolais wine. The French commemorate holidays by eating festive foods, but they also commemorate important foods with festive holidays, with celebrations dedicated to truffles, citrus fruit, and crepes, for example. Whatever the holiday, France and the French territories celebrate in style with traditional dishes and special drinks to mark the occasion.

Religious Holidays

To celebrate Christmas, some regions of France keep religious-inspired culinary traditions. In Provence, those who honor the traditional Christmas Eve dinner serve seven dishes representing the seven marks of stigmata on Christ's body. The meal begins with a traditional garlic soup and includes various fish and vegetable dishes but no meat dishes, as well as 13 small loaves of bread representing the 12 apostles and Jesus. After the 7-course dinner, there are 13 desserts, a tradition that is part of the folklore in Provence but that likely took hold only in the twentieth century. As early as the seventeenth century, texts indicate that Christmas dessert in Provence featured a vast selection of treats but do not specify 13 dishes (Brégeon-Poli 1995, 150). Traditional dessert items in the array included almonds, hazelnuts, figs, and raisins (each one representing one of the four religious orders for Catholic priests), as well as other dried and fresh fruits. The *fougasse* or *pompe à l'huile* pastry made from olive oil and orange-flower water plays an important role in the feast, and the recipe dates to the seventeenth century, but the tradition of serving *pompe à l'huile* is not widespread in more rural parts of Provence (Brégeon-Poli 1995, 148). Nearly all families in Provence serve nougats made from egg whites, honey, and almonds that were homemade in the past but are now almost certainly store-bought. This tradition dates to at least the eighteenth century.

Some families in Provence ban "exotic" fruits, such as kiwis or pineapple, from the dessert display, in the belief that only local fruits should be served. Since Provence is in the South of France, oranges, mandarin oranges, figs, and dates have local standing and still play a part in Christmas dessert today. Children all over France receive oranges and mandarin oranges as a symbolic gift at Christmas. Although the *bûche de Noël* cake (Yule log) is a mandatory part of Christmas in the rest of France, in Provence it is prohibited from the dessert table. The items chosen for Christmas dessert must be celebratory and out of the ordinary; fruit preserves from the cellar are not acceptable, but fresh fruit or dried fruit preserved for the occasion fit the bill. A celebratory meal deserves a celebratory drink: the traditional choice in Provence is mulled wine, but many prefer champagne.

Champagne is a must-have at most French holiday celebrations, as well as birthdays, graduations, christenings and all other festive occasions. Champagne became the wine of celebrations in the late nineteenth century, when the wines of the Champagne region were given a special status. In 1887 the name *champagne* legally defined a natural product of the Champagne region that became bubbly (*mousseux*) in a second processing phase (Guy 2003, 26). Other types of sparkling wine, inside and outside of France, turned bubbly from the same second fermentation technique, but the name *champagne* designated only the wine of this region produced by this technique. Champagne then became a symbol of celebration and is now an inseparable part of French holidays. At Christmas, for example, a glass of champagne opens the festivities on Christmas Eve, to start the evening of feasting called the *réveillon* (vigil). Generally, the French eat Christmas dinner on Christmas Eve, followed by a day of rest on December 25. Unlike most of Europe, the French return to work on December 26.

Holidays and Special Occasions

Christmas in France brings the whole family together at home for an enormous feast beginning at the dinner hour (8:00 p.m.) on December 24 and ending at midnight, when some families attend midnight Christmas mass, although the feast sometimes continues for several more hours. On a very traditional menu, the meal begins with oysters, caviar, scallops, or other seafood; and foie gras in Armagnac (brandy).

Foie gras (fattened goose or duck liver) belongs to fine cuisine and came of age in the nineteenth century as a sought-after specialty. Food writer Alexandre-Laurent Grimod de la Reynière praised foie gras and named the best shops in Paris to buy it in his *Almanach des gourmands* (1804). Recipes for pâtés made of foie gras appear in the most notable cookbooks for elite cuisine, such as Carême's *Pâtissier royal parisien* (1815). The popularity of foie gras in France grew even more as preserved (canned) foie gras became available in the 1850s and 1860s. Shelf-stable foie gras meant consumers could access the luxury product year-round, and chefs expressed a preference for prepared foie gras over fresh goose liver

---

Coquilles St. Jacques (Scallops with Cream Sauce) for Christmas

Yield: Serves 4

Ingredients
2 Tbsp unsalted butter
Salt, pepper to taste
16 fresh sea scallops
2 shallots, minced
1 Tbsp fresh parsley, chopped
¼ cup heavy cream

1. Melt 1 tablespoon butter over medium-high heat in a nonstick pan. Dry scallops with a paper towel and sprinkle with salt. Fry scallops until browned, 2 minutes per side. Set aside.
2. Melt remaining butter in a nonstick pan over medium heat. Add minced shallots and cook, stirring often, until softened. Add parsley and cook until fragrant, about 1 minute. Add heavy cream and cook until slightly thickened, about 2 minutes. Sprinkle with pepper to taste.
3. Heat the oven to 450 degrees. Place four scallops on each of four small, oven-safe dishes (or scallop shells, if you can find them). Divide the sauce evenly over the scallops. Bake until browned. Serve.

> ### The Pause during the Feast
>
> The French are known for spending hours at the table to enjoy a meal. Holiday and celebratory meals, such as the Christmas réveillon and wedding feasts, can last six hours or more. In the middle of an extended celebratory meal, the French observe a ritual called the *trou normand* (Norman pause), originally a shot of strong liquor or cognac and now more likely a scoop of sorbet or ice cream that acts as a refreshing palate cleanser. The *trou Normand*, and the pause that accompanies it, enables French revelers to continue feasting well into the night.

(Mognard 2011). Most chefs now prefer fresh goose liver. The vogue for foie gras in Paris soon passed to the entire country and abroad. To provide foie gras for all those who want to buy it in France, production of foie gras is divided between artisanal producers in Alsace and the southwest and industrial production in the Loire Valley, Brittany, and foreign sources in Bulgaria and Hungary.

Regional specialties also appear on the Christmas menu in some areas of France. Families may serve escargots in butter (in Burgundy) or *boudin blanc*, white sausage made with pork or chicken and truffles or morel mushrooms (in Alsace). More modern menus include smoked salmon, shrimp, or vegetarian dishes.

The feasting continues with the main course; traditionally, French families insist on turkey with chestnut stuffing, the classic Christmas dish. If turkey seems too staid, ambitious cooks serve duck breast, *pintade* (guinea fowl), goose, or other fancy fowl roasted with herbs and accompanied by turned vegetables, that is, carrots and potatoes carved into uniform oval shapes. The practice of eating turkey or other poultry re-creates in miniature the aristocratic feasts of the previous centuries, where poultry was the most esteemed meat. Turkey belongs to the modern era, of course; before the eighteenth century, holiday feasts in France featured *boudin* sausages, pork or ham, or roast beef. In her novel *Nanon* (1872), written just after the Prussian siege that left Paris in the grip of famine, George Sand describes a Christmas *réveillon* in the mountains where the family of modest means burns a Yule log in the fireplace and enjoys a brace of roasted larks, a pile of roasted chestnuts, and goat cheese made from the family goat (1872, 236).

For dessert, the *bûche de Noël* (Yule log) is inescapable in France; it is made of sponge cake rolled around a soft filling and decorated to look like a log, complete with meringue mushrooms. The Yule log cake has a fairly recent history as well, likely becoming popular in the nineteenth century. It came out of the tradition of burning a large log in the fireplace on Christmas Eve in the Middle Ages, when homes were heated by a central fireplace, and eventually the practice developed into eating the log in the form of cake. Pastry shops in France prepare for the Christmas rush weeks in advance, and most families purchase their *bûche* from the local patisserie, but some ambitious bakers create them at home. Chocolate and hazelnut or chestnut are the most common flavors for the Christmas *bûche*, but there are endless variations, such as those made with vanilla, bananas and rum, or berries, for example. Christmas desserts before the *bûche de Noël* resembled the Provençal tradition of dried and fresh fruit or cakes and pastries like the *gâteau de Savoie*. After the *bûche de Noël* in modern-day France come chocolate truffles, roasted chestnuts, jellied fruit candies called *pâtes de fruits*, and a long nap.

For the feast of the Epiphany on January 6, another dessert takes center stage: the *galette des rois* or king cake. Epiphany commemorates another Catholic holiday, the day the three kings visited Jesus in the manger. Traditionally made with flaky pastry and a layer of marzipan, the king cake contains a *fève* (a dried bean or other small item) baked inside the cake. The practice of electing a king by means of a cake dates to Roman times during the Saturnalia feast days at the beginning of January, when a servant became king for a day. Like other Christian holidays, this tradition commemorates what was originally a pagan feast. In French practice, the youngest member of the family distributes a slice of cake to each person, and the lucky one who finds the bean becomes king (or queen) for the day and is awarded a paper crown to wear.

To combat the pagan aspects of the feast, church authorities in France encouraged bakers to replace the bean with a porcelain figure of baby Jesus. The *fève* evolved from a bean to a porcelain figure to the plastic items used today; during the Revolution, the Phrygian bonnet replaced the baby Jesus, and *fèves* come in all kinds of shapes today. After the French Revolution, the revolutionary government, opposed to any mention of the monarchy, attempted to ban the *galette des rois* entirely in 1791, but managed only to change its name from "king's cake" to "equality cake" (Armengaud 2000, 144). The change lasted only a short time before the traditional name and cake returned. The *galette des rois* practice spans the French-speaking world, from France, Belgium, and Switzerland to Louisiana in the United States. Most French families purchase their Epiphany cakes from a pastry shop.

> ### The President and Kings Cake
>
> The president of France participates in the January 6 tradition every year, with some modifications. Since 1975 the Elysée palace has accepted delivery of a *galette des rois* for the enjoyment of the presidential family. However, the cake does not contain a *fève* because the French president could certainly never be king (Ribaut 2010).

Between Epiphany and Easter, the feast of Mardi Gras (Fat Tuesday) precedes the Christian observation of 40 days of Lent. The celebration of Carnival takes place in Nice and most famously in the overseas French territory of Guadeloupe, at the end of January or beginning of February, depending on the calendar. In terms of food, Carnival is best known for beignets, fried dough lightly sweetened with sugar. Traditionally, beignets and other fritter-type foods served to use up cooking fat (and make a celebratory treat) in advance of the period of abstinence from meat and fat during Lent. Today they are a delicious warm snack and part of a festive celebration with floats, costumes, and music.

In the French Caribbean islands, including Martinique and Guadeloupe, crab is the symbol of the Easter holiday. *Dombrés* (or *dombwés*) *au crabe*, crab stew with flour dumplings, always graces the Easter table in Guadeloupe. In Martinique, the *matatou au crabe* (whole crabs in a spicy stew) carries the same importance: a must-have on the Easter holiday, served with rice and vegetables. The dish is called *matété* in Guadeloupe and uses the same spice mixture that flavors *colombo de cabri*, the national dish. Stuffed crab (*crabe farci*) combines crab meat with spices, lime juice, and bread crumbs baked and served in the cleaned crab shell. A specialty in Guadeloupe and Martinique, it is often served with *accras de morue*, or salt-cod fritters.

The tradition of eating crab and fish relates to religious observance as well as to the history of the islands. On Good Friday, a day of abstinence from meat in Catholicism, Martinicans and Guadeloupeans serve *accras* made with fish or vegetables. On the Monday after Easter, a day of celebration and the end of the Lenten period, crab stews are the main attraction. The holiday falls at the beginning of crab season, when mature crabs emerge from their spring hiding places. In the French Caribbean, many families go on vacation during the Easter holiday to campgrounds near the ocean, where they participate in gathering fresh crabs for the meal. But

Dombrés aux Crabes for Easter
(Easter Crab Stew with Dumplings)

Yield: Serves 4

Ingredients for the stew:
2 pounds fresh crabs
2 limes
1 tsp cayenne pepper
Salt, pepper
1 Tbsp vegetable oil
4 slices bacon, cut into ½-inch pieces
1 yellow onion, chopped fine
2 garlic cloves, minced
½ cup chopped chives
1 tsp dried thyme or a branch of fresh thyme
½ cup fresh parsley, chopped
1 Tbsp tomato paste
1 bay leaf
1 jalapeño pepper, sliced

Ingredients for the dumplings:
2 ½ cups all-purpose flour
1 cup seltzer water
Pinch of salt

1. Marinate the crabs with the juice of one lime, cayenne pepper, 1 teaspoon of salt and ½ teaspoon of pepper. Refrigerate for several hours or overnight.
2. Make the dumplings. Mix the flour, seltzer, and salt. Form into ½ inch balls on a lightly floured surface.
3. In a large pan, heat oil over high heat until shimmering. Sauté crabs over high heat until they turn red. Add bacon and sauté until browned. Add onion, garlic, chives, thyme, and parsley and mix well. Add the tomato paste, bay leaf, jalapeño pepper and enough water just to cover crabs. Cover and simmer on medium-low heat for 45 minutes.
4. Add the flour dumplings and simmer uncovered for 15–20 minutes, stirring occasionally. Season to taste with lime juice, salt, and pepper. Serve hot.

Adapted from Leslie, "Dombrés aux crabes," *Je Cuisine Créole*, March 26, 2017. https://cuisine-creole.com/dombres-aux-crabes.

crab as a food item has an important heritage in Guadeloupe and Martinique for its connection to slavery. The slave trade brought Africans to the islands, and native peoples were also enslaved there. Plantation owners often did not provide enough food to their slaves, and crabs were easy to find and plentiful in the area. Since the Easter holiday was a day of rest, slaves had the opportunity to gather crabs during the day and feast on them. After slavery was abolished, freed peoples gathered crabs to sell as a reliable source of income. Today, stewed crabs and dishes made with crab have become a positive symbol of the island, especially in the Easter season.

In France, Easter dinner means leg of lamb. Just as Christmas requires roast turkey, Easter and lamb go together in France. By far the most popular main dish at Easter, lamb has a smaller presence on French tables the rest of the year except as a special occasion main dish. At Mont-St-Michel, in Brittany, herds of sheep that graze on the grassy fields blown by the salty ocean breeze, called *agneau prés-salés* (lamb from salted prairies), are especially prized. Their meat has a particular flavor sought after by connoisseurs, but *prés-salés* lambs are not usually available for sale until late May, usually after Easter has passed. Roast leg of lamb with spring vegetables is the most typical Easter main dish, but lamb shoulder or braised lamb also appear on the French Easter table, as does the classic *navarin d'agneau*, lamb stew.

Newly arrived spring vegetables like asparagus, fresh peas, and new carrots showcase the bounty of the season at Easter. In Burgundy, ham (not lamb) is the prized ingredient in the traditional *jambon persillé* (ham with parsley) served on Easter Sunday. The finest quality ham is cut into cubes, encased in herb-infused aspic, then chilled in a terrine, and served as a first course. The *pâté de Pâques* (Easter pastry) found in Berry, in central France, encloses hard-cooked eggs and a filling of minced pork or veal with herbs in a rich pastry shell to create an Easter version of *pâté en croûte* (pâté in pastry). Eggs carry Christian symbolism for the holiday, and they appear in various first-course dishes on Easter like baked eggs (*oeufs cocotte*) with smoked salmon or morel mushrooms, and in the form of traditional Easter brioche, a rich bread made with eggs and milk. For dessert, brioche with chocolate or chocolate eggs round out the meal. The Monday following Easter is also a day for eggs in many parts of France. Families take a picnic lunch of hard-boiled eggs or deviled eggs to the park or prepare an omelet for lunch. In the Pyrenees region in southwestern France, the tradition of making an enormous omelet on Easter Monday with leftover Easter eggs is called the *pâquette* (little Easter).

Holidays and Special Occasions

Brioches de Pâques (Brioche Rolls for Easter)

Yield: Makes 12 rolls

Ingredients
1 packet yeast
3 ½ cups all-purpose flour
½ cup granulated sugar
¾ teaspoon salt
½ cup whole milk, slightly warmed
3 eggs, lightly beaten
4 Tbsp unsalted butter, melted and cooled

1. Mix the yeast with 3 tablespoons of warm (100 degrees or body temperature) water. Let rest for 15 minutes.
2. Combine the flour, sugar, and salt in a bowl. In a stand mixer on low speed or by hand, mix the yeast with the flour mixture until combined. On medium speed, slowly add the milk, eggs, and butter. Mix until the dough comes together and forms a ball.
3. Knead gently on a lightly floured surface until the dough is smooth. Divide into twelve equal portions. Roll each portion gently into a rounded shape.
4. Place the rounds into a lightly greased baking pan and cover with lightly greased plastic wrap. Let rise in a warm place until doubled (about one hour).
5. Heat oven to 350 degrees. Bake brioches for 15–20 minutes or until golden. Serve warm.

Adapted from Marie-Laure Tombini, "Petites brioches de Pâques," Ôdélices, accessed May 8, 2020, https://odelices.ouest-france.fr/recette/petites-brioches-de-paques-map-r3006.

National Holidays

On December 31, the French celebrate the new year with a *réveillon* feast, given the same name as the Christmas Eve feast. The celebration is called the feast of Saint-Sylvestre in France—named for Pope Sylvester, who died December 31, 314 CE—but the holiday was originally a pagan feast day. The *réveillon* dinner on New Year's Eve brings together friends for an elegant selection of expensive items. Champagne, foie gras, oysters, and caviar appear on most

Saint-Sylvestre menus, as does smoked or poached salmon and other seafood dishes. Since the New Year's Eve celebration takes place over an entire evening, most dishes are prepared ahead and served cold. Less elaborate *réveillon* choices for a more casual evening include *gougères* (cheese puffs), quiches, olive tapenade spread on bread, pâtés made of pork or other cured meats, and a selection of cheeses. For a very modern take on the New Year's Eve meal, some cooks prepare savory *cakes* (loaf cakes) with seafood, or *verrines* (parfaits) of marinated vegetables. More formal

---

Cake de Gascogne (Savory Gascony Loaf Cake) for New Year's Eve

Yield: Serves 6

Ingredients
3 eggs
1 ¼ cups all-purpose flour
1 packet yeast
Salt, pepper
½ cup vegetable oil
½ cup whole milk, warmed
1 cup shredded Swiss cheese
1 cup cubed ham, or 4 slices bacon, cut into ½-inch pieces
¾ cup of dried prunes (preferably *pruneaux d'Agen*), cut in ¼-inch strips
½ cup of crushed hazelnuts

1. Heat oven to 350 degrees. In a large bowl, whisk eggs until lightly beaten. Mix flour, yeast, ½ teaspoon salt, and ¼ teaspoon pepper in a separate bowl. Add the flour mixture to the eggs and stir until well mixed. Slowly add oil and milk to the flour mixture and mix until combined. Gently stir in shredded cheese.
2. Fry the ham until lightly browned or bacon until crisp. Drain on paper towels. Stir ham or bacon, prunes, and hazelnuts into the flour mixture. Spread into an ungreased 4-inch loaf pan.
3. Bake for 45 minutes or until toothpick inserted into center of loaf comes out clean. Let cool for at least one hour. Slice and serve warm or at room temperature.

Adapted from "Cake de Gascogne," Cuisine à la française, accessed May 7, 2020, https://www.cuisinealafrancaise.com/fr/recettes/aperitif-et-entrees/aperitif-et-tartines/cake-de-gascogne.

réveillon dinners involve a multicourse meal, but casual gatherings for a younger crowd offer a buffet of carefully selected dishes.

Candlemas Day (la Chandeleur) is a day for eating crepes. The holiday is celebrated on the same day as Groundhog Day in the United States (February 2) and had a similar meaning at its origin: a celebration in the hope that spring was on its way and the new crops of food would soon be ready. The feast day began in the Middle Ages in early Christian France. Pope Gelasius I (who governed the Catholic Church from 492–496 CE) sought to replace the pagan holiday dedicated to Lupercus (the god Pan) in February by a day to commemorate the presentation of Jesus at the Temple of Jerusalem. He created the feast of "la chandeleur," or Candlemas, as a celebration of Christ as the "light of the world" and introduced the tradition of eating crepes as nourishment for pilgrims coming to worship in Rome. If the previous year's harvest had been successful and there was plenty of grain left in reserve, people celebrated with crepes and other baked goods. If stocks were low due to a bad harvest, worshipers went to church instead (Wagda 2005, 131). The crepes promoted by Gelasius were flat disks made of flour, salt, and water with perhaps a touch of oil or fat. They took the form of a circle, representing the sun and by extension the light of Christ.

It is possible to reproduce the original Candlemas experience with a thick crepe dough made of flour, water, and a little oil. Cooked on a nonstick pan, the crepes are easy to make but are heavier and tougher than modern crepes. When covered with toppings (savory, since sugar was not available to most consumers until the eighteenth century), the modern cook can re-create the original Candlemas (Wagda 2005, 132). Today's traditions have deviated from a religious emphasis and are more family-oriented. In modern France, many French people buy premade crepes at the supermarket for Candlemas rather than making them at home. According to tradition, if you can successfully flip a crepe while holding a coin in your flipping hand, you will have good luck all year. Whether they make their own crepes or buy them for the holiday, French households buy twice as many jars of Nutella in the two weeks preceding Candlemas as compared to the rest of the year, and 50 percent more jars of jam and bottles of cider (the traditional accompaniment to crepes) for Candlemas (Levy 2019).

On July 14, the French nation celebrates the *Fête Nationale*, known in the United States as Bastille Day but never by that name in France. On this summer holiday, the French commemorate the formation of the French republic during the Revolution. On this date in 1789 citizens liberated the remaining residents in the Bastille prison and symbolically overturned the monarchy. On the same date in 1790 France celebrated the *Fête de la Fédération*, inaugurating the new constitution of the French republic. At the Feast of the Federation, 20,000 citizens participated in a *repas civique* (common meal) on the Champ de Mars in Paris that resembled those held during the Revolution to create community among the French by inviting them to break bread together. The holiday officially became France's national holiday in 1880. On July 14, France celebrates with foods appropriate for summer and with dishes that have a French heritage. Classic quiche lorraine or coq au vin (chicken in red wine) honor the French culinary traditions, as does the *gâteau Saint-Honoré*, a common choice for dessert. Some families celebrate the holiday with a picnic and easy-to-transport foods like tomato salads and sandwiches on baguettes, and many towns still hold *repas civiques* with communal tables for a shared meal. Desserts and beverages on the holiday model the French flag with red, white, and blue colors, such as strawberry *fraisier* (icebox cake) or blueberry macarons.

Summer holidays in the French Caribbean include the tradition of *ti-punch*, a rum-based cocktail with fresh lime juice, created (as the story goes) when newly freed slaves celebrated by drinking the stocks of rum and sugar left by the departed plantation owners. The major agricultural crop on the island was sugarcane, which was made into refined sugar and rum. In the present day, partygoers enjoy *ti-punch* made with local rum, sugarcane juice, and lime juice as part of any celebration, usually accompanied by *accras de morue, boudin,* or other snacks.

The *Fête de la gastronomie* (Day of Gastronomy) is a new national holiday, created in 2011 after UNESCO recognized the "gastronomic meal of the French" as part of the "Intangible Cultural Heritage of Humanity" in 2010. The UNESCO list honors cultural traditions around the world that are deserving of preservation. The French won the honor by demonstrating that their practice of gathering for a festive meal with at least four courses and wine pairings "emphasizes togetherness, the pleasure of taste, and the balance between human beings and the products of nature" (UNESCO n.d.). To commemorate the UNESCO honor, the French Ministry of the Economy in 2011 designated the last weekend of September as the Day of Gastronomy, with a selected theme each year. All over France, restaurants offer special meals, and French government offices host tastings and workshops to cultivate interest in local products and teach residents, particularly children, about the wonders of French gastronomy and the savoir faire (know-how) of French cooks. In order to provide access to French gastronomy to people of all ages and incomes, chefs who participate in the *Tous au restaurant* (Restaurants for All) event reserve a certain

Holidays and Special Occasions

Fraisier (Strawberry Cake) for Fête Nationale (July 14)

Yield: Serves 6

Ingredients
6 eggs
¾ cup granulated sugar
1 cup all-purpose flour
1 cup mascarpone cheese or whipped cream cheese
2 cups heavy cream
6 rounded Tbsp powdered sugar
10-oz. package of ripe strawberries, washed and stemmed

1. Heat oven to 350 degrees. Separate eggs, reserving whites in a very clean bowl. With a hand mixer, beat egg yolks with granulated sugar on high speed until light and frothy. Reduce speed to low and gradually beat in flour.
2. In another bowl, using clean beaters, beat egg whites until stiff peaks form. Gently fold egg whites into flour mixture. Spread batter into a jelly roll or half sheet pan (13"x18") lined with greased parchment paper. Bake for 12–15 minutes or until golden brown. Let cool completely.
3. Meanwhile, make whipped cream. Beat mascarpone cheese and heavy cream in a mixer on high speed until fluffy, adding powdered sugar one tablespoon at a time while mixing.
4. Lightly butter a 9-inch square cake pan. Cut two 9-inch squares from the cooled cake. Place one square on the bottom of prepared pan. Cut a few strawberries into slices (enough to line the prepared pan) and cut the rest in half. Stand the strawberry slices upright around all four sides of the pan. Fill the pan with whipped cream and layer the halved strawberries on the cream. Place the second cake square on top. Press gently and cover with plastic wrap.
5. Chill for at least 2 hours. Unmold onto a platter and garnish with powdered sugar. Cut into slices to serve.

Adapted from Sybille Joubert, "Fraisier facile," *Cuisine actuelle*, accessed May 8, 2020, https://www.cuisineactuelle.fr/recettes/fraisier-facile-117781.

number of tables for two-for-one meals and cooking demonstrations. The event includes restaurants ranging from the highest Michelin-starred establishments to modest local eateries, with the goal of inviting a larger public to the gastronomic table.

Celebrations of Agriculture

To commemorate the new vintage of Beaujolais wine, the *Fête du Beaujolais nouveau* on the third Thursday in November marks the end of fermentation of a new vintage of this fruity red wine from the Rhone valley in southeastern France. It is celebrated all over France with the opening of bottles of new Beaujolais wine and a good meal, and in the region where the wine is produced, the celebrations include a parade of wagons filled with Beaujolais vines that are set aflame. At the stroke of midnight, winemakers tap the barrels of new Beaujolais, and the celebration begins. Wineries open their doors to revelers for tastings, and nearby restaurants offer Beaujolais-themed menus for residents and tourists.

In Espelette, a small village on the French border with Spain in extreme southwestern France, visitors from all over France and parts of Europe gather on the last weekend in October to celebrate the Espelette pepper. The *Fête du Piment* (Feast of the Pepper), begun in 1968, honors the spicy red pepper grown in the village since the seventeenth century that now carries an AOC (*Appellation d'origine contrôlée*) label that confirms its authenticity and protects the Espelette name from imitators. On the opposite side of France, in Menton, near the Mediterranean Sea, the *Fête du citron* (Citrus Festival) celebrates the warm climate of the region that produces lemons, oranges, and other citrus fruits. Menton boasts its own locally grown treasure, the Menton lemon, grown in the region since the seventeenth century and still harvested by hand (APCM n.d.). Inaugurated in 1934, the Citrus Festival runs from mid-February through early March and features parades with floats made from citrus fruits, the mascot Citrus Limonia, and giant sculptures made from lemons and oranges. More than 200,000 visitors enjoy the celebration, and the festival uses 180 tons of citrus fruit each year, mainly imported from nearby Spain (Fête du Citron n.d.).

Other regions offer food-themed festivals to celebrate and promote their famous food products. In the Périgord region of the southwest, the Truffle Festival in mid-January brings truffle fanatics together to learn about truffle cultivation and meet truffle hunters. Visitors enjoy truffle tastings and celebratory truffle-themed menus at local restaurants, along with foie gras (fattened goose liver) and the other gastronomic specialties of food-centric Périgord. After the Truffle Festival comes the Goose Festival (*Fest'Oie*) in Périgord in March, to honor the source of foie gras and other succulent products produced in the region from the local flocks of geese. After a free serving of goose broth for all visitors to the festival marketplace, brave (and hungry) diners can participate in an all-you-can-eat foie gras banquet, offering other delicious dishes made with goose, including stuffed goose neck and goose pot-au-feu (boiled stew).

The nearby town of Agen is known all over France for its prunes (dried plums), eaten as a snack or used in recipes like braised chicken with prunes. The Prune Festival celebrates this humble fruit at the end of August with three days of music, dancing, and samples of the famous Agen fruit. In Metz, on the eastern border with Germany, the Mirabelle plum has its own festival during two weeks in August, an annual tradition since 1954. The sweet orange-yellow fruit used in jams and tarts becomes the center of attention for local pastry chefs and chocolate makers. Thousands of visitors choose the Queen of the Plums at the festival and enjoy a hot-air balloon show over the city.

Family Celebrations

Weddings in France follow the rule of elegant cuisine at important celebrations. At most weddings, guests enjoy foie gras and champagne, of course, and traditionally a fish course followed by a meat course. A cheese platter of carefully selected cheeses finishes the meal. For dessert, a *pièce montée*, or tiered dessert, usually a *croquembouche* of cream puffs decorated with the wedding colors, is almost guaranteed. Modern weddings sometimes offer layered wedding cakes, but the *pièce montée* has a justifiably loyal following. At the end of the wedding celebration, some couples serve French onion soup to their guests to revive them after a long night of revelry. An older tradition from the twentieth century, particularly in rural areas, offered both a luncheon and a dinner on the day of the wedding, both extended meals interrupted by the *trou normand* to offer guests a glass of strong liquor and a pause between courses. In the two-meal tradition, wedding lunches ended with cookies and fruit, and the *pièce montée* appeared at the end of the wedding dinner. In the nineteenth century in rural northern Brittany, newly married couples shared a ceremonial loaf of bread and cup of cider in front of their entire village, and the gathered crowd then drank a toast in their honor (Chesnel 1846, 192). In Burgundian villages in northeastern France, newlyweds left the church and went directly to the village cemetery where an enormous cauldron of soup awaited them. Each spouse ate a few spoonsful, and all of the wedding guests did the same; the tradition symbolized the equality that they would enjoy in their marriage (Chesnel 1846, 290).

Famous French weddings, both real and fictional, demonstrate that weddings in France demand an out-of-the-ordinary banquet and usually a high price tag. In Gustave Flaubert's 1857 novel, *Madame Bovary*, main characters Charles and Emma host a wedding banquet in the country that lasts 16 hours. Guests feast on fillet of beef, chicken in fricassée, three legs of lamb, and an enormous suckling pig. The extravagant many-layered wedding cake included a *gâteau de Savoie*, a pastry castle, and lakes made of jam ([1857] 1945, 30–31). For the wedding of Napoleon Bonaparte to his second wife, Marie-Louise of Austria, in 1810, nearly 3,000 guests attended the banquet held in the Tuileries Palace in Paris near the Louvre. No records remain of the dishes served at the wedding banquet, but historians suggest that it was likely similar to the Sunday dinners enjoyed by the ruling family at the time: two soups, four first course dishes, two kinds of roast meat, two vegetable dishes and four sweet dishes (Boudon 2016, 78–79). Napoleon I had a reputation for eating quickly. It was rumored that his wedding feast lasted no more than 20 minutes.

Mother's Day, the last Sunday in May, is a springtime holiday with a menu to match. French families honor their mothers with a new practice borrowed from the United States: brunch. The word *brunch* does not exist in the French language, but the French use the English word and have adopted lighter dishes served as a late-morning meal for Mother's Day. Fresh spring fruits and vegetables dominate the menu, from asparagus with hollandaise to strawberry cake (the light and sweet *fraisier*). Since the term *brunch* is borrowed, many of the dishes come from American cooking as well. For Mother's Day, French families serve pancakes and waffles, pasta salads, and even smoothies. There are no classic foods associated with Mother's Day in France, but fresh seasonal ingredients are the common denominator in the dishes prepared for French mothers.

Baptisms in France are an important occasion for a family gathering after the church service. The menu varies according to the family and the time of year, but the celebration always includes *dragées* (candy-coated almonds in pastel colors) at the church and a *pièce montée* (a tiered cake or pastry) for dessert. Candy *dragées* serve as a thank-you gift to guests at baptisms, a practice that dates to the sixteenth century, when almonds were distributed to attendees. In the modern tradition, sugared almonds in decorative pouches are considered a required part of the baptismal celebration. They also appear at French weddings as a gift to guests.

The *pièce montée* originated in the eighteenth century and is a key component of important celebrations like baptisms and weddings today for the same reason as three centuries earlier: it makes an impression. The towering confection demonstrates the skill of the baker and requires creativity in its decorative elements. Most French families order the baptismal *pièce montée* from a caterer or a pastry shop. In its most classic form, the *pièce montée* is a pyramid of cream puffs covered with spun sugar, but

Holidays and Special Occasions

modern displays might take the shape of a basket, a church, or even a carousel. A baptismal *pièce montée* from a pastry shop can cost more than $100, a demonstration of the importance of the dessert and the skill required to make it. In Guadeloupe and Martinique, baptisms traditionally feature brioches (breads made with egg and milk), *gâteau fouetté* (a light cake leavened with egg whites, similar to angel food cake) and a festive beverage called *chodo*, similar to eggnog. For some families in France and in the overseas departments, first communions are celebrated in a similar way, with a grand feast and a *pièce montée* or a special dessert.

For the French and the French overseas departments, celebratory meals to mark a holiday vary immensely with family traditions, seasonality, and regional specialties. Apart from Christmas turkey and Easter lamb (and even these rules have exceptions), there are few absolutes in terms of the dishes that appear on holiday tables. One principle does hold true for all holiday feasts in France and abroad, however: these dishes cast aside the foods common in daily meals and replace them with special ingredients, usually more expensive and reserved for rare occasions. Foie gras and truffles are decadent treats at Christmas and New Year's precisely because they are not part of weekly Sunday lunches. An extravagant *pièce montée* belongs to a baptism or wedding celebration but would be out of place on a dessert menu in a bistro. Finally, the French and French overseas territories preserve and showcase their culinary traditions purposefully with holiday meals, intentionally selecting recipes that have a meaningful history. In this way, celebrations act as a remembrance of the proud heritage of these dishes and a continuous celebration of holidays enjoyed over generations.

Further Reading

APCM (Association pour la Promotion du Citron de Menton). n.d. "Le Citron de Menton." Accessed May 6, 2020. https://www.lecitrondementon.org.

Armengaud, Christine. 2000. *Le Diable sucré*. Paris: La Martinière.

Boudon, Jacques-Olivier. 2016. "A la recherche d'un héritier. Le mariage de Napoléon Ier avec Marie-Louise d'Autriche. 1er et 2 avril 1810." In *A la Table des diplomates*, edited by Laurent Stefanini, 71–79. Paris: Iconoclaste.

Brégeon-Poli, Brigitte. 1995. "'Va pour treize!' La 'tradition' des desserts de Noël en Provence." *Terrain*, no. 24, 145–52.

Chesnel, Adolphe de la. 1846. *Coutumes, mythes et traditions des provinces de France*. Paris: Périsse.

Davidson, Alan, and Tom Jaine. 2014. *The Oxford Companion to Food*. Oxford: Oxford University Press.

Ferguson, Priscilla Parkhurst. 2006. *Accounting for Taste: The Triumph of French Cuisine*. Chicago: University of Chicago Press.

Fête du Citron. n.d. "87ème Fête Du Citron Menton." Accessed July 24, 2020. https://www.fete-du-citron.com.

Flaubert, Gustave. (1857) 1945. *Madame Bovary*. Edited by R. Dumesnil. Paris: Belles Lettres.

Guy, Kolleen. 2003. *When Champagne Became French*. Baltimore, MD: Johns Hopkins University Press.

Levy, Armelle. 2019. "Chandeleur: Les Français mangent de plus en plus de crêpes industrielles." *RTL*, February 2, 2019. https://www.rtl.fr/actu/conso/chandeleur-les-francais-mangent-de-plus-en-plus-de-crepes-industrielles-7796418658.

Mognard, Elise. 2011. "Les trois traditions du foie gras dans la gastronomie française." *Anthropology of Food* (Online) 8 (May 12). http://journals.openedition.org/aof/6789. https://doi.org/10.4000/aof.6789.

Ribaut, Jean-Claude. 2010. "La galette des Rois, une tradition congelée." *Le Monde*, January 1, 2010. https://www.lemonde.fr/vous/article/2010/01/01/la-galette-des-rois-une-tradition-congelee_1286565_3238.html.

Root, Waverley. 1970. *The Food of France*. New York: Alfred A. Knopf.

Sand, George. 1872. *Nanon*. Paris: Michel Levy.

Toussaint-Samat, Maguelonne. 2009. *A History of Food*. West Sussex, UK: Wiley-Blackwell.

UNESCO. n.d. "Gastronomic Meal of the French." Accessed May 6, 2020. https://ich.unesco.org/en/RL/gastronomic-meal-of-the-french-00437.

Wagda, Marin. 2005. "A l'origine était la crêpe." *Hommes et Migrations* 1254 (March–April): 130–33.

CHAPTER EIGHT

Street Food and Snacks

The French meal system of a small breakfast, a multicourse lunch, and a simple evening meal is heavily embedded in the modern French approach to eating. Between-meal snacks are unusual in the French tradition, and the French claim that they rarely eat outside of formal mealtimes. The verb for snacking in French is *grignoter*, meaning "to nibble." Nevertheless, the French meal system includes an after-school snack for children, the *goûter*, so institutionalized that it has a name and a common menu, usually a *tartine* of toast and jam or Nutella, a chocolate hazelnut spread that originated in Italy. The midday snack has a long history among the working class, and other between-meal foods are certainly part of French traditions. Many treats to-go can be purchased in French cities and towns for a quick bite, from ice cream to kebabs, many of them borrowed from other cultures and shaped by immigration. Young people in France have increasingly begun to consume small meals and snacks in imitation of American culture as more American chains become established in France.

Original Street Food

As with much of French food culture, street food began with bread in the Middle Ages. Outside of churches in medieval cities in France, street vendors sold unconsecrated hosts (the bread wafers used in the Catholic ceremony of the Eucharist to represent the body of Christ) called *oublies*. These unleavened wafers were cooked between two iron plates heated over a flame, a sort of rudimentary waffle iron. Bake shops in the Middle Ages did not sell cakes or sweet pastries but cooked meats wrapped in dough (like those called *pâté en croûte* that we know today) (Desportes 1987, 80). In fourteenth-century Paris, pastry shops sold their wares in taverns or on the street, offering flan (baked custard), pâtés, cheese tarts, turnovers filled with pork or veal, and other savory pastries (Laurioux

1999, 94). In response to the demands of professional guilds and associations, the French government developed strict rules as to which institutions had the right to serve hot food. In order to protect their business, *traiteurs* who acted as caterers to supply fully cooked meals wished to prevent other businesses from selling food to be eaten on-site. For this reason, food sales in France tended to remain part of the meal system, with little opportunity for purchasing a bite to eat or a snack to go.

In the seventeenth century, drinking chocolate became fashionable among the nobles, who might sip a cup of chocolate as mid-morning indulgence or as a replacement for a meal. Hot chocolate, when it first appeared in France, contained very little sugar—sugar was a rare and expensive commodity—and was thick and bitter, much like the original beverage created in the Americas. Eighteenth-century workers used café au lait, purchased from street vendors and consumed on the spot, as an easy and inexpensive way to replace a meal. In the nineteenth century, when meal times in Paris were shifting from a late lunch and even later supper to a midday lunch and evening dinner, fashionable members of society might drink a cup of hot chocolate to stave off hunger or resort to smaller in-between meals. Coffee breaks became a common practice in late nineteenth-century Paris, as working men and women stopped in a café for their daily coffee, which they took while standing at the counter (Montorgueil 1899, 90). In the twentieth century, a daily newspaper featured an image of middle-class workers eating breakfast outside on the way to work: a bowl of coffee and a roll, with the female proprietor supplying the bowl (Bruegel 2015, 259). To this day, the most popular item purchased from vending machines in France is coffee.

More substantial street food came of age in nineteenth-century Paris as more workers flocked to the capital. Since they lived at a distance from their workplaces and had very little money to spend on a proper lunch, these young workers sustained themselves on simple foods. Common street foods included soup, fried potatoes, fried tripe, and boudin sausages (Bruegel 2015, 276). Emile Zola's novel *L'Assommoir* (*The Drinking Den*), offers a scene of various lunchtime customers who purchase quick snacks from street vendors selling cones of French fries, cups of mussels in broth, and bunches of radishes. Small children enjoy a hot boudin sausage or a breaded cutlet of meat (Zola [1877] 1961, 2: 406). Near the central food market in Paris, called Les Halles, food resellers offered mobile food to workers who had neither the time nor the money to buy a whole meal. Mobile vendors, often women, with portable stoves served bowls of cooked tripe (cow stomach), soups, or stews to merchants and

Street Food and Snacks

shoppers, a phenomenon one author said was "common only in Paris" (Briffault 1846, 62).

Depending on the physical effort required for their jobs, some workers in the nineteenth and early twentieth centuries might have taken several snack breaks during the day: often a little bread, a bit of meat, and some wine or liquor. These snacks were called *casse-croûte* (literally, "breaking of bread") perhaps because they often consisted of bread or a sandwich. Occasionally, a worker might save some bread or meat from the lunchtime meal to consume later in the day. Sandwiches made of a baguette sliced lengthwise and filled with meat or cheese remain a common meal on the go in France, sold from bakeries at lunchtime and featuring classic combinations like ham and butter or pâté and cornichons (small, sour pickles) or newer flavors, like curried chicken.

Food Trucks

Much more recently, Paris has become home to food trucks that offer street food from all sorts of national cuisines. The concept is so American that it carries the name *le food truck*, even in French. The first food truck in Paris opened for business in 2011, run by Kristin Frederick, a

---

Sandwich Pâté Cornichons (Pickle-Pâté Sandwich)

Yield: Serves 2

Ingredients
1 baguette
2 tsp Dijon mustard
4 oz. pâté de campagne (country-style pâté, found in deli case)
¼ cup French cornichons (sour gherkin pickles), cut lengthwise into slices
Frisée lettuce (also known as curly endive), optional

1. Cut baguette in two and then cut each half-baguette lengthwise
2. Spread mustard on cut sides of each baguette.
3. Slice the pâté into pieces that will fit onto the baguette without overhanging the sides. Place pâté slices evenly onto the bottom half of each sandwich.
4. Place sliced cornichons on pâté, distributing evenly.
5. Add lettuce, if using.
6. Top with baguette half and serve.

Californian who named her truck *Le Camion qui Fume* (The Smoking Truck). Her American-style burgers found a following because the French are enamored with American culture but also because she used locally sourced ingredients including French beef and buns from a neighborhood pastry shop. Her well-made burgers coincided with a burger fad in Paris, when chefs applied their skills to this American classic and made it Parisian. Other popular Parisian food trucks serve British fish and chips, tacos, and Thai food. The gourmet food truck in France began as a Parisian phenomenon, but some estimate that about 400 food trucks were in operation across the country in 2015, although the majority were in Paris. By 2017, the number of food trucks in Paris had dropped from an estimated 200 to less than 40 (Kindermans and Delpont 2017).

The food truck phenomenon has not been without its critics, however, and these new street vendors have to conform to strict rules in order to remain in business. Because food is so important in Paris and because restaurants there are of immense economic and cultural importance, local and national government regulations first tried to limit growth of these businesses by restricting the hours they could be open and giving permits in some areas of the city but not in others. By 2015, however, the French government recognized the popularity of the food truck for tourism. France is the most visited country in the world, and tourist spending represents one of the most important segments of the French economy.

An open call for food truck applications managed by the Office of the Mayor of Paris in 2015 drew 160 applicants; 56 were selected and given licenses to operate for one year in a limited range of 10 *arrondissements* (sections) of the city (Méreuze 2015). After a year, none of the new applicants' licenses were renewed, and the mayor of Paris revisited the rules for opening food trucks once more in 2017. Of the successful food truck businesses, most rely on a brick-and-mortar restaurant to earn a living; the food truck is a sort of accessory. Frederick recently became the head of an association called *Street Food En Mouvement*, founded in 2012, that aims to help potential "food truckers" start a successful business and to promote food trucks and quality street food across France. Their association claims 120 food truck owners as members and seeks to make street food a healthy, locally sourced alternative to what the French call *malbouffe*, or bad eating, usually associated with fast food.

Le Tricycle

Vegetarian hot dogs have become one of the most fashionable street foods in Paris. They are served from a street cart called Le Tricycle, which features menu items named Le Snoop Dogg and Le Dogtor Dre. Coralie Jouhier, with roots in France and Martinique, was a fashion model before she created the hot dog cart with her partner, Daqui Gomis, to share her family's traditions of healthy, plant-based eating. Le Tricycle has expanded into a small restaurant for vegetarian and vegan food (Carlos 2019).

Le Goûter

In 2013 a survey showed that 99 percent of French households participated in the after-school *goûter* or afternoon snack (Bonora 2013). Children generally pause at around 4:30 p.m. for a snack of fruit juice, a slice of bread with jam or Nutella, and perhaps a cookie or pastry. For many families, the *goûter* is not a to-go snack but a moment to sit around the table and enjoy a treat in the company of the family. Of course, in families where both parents work, such a practice is difficult to accomplish, but the afternoon snack break is still valued as an ideal, keeping a long-held tradition. The *goûter* dates to before the French Revolution (and likely much earlier), when religious boarding schools had a snack break at 4:30 p.m. between lunch at noon and dinner at 7:15 p.m. (Grignon 1993, 278).

In a twentieth-century survey, university students reported that they continued to take a *goûter* in the afternoon about 25 percent of the time, eating bread and jam in the traditional model or yogurt and fruit in a more modern version of the afternoon snack. Their morning coffee break was similarly regimented: for female students it might consist of a cup of tea and an apple or a cookie and, for male students, some bread and a bit of chocolate (Grignon 1993, 325). In 1993 about 32 percent of university students in the study reported that they did not eat anything outside of formal meals, compared to 43 percent of adults in a 1988 study (Herpin 1988, 513). Many adults continue to take a morning snack break (a *casse-croûte*) or an afternoon *goûter* of a pastry or a piece of fruit. One popular and traditional sweet treat is flan, a custard pie made with eggs, milk, flour, and a little vanilla that is traditionally sold at bread shops (*boulangeries*) rather than pastry shops (patisseries) because it is fairly simple and not very sweet. Once chilled, the pie-shaped custard is cut into slices and sold for about two dollars a slice, making for a filling snack that is easy to eat while walking.

Perhaps the most recognizable French after-school snack is a *tartine* (slice of bread) or two with Nutella spread. Nutella, a chocolate-hazelnut spread that may be considered comparable to peanut butter in the United States, is so important to the French household routine that near riots broke out in 2018 when the supermarket chain Intermarché put it on sale at 70 percent off—less than €1.50 for a 950-gram jar that normally sold for €4.70. Hundreds of shoppers all over France stormed the aisles, and some customers resorted to violence when supplies ran out. Some analysts attributed the surprising response to high unemployment rates in the regions where the conflicts erupted, economically depressed areas in the industrial north and rural southwest that had 20–30 percent unemployment in 2014 surveys. Lower-income households, it was argued, would be driven to take advantage of a steep discount on an everyday staple. Others noted that populations in these areas tended to be less educated and thus more susceptible to marketing of industrial foods like Nutella (Rondeau 2018). Both arguments demonstrate that the French make associations between the kinds of food consumers eat and their class status or social rank, even if many French households buy and use Nutella regularly. France is home to the largest Nutella factory in the world, and the French buy more Nutella than any other country.

Aperitif

Very different from the afternoon *goûter*, French adults often take an aperitif before dinner: a drink and a few small, salty snacks such as nuts or even potato chips. The aperitif or *apéro* functions as a moment for family or

---

Tartine pour Goûter (After-School Snack)

Yield: Serves 1

Ingredients
1 slice crusty bread (large loaf or 2 slices of baguette)
1 Tbsp Nutella

1. Toast bread lightly.
2. Spread Nutella on bread. Serve with a glass of juice or a cup of hot chocolate.

> **Feuilletés au Fromage (Cheese Twists)**
>
> *Yield:* Serves 6 as an aperitif
>
> 1 package puff pastry (fresh or frozen)
> 1 egg, beaten
> 1 cup shredded hard cheese (Comté, Emmental, or Parmesan)
>
> 1. Preheat oven to 375 degrees.
> 2. Thaw puff pastry if frozen. When thawed (or if using fresh), unroll into a flat rectangle. Cut into ½ inch strips with a pizza cutter.
> 3. Place the strips carefully onto a baking pan covered with parchment paper. Brush with beaten egg.
> 4. Sprinkle the strips with cheese. Twist them carefully into spiral shapes.
> 5. Bake for 12–15 minutes, checking carefully so that the cheese does not burn. When golden brown, remove from the oven and serve immediately.

guests to gather before a meal to enjoy a glass of juice, soda, or a cocktail and a few crackers or small bites as a way of opening up the appetite for a meal. (The term *apéritif* comes from the Latin word for "opening.") In cities, many people use the hour or so before dinner (around six or seven o'clock) to socialize and have a glass of wine or a cold beverage at a café. More recently, the aperitif has turned into an *apéro-dinatoire*, or a more substantial cocktail-dinner hour, with a selection of small plates including olives, prosciutto or other charcuterie, a number of cheeses or pâtés, and perhaps some small cooked dishes. Younger French people have begun to revive the aperitif tradition as a way of finding community and enjoying time with friends. At a café or bistro or even at home, the aperitif may include a cheese platter and some charcuterie (cured meats like salami or prosciutto), smoked fish spreads or mousses, or raw vegetables with a dipping sauce.

Le Snacking

Between-meal snacks have become more common as the French imitate North American eating habits, and the term *le snacking* has entered the lexicon, to designate the consumption of ready-made, industrial foods, such as those purchased at a convenience store. As defined by a French geographer, *le snacking* is made up of "mobile products, accessible day and night" (Fumey 2006, 237) and certainly has a different connotation

Le Snack

The term *le snack* in French is not the name of a food but the word for a modest restaurant or "snack bar." These establishments are often the only food-service businesses open late in many French cities, and they serve inexpensive meals, often to a mostly immigrant clientèle. Many of the snack bars in Marseilles, on the southern coast of France, are run by Egyptian immigrants. These businesses serve halal food and no alcohol and are safe havens for Muslim residents of the city (Bouillon 2000, 44–45).

from the *goûter* eaten at home, both in the quality of the food and drink and the symbolism attached to the practice. While the *goûter* for children very often consists of bread with jam or Nutella, "mobile snacks" include prepackaged sandwiches, salads, and cut vegetables as well as candy and ice cream. Hot food eaten as a snack in France more likely takes the form of a kebab, a cone of fries, or a slice of pizza and is usually consumed by young people.

The kebab sandwich or *döner kebab*, an import from Turkey and similar to the Greek gyro sandwich, can be found in most cities in France. In France, a kebab consists of marinated meat cooked on a spit, shaved onto bread, and then topped with fries, a French innovation. Kebabs usually include lettuce, tomato, and onion and may be garnished with mayonnaise, harissa (a spicy, tomato-based sauce), or a combination. They are normally eaten on the go or by those looking for a hearty meal for very little money. Young people particularly appreciate kebabs, and their growth in France has been bound up with worries about immigration and cultural change. Kebab restaurants arrived in France in the 1980s in Alsace, a region that borders Germany, where kebabs had already become popular. They began to find widespread acceptance in the 1990s.

Despite the origins of the dish in Turkish cuisine and an influx of Turkish immigrants at the moment that kebab restaurants became popular, kebabs in France are commonly associated with North African immigrants. The relationship in the French mind between kebabs and immigrants from the Maghreb is motivated by politics, since this "foreign" food is seen as a threat to French culinary identity. The spread of kebab restaurants is seen as a sign of the "Islamization" of France, since both Turkey and North Africa have large Muslim populations. In reality, these restaurants have sprung up in city centers with large populations of immigrants, in neighborhoods where

Street Food and Snacks

there are not many restaurants or cafés. As such, the kebab restaurants serve an important social role as a community gathering place. But they are also popular as cheap lunch spots in big cities, particularly those with large universities, and as part of the nightlife in cities where young people might want to buy a snack after an evening out at bars or clubs.

Kebab sellers have also become common in small towns and midsize cities suffering from economic decline and the departure of small businesses that were formerly the center of shopping and food consumption (Cassely et al. 2019, 9). Smaller towns, especially in the far north and southwest of France, have seen steep declines in the number of restaurants and small shops in their city centers due to both the growth of large supermarkets and discount chains on the outskirts of town and a persistently difficult economic climate. Kebab shops fill a role once held by these family-run establishments, and the French have not always welcomed the change, viewing these shops and their often immigrant owners with suspicion and wistfulness for the past. Nevertheless, in 2017 French diners bought an estimated 350 million kebabs and were the second-largest consumers of kebabs in Europe, after Germany (Vovos 2019).

For a quick bite, the classic French *jambon-beurre* (ham and butter on a baguette) sandwich has an enduring history, but it has recently seen a drop in popularity due to an influx of American foods like bagels and

---

Sandwich Jambon-Beurre (Ham-Butter Sandwich)

Yield: Serves 2

Ingredients
1 baguette
1 tsp Dijon mustard
4 Tbsp salted butter, softened
4 slices deli ham
1 ripe tomato, sliced (optional)
Lettuce (optional)

1. Cut baguette in two and then cut each half-baguette lengthwise.
2. Spread mustard on the cut side of the top half of each sandwich.
3. Spread butter evenly on both halves of each split baguette.
4. Layer ham evenly over butter on the bottom half of each sandwich.
5. Layer tomato and lettuce on ham, if using.
6. Place the buttered top on the sandwich. Serve.

hamburgers. French consumers purchased more than a billion *jambon-beurre* sandwiches in 2016, representing 51 percent of all takeout sandwiches ("Jambon-beurre" 2017). But sales dropped by nearly 3 percent compared to the previous year and were significantly lower than in 2012, when 62 percent of sandwiches sold in France were *jambon-beurre*. The classic *jambon-beurre* sandwich has declined in popularity due to a rise in price and the appearance of some more elegant versions. The average price for a premade ham-butter sandwich in 2017 was €2.93, more expensive in large cities like Paris and in cafés and restaurants but less expensive in small towns and in mini-markets offering prepackaged food. The *jambon-beurre* sandwich could be considered the equivalent of the hamburger in the United States, since it is available in every French town and uses two ingredients very important to French culture: a baguette and good butter.

Gira Consulting, an industry research group, confirmed the importance of the *jambon-beurre* sandwich when it created the "ham-butter index" in 2008 to show the price and availability of this sandwich compared to others in France and to the cost of living in different parts of France.

In 2018 Gira Consulting reported that for the first time, hamburgers had become more popular by sales in France than the *jambon-beurre* sandwich. In 2018 the French consumed 1.7 billion hamburgers (Gira Conseil 2019). Pizza is not far behind, as a snack food with a newly growing fan base. The French are second only to the United States in pizza consumption per capita in the world, with more than a million pizzas sold in 2018. Domino's Pizza opened its first restaurants in France in 1989 and, according to Domino's in France, the most popular toppings in the country are goat cheese, ham, and potatoes. American-style pizza became popular in France in the early 1990s and currently exists alongside Italian-style pizza, which was introduced to France by Neapolitan immigrants in the early twentieth century. Pizza chains like Domino's, Pizza Hut, and McCain (from Canada) dominate the American-style pizza market and serve a standardized product, but Italian-style pizza remains an artisanal, handmade food.

In Provence and particularly in Marseille in the South of France, pizza makers created mobile wood-burning pizza ovens in the 1960s to sell Neapolitan-style pizza (Sanchez 2005, 128). Marseille sits on the Mediterranean Sea and has long served as a crossroads for different cultures; in this case, nearby Italians brought ingredients from Sicily (like anchovies) and techniques from Naples (like white pizza) to create a new type of wood-fired pizza in France. Sylvie Sanchez identifies a "line of demarcation" for pizza in France: from Nantes, on the Atlantic coast, to Besançon, on the border with Switzerland. North of this line, American chains dominate the pizza market, and there are very few artisanal "pizza trucks"; and

Street Food and Snacks

"French-Style" Pizza

Yield: Serves 4

Ingredients
1 medium white or Yukon Gold potato
1 premade pizza crust
½ cup prepared pizza sauce
4 thin slices of deli ham or prosciutto
4 oz. goat cheese
1 Tbsp olive oil

1. Place potato in a small saucepan with 1 teaspoon salt and cover with water. Bring to a boil and cook until tender. Check by piercing with a fork or the tip of a knife. Drain and let cool.
2. Place the pizza crust on a baking sheet. Spread a thin layer of tomato sauce over the crust. Layer the ham over the tomato sauce. Preheat the oven to 400 degrees.
3. Cut the potato into thin slices and layer over and around the ham. You may not need the whole potato.
4. Cut the goat cheese into ¼-inch thick rounds, or break up into pieces about the size of a quarter. Sprinkle the cheese over the ham and potato.
5. Drizzle the olive oil over the entire pizza. Bake at 400 degrees for 15 minutes or until bubbling and the cheese is starting to brown.
6. Cut into four pieces and serve hot.

---

in the South of France, the reverse is true (Sanchez 2005, 128). Pizza toppings in France also follow regional preferences. In the north, customers prefer ham, eggs, onions, and cream on pizzas, similar to the ingredients they might put on a crepe; and in the south, preferences lean toward tomatoes, olives, and sausages. The Alsatian specialty *flammekueche* (*tarte*

Pizza-Vending Machines

Motivated by the growing popularity of takeout pizza in France, the chain Tutti Pizza (in Toulouse) has (as of 2020) installed nine pizza-vending machines, called "TuttiMatic," in southwestern France. These machines offer fresh pizza in three minutes, 24 hours a day. Selections include kebab and curry pizzas as well as pizzas with standard toppings, and each pizza costs between eight and 11 euros (about 10 dollars).

flambée in French, or "flamed tart," because it is cooked over a wood fire) is similar to a thin-crust pizza, topped with cream, onions, and ham, and served as an appetizer.

New Trends

The growth of kebabs, hamburgers, and pizzas as snack foods can certainly be linked to the youth market. Although fast food has declined in France recently, prompting McDonald's to change its logo from bright red to "healthy" green and to offer more salads and table service, young people in France still want a quick meal or snack for a low price. The average French consumer visits fast-food restaurants much less frequently, preferring a high-end burger or classic French dish at a bistro or the stylish and more expensive food offered by food trucks. In 2019, 91 percent of young people ages 18–24 visited a fast-food restaurant compared to 63 percent of the general population, and 54 percent of young people ate at a kebab restaurant compared to 46 percent of the French in general (Cassely et al. 2019, 18).

The new wave in fast food is taco restaurants, which have seen an enormous increase in popularity. The chain O'Tacos had opened 186 stores in France by the end of 2018, after just five years in business, and 57 percent of people under the age of 25 responded to a survey saying that they had eaten at a taco restaurant (compared to 28 percent of the general French population) (Cassely et al. 2019, 27). By comparison, Starbucks sales grew by 48 percent in France between 2017 and 2018, and O'Tacos sales grew by 78 percent ("France Rapide" 2019, 46). French-influenced tacos at these new fast-food restaurants may include fries or other local ingredients. O'Tacos recently added milkshakes and ice cream to the menu. Compared to the kebab, tacos in France are perhaps less suspicious as a foreign food because Tex-Mex cuisine is not well known there. The French do not view Mexican food as threatening because it is not attached to a wave of immigration, as is North African cuisine, and because these are "French tacos" with French ingredients. In fact, "French tacos" are not really tacos at all but resemble grilled burritos or wraps: a wheat wrap enclosing ground meat, fries, and a cheese sauce is folded into a rectangle and grilled. The phenomenon began in Lyon and then traveled across the country. In French, the treat is called a *matelas*, or "mattress," due to its shape. Bagels are also becoming more popular in France, with five million bagels sold in 2018 across France ("France Rapide" 2019, 45). Bagel shops in France do not limit themselves to

> ### "French" Tacos
>
> *Yield:* Serves 4
>
> *Ingredients*
> 1 bag frozen French fries
> 1 tsp vegetable oil plus more for oiling pan
> 1 pound ground beef
> Salt, pepper
> 2 Tbsp butter
> 2 Tbsp flour
> 1 cup whole milk
> 1 cup shredded cheddar cheese
> 4 flour tortillas (10-inch-burrito size)
> Barbecue sauce (or your favorite sauce), optional
>
> 1. Bake French fries as package directs until golden brown. Set aside.
> 2. Add oil to a large skillet over medium-high heat. Cook ground beef until no longer pink. Add salt and pepper to taste.
> 3. In a small saucepan, melt the butter over medium heat until foaming. Add the flour, and stir constantly until bubbly and light golden. Add the milk, and whisk constantly until smooth. Turn heat to low, add the shredded cheese, and stir until smooth.
> 4. Assemble the "tacos": place a tortilla on a plate. Spread with cheese sauce and place one-fourth of the ground beef and a handful of fries in the center of the tortilla. Add barbecue sauce if desired. Fold the tortilla into a rectangular shape by folding the short sides in first and then the long sides. Continue with the remaining tortillas.
> 5. Heat a panini press or a grill pan (or a heavy frying pan) over medium-high heat. Oil the press or pan lightly with vegetable oil. Grill the "tacos" for 2–3 minutes on each side or until browned. Serve immediately.
>
> Adapted from Lex 1812, "French Tacos," Marmiton, accessed February 22, 2020, https://www.marmiton.org/recettes/recette_french-tacos_349386.aspx.

toasted bagels for breakfast, offering pancakes and gourmet coffees as well as local beers and shared bagels in the evening for aperitif time before dinner.

Among the more traditional snacks are crepes, thin, sweet pancakes filled with jam or Nutella and purchased from street vendors or at the takeout window of sit-down crepe restaurants. Crepes have their own holiday in France, called *fête de la chandeleur*, or Candlemas Day, February 2, when families eat crepes together. When crepes were first part of the Candlemas celebration in the fifth century, they were made simply of flour, water, and salt, and more prosperous families might have added a bit of oil or fat to grease the pan. Only the very wealthy would have added eggs or milk, and these early crepes would not have been served with jam, since sugar was an expensive and rare commodity for anyone but the richest consumers until at least the eighteenth century. In the Middle Ages, the northern regions of France began to cultivate buckwheat flour, and this grain became the common flour for crepes from Brittany, famous for the best crepes. Medieval crepe recipes from Brittany call for only three ingredients: buckwheat flour, water, and gray sea salt, stirred for a long time with a wooden spoon or with the hands (Wagda 2005, 132). Variations on the recipe might have added buttermilk or milk in place of water, or even mashed potatoes to thicken the batter. In the early nineteenth century, it became common for cooks to add eggs and milk to crepe batter, producing the crepes we recognize today.

In Brittany, in the early days as now, crepes (called galettes if made of buckwheat and crepes if made of white flour) are cooked on a large, circular flat griddle called a *billig* or *pillig*, in the Breton dialect; it was originally made of terracotta and later of iron or steel. Crepe making in the traditional way involves specialized equipment: the *rouable*, a wooden scraper to spread the batter across the *billig* in a thin layer; the *tournette*, a spatula for flipping the crepe; and a "mop" of fabric strips for greasing the *billig* with oil (Wagda 2005, 133). In Brittany, more than 1,300 *crêperies* serve tourists and locals alike, with crepes of all kinds but particularly the well-loved *galette-saucisse* or sausage crepe, also known as the "Breton hot dog." In Rennes, in northwest France, this combination, served by street vendors at open markets and outside soccer stadiums, has become so popular that fans of the Rennes soccer team sing, "Galette-saucisse, je t'aime" (Sausage crepe, I love you) as a rallying cry at every game. Defenders of the tradition insist that an authentic *galette-saucisse* has a grilled pork sausage in a cold galette, with no mustard or sauce of any kind, and must be eaten with the hands. Another popular snack item in Brittany is simply a galette with melted butter, folded in fourths and eaten out of hand. In Corsica, similar pancakes can be found in street markets; made of chestnut flour, they are called *castagnacci*. In Nice, those made of chickpea flour are called *socca*. The city of Nice is famous for other traditional street foods as well, including the *pan bagnat*, a tuna sandwich dripping with good olive oil, and the *pissaladière*, a thin pizza-like crust topped with a thick layer of caramelized onions and anchovy paste. Anchovies, olives, and olive oil are signature ingredients of this region.

In other parts of France, crepes and galettes are sold at street markets and restaurants, such as the P'tit Grec restaurant on the rue Mouffetard in the center of Paris, which is known for its boisterous vegetable and fruit markets. This creperie has been serving enormous filled crepes since 1981 to a crowd of students, tourists, and native Parisians. The new trend in crepes as street food have more in common with fast food than with the long-standing traditional recipe. The chain *Fête à crêpe* opened its first shop in 2014 outside of Paris and by 2018 had 36 stores across France and as far away as Montreal (Lebelle 2018). Customers select their own fillings from a menu that includes M&Ms, brownies, and strawberry gummies for sweet crepes, a far distance from traditional fruit jams or fresh fruit. For savory crepes, the menu offers chicken tenders, ground beef, jalapeños, and blue cheese (among others). None of the meats is pork-based (including turkey bacon, for example), making the restaurant friendly to Muslim diners, an increasingly important segment in France. Students taking their *goûter* can enjoy a crepe with a milkshake or a soda, and the founder of the company positioned his business deliberately as an "alternative to kebabs, pizzas, and sandwiches" (Lebelle 2018).

Another snacking trend driven by young people in France is the rise in popcorn sales at the movies. Americans take snacking during films for granted, since popcorn has been sold in American theaters since the 1930s, but French filmgoers resisted the trend wholeheartedly until very recently. The French attitude toward meals and their high respect for the art of cinema made snacking at movie theaters incomprehensible to most French people. This attitude persists in the older generations, even as popcorn and other snacks are becoming more common at the movies. In 2019 half of all French cinemagoers purchased snacks or drinks (the figure rises above 60 percent for those younger than 24), and popcorn was by far the most popular choice, selected by 32.7 percent of all audiences and 52.3 percent of those ages 15–24 (CNC 2019, 48).

Even if the French imitate the American practice of eating popcorn, their habits are still unique. French movie popcorn is often sweetened with sugar or caramel, not salt. Other packaged snacks in France come in flavors that reflect local preferences, such as peanut-flavored corn puffs and potato chips with paprika, roast chicken, or sausage flavor, although the most popular kind of potato chips is plain. In contrast to other countries, the French generally eat potato chips with a meal or as part of the aperitif rather than as a between-meal snack. The market for potato chips, particularly for flavored chips, is growing in France, but the French still consume less than two pounds of potato chips per person per year compared to more than twice that amount in Spain or Germany (Lentschner 2014).

Snacks and street food in France have undergone a dramatic evolution since the Middle Ages and their simple, baked, flour-based treats. Young people in France today, with their purchasing power and their admiration of American culture, have created fads for bagels, tacos, kebabs, and more, while the standard forms of snacking diminish in popularity. Pride in French gastronomy will not allow a wholesale American takeover, however, even of the marginal practice of snacks in France, and entrepreneurs market their new snacking items as healthy and fresh as well as inventive. Even celebrated chefs participate in creating quality takeout food and small plates so as not to be left out of the trend. On the whole, the new snack items have had an effect on French culinary practices, but the old-fashioned *jambon-beurre* sandwich and the entrenched *galette-saucisse* will never really disappear. Around the December holidays, street vendors sell warm roasted chestnuts to shoppers, filling the streets with a welcome scent. In the summer, many French people enjoy a cone of ice cream or gelato on an evening stroll, or a piece of flan—a slice of eggy custard—purchased from a bakery window. The French way of snacking is their own, and it is as important as the defined meals they share together.

Further Reading

Bonora, Tancrède. 2013. "Le goûter, c'est sacré . . ." *Le Parisien*, March 13, 2013.
Bouillon, Florence. 2000. "Des escales dans la nuit: Les snacks égyptiens à Marseille." *Les Annales de la Recherche Urbaine* 87 (1): 43–51.
Briffault, Eugène. 1846. *Paris à table*. Paris: Hetzel.
Bruegel, Martin. 2015. "Workers' Lunch Away from Home in the Paris of the Belle Epoque: The French Model of Meals as Norm and Practice." *French Historical Studies* 38, no. 2 (April 1): 253–80.
Carlos, Marjon. 2015. "A French Caribbean Chef Talks Fashion and Vegetarian Cuisine." *Vogue*, September 30, 2015.
Cassely, Jean-Laurent, Jérôme Fourquet, and Sylvain Manternach. 2019. "Des Dimensions politique, socioculturelle et territoriale du kebab en France." Fondation Jean-Jaurès, October 5, 2019. https://jean-jaures.org/nos-productions/des-dimensions-politique-socioculturelle-et-territoriale-du-kebab-en-france.
CNC (Centre National du Cinéma). 2019. "Géographie du cinéma 2018." *Dossiers du CNC* 341 (September).
Desportes, Françoise. 1987. *Le Pain Au Moyen Âge*. Paris: Orban.

Flandrin, Jean-Louis, Massimo Montanari, and Albert Sonnenfeld, eds. 2013. *Food: A Culinary History*. New York: Columbia University Press.

"France Rapide." 2019. *Snacking: Le magazine de l'alimentation rapide et fast casual* 53 (April–May): 42–53.

Fumey, Gilles. 2006. "Manger sur l'autoroute en France: Les pratiques alimentaires des touristes." *Collection EDYTEM. Cahiers de géographie* 4 (1): 231–38.

Gira Conseil. 2019. "Sandwich, Burger et Pizza, les stars du snacking en pleine forme en 2019." Snacking, September 19, 2019. https://www.snacking.fr/actualites/tendances/4440-Sandwich-Burger-et-Pizza-les-stars-du-snacking-en-pleine-forme-en-2019/.

Grignon, Claude. 1993. "La Règle, La Mode et Le Travail: La Genèse Sociale du Modèle des Repas Français Contemporain." In *Le Temps de Manger: Alimentation, Emploi du Temps et Rythmes Sociaux*, edited by Maurice Aymard and Françoise Sabban, 276–323. Paris: Éditions de la Maison des sciences de l'homme.

Herpin, Nicolas. 1988. "Le repas comme institution: Compte rendu d'une enquête exploratoire." *Revue française de sociologie* 29 (3): 503–21.

"Jambon-beurre: Le roi des sandwichs menacé par la concurrence." 2017. *Les Echos*, March 2, 2017. https://www.lesechos.fr/2017/03/jambon-beurre-le-roi-des-sandwichs-menace-par-la-concurrence-164087.

Katz, Solomon H., and William W. Weaver. 2003. *Encyclopedia of Food and Culture*. New York: Scribner.

Kindermans, Marion, and Lea Delpont. 2017. "Food-trucks: malgré l'effet de mode, un business pas si facile à tenir." *Les Echos*, February 8, 2017. https://www.lesechos.fr/2017/02/food-trucks-malgre-leffet-de-mode-un-business-pas-si-facile-a-tenir-154607.

Laurioux, Bruno. 1999. "Les repas en France et en Angleterre aux XIVe et XVe siècles." In *Tables D'hier, Tables D'ailleurs: Histoire et Ethnologie Du Repas*, edited by Jean-Louis Flandrin, 87–113. Paris: Jacob.

Lebelle, Aurélie. 2018. "Tacos, bagels, pad thaï. . . . Les nouvelles recettes street food qui cartonnent." *Le Parisien*, August 26, 2018.

Lentschner, Keren. 2014. "Les chips Vico partent à l'assaut de la forteresse Lay's." *Le Figaro*, March 15, 2014.

Méreuze, Didier. 2015. "Les 'food trucks' envahissent Paris." *La Croix*, June 28, 2015. https://www.la-croix.com/Culture/Cuisine/Les-food-trucks-envahissent-Paris-2015-06-28-1328814.

Montorgueil, Georges. 1899. *Les Minutes Parisiennes: Midi*. Paris: Paul Ollendorff.

Rondeau, Pierre. 2018. "Les émeutes pour du Nutella en promo en disent long sur l'état d'esprit des Français." Slate.fr, January 26, 2018.

Root, Waverley. 1970. *The Food of France*. New York: Alfred A. Knopf.

Sanchez, Sylvie. 2005. "Pizzas, crêpes et autres galettes." *Communications* 77: 127–48.

Schehr, Lawrence R. 2001. *French Food: On the Table, on the Page, and in French Culture*. New York: Routledge.

Vovos, Joffrey. 2019. "Sur la route des kebabs." *Le Parisien*, May 4, 2019. https://www.leparisien.fr/societe/sur-la-route-des-kebabs-le-sandwich-dont-les-francais-raffolent-04-05-2019-8065452.php.

Wagda, Marin. 2005. "A l'origine était la crêpe." *Hommes et Migrations* 1254 (March–April): 130–33.

Zola, Emile. (1877) 1961. *L'Assommoir*. Vol. 2. Edited by A. Lanoux and H. Mitterand. Paris: Gallimard.

CHAPTER NINE

Dining Out

It is strange to imagine a world without restaurants, but before the eighteenth century, there was nowhere in the world to sit down and order an individual meal at a private table outside the home. The restaurant as we know it was invented in Paris. But before the restaurant, there were many options for dining out if the diner belonged to the upper classes. Aristocratic banquets from the Middle Ages onward brought together power brokers and allowed hosts to show their wealth with expensive feasts. Taverns and inns offered simple meals at communal tables for travelers, and coffee shops popped up in Paris in the seventeenth century, later to become meeting places for philosophers, revolutionaries, and the common people. Finally, in the eighteenth century, came the development of the modern restaurant, followed by all of the many ways it is possible to eat food away from home today. Of about 175,000 restaurants currently open in France, the average size is 100 seats (60 inside and 40 on the outdoor patio), and 37 percent are fast-food or quick-service restaurants. French restaurants are busiest at lunchtime, and most are open on Sunday, their most popular day. This chapter describes what eating out means in France, from a simple cup of coffee to an elaborate multicourse meal.

Banquets: Gaul, Medieval and Renaissance France to the Eighteenth Century

An invitation to a banquet in ancient Gaul meant that the guest belonged to the elite. Wealthy patrons used banquets to create divisions between the upper and lower classes, and food played a major role. The kinds of foods served at aristocratic banquets and the way diners consumed these foods distinguished one class of eater from another. In Roman Gaul, "good eaters" were different from "bad eaters," but not in terms of health or nutrition. The first group was "cultivated," and the second was "uncivilized."

Sidoine Apollinaire, a writer in the fifth century, gave the label of "onion eaters" to the poor because the lower classes often had only vegetables to eat (and root vegetables were considered the lowest kind of eating), while those who attended banquets ate meat, an expensive commodity (Ariès 2016, 290). Meat was the food of the powerful, and banquets consisted of platter after platter of roasted, boiled, and stewed meat. Quantity was important, but some kinds of meat were considered more elite than others. Animals that grazed were associated with the earth and were less valued than water dwellers or animals that flew in the air: the most esteemed meats were fowl, especially pigeons, swans, cranes, peacocks, and storks. Fish was prized as well, due to its scarcity and expense. To create an impressive presentation, cooks reassembled large birds after cooking and decorated them with feathers so that they appeared just as they were when alive.

In the Middle Ages and the Renaissance, court banquets continued to feature meat and fowl but rarely beef or mutton since these meats were considered too common. Exotic birds like swans, cormorants, and herons disappeared from banquet tables, but table decorations like wine fountains, sculptures, and even orange trees gave the diners a sense of the importance of the occasion and of the host's budget. At large aristocratic functions, balconies above the dining area gave visitors (who were not invited to eat) a view of the ostentatious table settings and displays of expensive foods. In the midst of this display of great wealth, the table manners of the guests were far below the standards of the modern diner. Although serving forks were used for meat, individual forks were rarely used in France until the seventeenth century, and Louis XIV once banned them from his royal tables since he preferred to eat with his hands and did not want to be shown up by his guests. Banquet guests brought their own knives and often shared drinking goblets for water or wine. Spoons on the table, often made of wood, could be used for serving from the communal dishes and eating, meaning that they were not sanitary. Only hosts, and

Dining Plates

Metal or ceramic plates did not appear on French dining tables until the Renaissance. In the Middle Ages, diners used a thick slice of twice-baked bread called a *tranchoir* as a "plate" for meat or fish. Sometimes two guests sitting side by side shared a single *tranchoir*. At the end of the meal, the bread soaked with juices was offered to the poor (Laurioux 2013, 222).

certainly the king at a royal banquet, had their own sets of utensils, housed in an ornamental *nef* (or nave) often covered with jewels. The *nef de table* contained the host's knife, spoons, salt and spices, and a piece of narwhal horn used to test wine for poison.

Unlike modern restaurants, diners at formal banquets in France before the eighteenth century were presented with all of the dishes for each course at once, a system called *service à la française* (French service). Diners would enjoy a succession of courses from soups and stews to roasts to fish, interspersed with *entremets* (in-between courses) of dried fruit or spiced nuts. Hierarchy of class and rank dictated the seating arrangement around a U-shaped table, and servers placed more expensive or more extravagant dishes near the most important diners. All diners served themselves or offered to serve nearby diners. This required aristocratic men (women would eat separately or wait to be served) to know how to carve roasts and serve various dishes gracefully and with attention to the importance of the people seated near them. If called upon to carve a roast, for example, the nobleman needed to carve the meat expertly and serve the best cuts to the highest-ranking diner first, before taking the less-desirable cuts for himself. Manuals for table service from the seventeenth century gave instructions on how to carve meat and serve the dishes that accompanied it, as well as guidance on which utensil to use for different foods. Olives, for example, had to be served with a spoon and never a serving fork. In a guide to noble behavior, Antoine de Courtin instructed readers not to wipe their hands on the bread or make their napkin too dirty, not to lick their fingers or knife, and not to eat directly out of the serving dish but to take a portion on their own plate, among other instructions that seem obvious to the modern reader but were new codes of conduct to those arriving at court (Courtin 1681, 121–24).

After the French Revolution and over the first half of the nineteenth century, *service à la française* fell out of favor, to be replaced by *service à la russe* (Russian service), adopted from the Russian courts, in which each diner received each course on an individual plate. Each style had its defenders: some claimed that French service was more egalitarian since diners could choose what they liked from large platters, and more ceremonial as large roasts arrived at table intact. Others argued that Russian service had the advantage of being faster and providing diners with hot food. Private banquets in elegant homes through the nineteenth century continued to practice *service à la française*, and it was, ironically, the standard in European courts outside of France, but restaurants favored Russian-style service. Above all, the French meal has always had a clear structure from beginning to end, with defined courses and the expectation that guests

The Age of the Restaurant

Restaurants were born in Paris in the form of bouillon shops serving meat broths called *restaurants* (restoratives) in the 1760s. As noted in chapter 1, an enterprising businessman named Mathurin Roze de Chantoiseau opened a bouillon shop in 1768 and used his license as a *traiteur* (cook-caterer) to gain access to the market for selling hot broth to Parisians. He advertised his bouillon shop in a commercial guide for visitors to Paris that he wrote and published himself, and as bouillon shops gained a following, the owners encouraged their customers to sit at a table and drink their cup of broth instead of taking it with them (Spang 2001, 24). Bouillon shops were allowed to stay open later than other food shops, and each restaurant offered patrons a menu of dishes to choose from, eventually expanding beyond meat broths to include light snacks. As far back as the fourteenth century, urban residents of France bought cooked meat (usually poultry) from roast shops since most homes did not have cooking equipment. Parisians and other city-dwellers could buy cooked food to take home from the *traiteur* or from a street vendor, or they could enjoy a hot drink at a café, but the novelty of the bouillon shops (both the drink and the shop were known as *restaurants*) was that they offered patrons a private table and an individual meal.

Other options available for dining out in Paris in the early eighteenth century included inns, taverns, and *tables d'hôte* (offering meals at a fixed price at a communal table), but none of these gave the diner a choice of dishes or a private space. They were also often crowded and unsafe for women traveling alone. The first restaurants in Paris quickly adopted the practices that we now take for granted: individual tables (taverns and boardinghouses offered only a communal table until the 1780s), printed menus offering the customer a selection of dishes (other eating venues had a fixed banquet menu and a fixed price), and single servings (taverns served food on shared platters, and *traiteurs* acted as caterers for groups or families). The concept of individual dining was so new that until nearly the end of the eighteenth century, menus specified that prices were for single servings only (Spang 2001, 76–77). By the 1790s all food businesses in Paris adopted the name "restaurant" even if they had not changed their services.

For the modern diner, the idea of a private table and separate meal seems commonplace, but this new way of dining clashed with the beliefs on which the French revolutionary movement was based. As it happened, the restaurant came into being in Paris at the same moment that the Revolution exploded: the fall of the Bastille occurred in 1789. In the midst of pledges of *liberté, égalité, and fraternité* ("freedom, equality, and brotherhood"), some restaurant owners were accused of being unpatriotic since they sold extravagant food to those who could pay for it instead of offering modest meals to all. In the immediate postrevolutionary moment, grand civic dinners were intended to reinforce the social and economic equality promoted by the new government. The Feast of the Federation on July 14, 1790, featured a dinner for all members of the National Assembly, and other associations promoted civic meals encouraging citizens to bring what they could and dine together. The Festival of the Supreme Being, celebrated across France in June 1794 and promoted by Robespierre himself, featured a communal supper of spartan fare at the Hôtel de Ville in Paris. Set against these ideals of communal dining, the restaurant took hold, of interest to those who wished to set themselves apart from the crowd.

The Rise of Gastronomy

The rise of the restaurant in Paris was helped along by another Parisian invention: gastronomy, or the love of good food. Previously, only wealthy nobles had access to elegant food and expensive ingredients. Only a household with significant means could maintain a kitchen staff and supply a larder sufficient to create dishes like those found on noble tables, but restaurants made these foods available to anyone with enough money for a single meal. Members of the bourgeoisie began to adopt noble habits of eating extravagant food in elegant settings. Gastronomic cuisine opened fine dining to the bourgeoisie, but it kept some remnants of aristocratic banquets. Beginning in the eighteenth century, the names of dishes and particularly sauces honored noble figures and royalty: cookbooks and menus featured sauces named for princes, princesses, dukes, and kings. Restaurant patrons were unfamiliar with this curious vocabulary of named dishes, sometimes called "menu French," and often may not have known what they had ordered, but they were entranced by the sophistication they saw in it. Menus featured long lists of different kinds of meats and sauces and seemed to offer unlimited variety, as the noble banquets had. Menus in fine restaurants were printed like newspapers with four columns in the early nineteenth century, as leather-bound booklets by midcentury, and then as a single sheet often decorated with drawings or flowers (Spang 2001, 186). To this day, French vocabulary permeates restaurant menus even in non-French-speaking countries. The French word for menu is *carte*, for example, and ordering a dish by itself is called *à la carte*. In France today, it is still common to order a three-course meal with a set price and limited choices; in French this is called a *prix fixe* menu, for "fixed price."

By the nineteenth century, restaurants and public venues for eating were not limited to the wealthy. In the urban context of Paris, meals for every budget were available in public spaces such as *gargotes* (cheap, working-class restaurants) and *crèmeries* ("cream shops," serving coffee with milk and simple lunches, like fried eggs); from ambulant vendors selling soup or cooked meats; tripe sellers, who were a regular feature outside meat markets; and drink shops offering coffee and hot chocolate. The wine shops (*marchands de vin*) gained the right to sell grilled meats to customers, to accompany their glass of wine or beer, taken on the way home from work. Restaurants and cafeterias sprang up in Paris in response to the wave of women working outside of the home in the late nineteenth century. Since these workers could not return home for lunch and earned very little, they needed a cheap meal in a safe place. Some companies opened on-site cafeterias, and many working-class restaurants served a standard meal called an *ordinaire* of broth, boiled beef and vegetables, and fruit for dessert, accompanied by bread and sometimes wine (Bruegel 2015, 265). The *ordinaire* followed the French structure of first course, main course, and cheese or dessert that has become universal in French meals. Workers could also choose one dish from the menu or buy only bread and cheese if they could afford nothing else.

For the most part, French restaurants and cafeterias, even in schools, replicate the three-course traditional structure of the French meal. Alexandre Lazareff, a cultural commentator, called the three-course meal the "symbol of French culinary culture" for both the quality of the food and the conviviality of eating with others (1998, 18). This symbol was recognized by UNESCO in 2010 as the "gastronomic meal of the French," and it is visible in the way the French structure meals at home and outside it. French elementary students are taught to eat "the French way" in school cafeterias that offer a three-course meal plus bread. School cafeteria menus feature the same kinds of dishes children might find at home, including a composed salad, meat with vegetables, a wedge of cheese and a fruit dessert. Sample menus from an elementary school in central France in 2017, for example, included green bean salad with shallots, beef stew, steamed potatoes and broccoli, Emmenthal cheese and fresh fruit on Monday; tomatoes in vinaigrette, veal with olives, sautéed zucchini, soft cheese and fruit salad on Tuesday; radishes and butter, quiche lorraine, beans with butter and

> ### Soupe à L'Oignon Gratinée (Onion Soup with Cheese Croutons)
>
> *Yield:* Serves 4–6
>
> *Ingredients*
> 2 pounds yellow onions
> 3 Tbsp olive oil, divided
> Salt
> 2 cups beef broth
> 4 cups water
> 1 bay leaf
> 5 whole peppercorns
> 1 baguette, sliced
> 2 cups Gruyère or Swiss cheese, shredded
>
> 1. Thinly slice the onions (about 8 medium onions). Add 1 tablespoon olive oil to a large, heavy soup pot, and turn heat to low. Add onions and ½ teaspoon salt. Cook onions slowly over low heat until golden, stirring occasionally.
> 2. Add beef broth, water, bay leaf, and whole peppercorns. Bring to a boil over medium-high heat, and then simmer over low heat until slightly reduced, about 1 hour.
> 3. For the croutons, slice baguette into ¾-inch slices. Brush with olive oil on both sides and toast in a 375-degree oven until light golden brown on both sides. Sprinkle with shredded cheese and bake until cheese melts.
> 4. Ladle soup into bowls and top with 1–2 croutons, cheese-side up. Serve hot.

parsley, and rice pudding on Wednesday ("Menus" 2017). At university dining halls and workplace cafeterias, the same structure can be found, with a fixed-price menu offering an *entrée*, a main dish, and a dessert.

Paris as the Center of Fine Dining

By the end of the nineteenth century, the "restaurant" was well known in Paris, and the concept had begun to spread to other cities in France. The center of fine dining was always Paris, however, and the temples of gastronomy remain Parisian for the most part. The restaurant Rocher de

Cancale, in the center of Paris, was named for the nearby coast, where perfect conditions produced the oysters consumed by the thousands there. Founded in 1804, the restaurant was a popular destination in the evening, after the theater or the opera, for wealthy patrons who ate dozens and dozens of oysters in one sitting, followed by a main dish and dessert, washed down with plenty of wine. La Tour d'Argent restaurant in Paris, founded in 1860, also gained fame for one ingredient: pressed duck, finished tableside. A chef in 1890 created the ritual for which the restaurant became famous: a waiter carves a roasted duck at the table and then uses a special press to extract all of the juices from the remaining carcass, which are then added to a simmering sauce of duck broth and liver, cognac, and madeira wine. Diners enjoy the duck breast and sauce as a first course, followed by duck legs and *pommes soufflées* (potato puffs).

Pommes Soufflées (Potato Puffs)

Yield: Serves 6 as an appetizer

Ingredients
4 russet potatoes, scrubbed
4 cups vegetable oil
Salt

1. Peel the potatoes and trim off the rounded edges to make them a rectangular shape. Using a mandoline or a sharp knife, slice the potatoes the long way into paper-thin slices, about ⅛-inch thick. Place on paper towels, and work quickly so that the potatoes do not discolor.
2. Add the oil to a heavy pan until it is at least 1½ inches deep. Heat to 300 degrees, using a meat or candy thermometer. Fry the potatoes in batches; avoid crowding them so that they do not stick together. The potatoes should be cooked through but not browned, about 2–3 minutes. Drain the potato slices on paper towels while you finish cooking the remaining raw potatoes.
3. For the second frying, heat the oil to 375 degrees. Add the potatoes in batches and cook until puffed and golden, 1–2 minutes. Flip each potato as it puffs so that both sides are browned. Not all of the slices will puff, but they are still fine to eat. Drain on paper towels, sprinkle with salt and serve immediately.

La Tour d'Argent served its 100,000th duck in 1929 and its millionth duck in 2003. The Jules Verne restaurant, opened in 1983, sits on the second level of the Eiffel Tower and offers a pricey menu of French classics enhanced by spectacular views. One of the earlier owners of the Jules Verne restaurant was Louis Vaudable, who owned another of the most famous restaurants in Paris: Maxim's. Maxim's was founded in 1893 and became one of the hottest addresses in Paris in the Belle Epoque of the late nineteenth and early twentieth centuries. Maxim's hosted the biggest names in art, music, and entertainment. It was the preferred restaurant of German officers under the Occupation in World War II, and under Vaudable's direction in the 1950s it became one of the most recognized and most expensive restaurants in the world (Hesse 2011, 59). After the Vaudable family sold the restaurant to designer Pierre Cardin in 1981, the Maxim's name became more important than the cuisine, and the restaurant (and its attached museum) now attracts tourists but is not known for excellent food.

One mark of quality for French restaurants is the number of stars accorded by the Michelin guide: one star indicates a very good restaurant in its category, two stars designate an excellent table worth a detour, and three stars guarantee remarkable cuisine worth a trip. In the 2019 Michelin guide, the city of Paris hosts nine three-starred Michelin restaurants compared to five in New York City (United States) and twelve in Tokyo (Japan). Overall, France is currently home to 26 three-star Michelin restaurants, 83 two-star, and 515 single-star restaurants, ahead of Germany but behind Japan in overall totals (Michelin Guide n.d.). Some top chefs have begun to refuse the Michelin classification, arguing that adhering to Michelin standards is distracting and very stressful and that the Michelin inspectors have too much power. To remain on the Michelin guide, restaurants must serve a high-end, creative, and expensive menu and constantly try to reinvent themselves. Jérôme Brochot, a chef in a small town in Burgundy, refused a Michelin star for his restaurant in 2017 because the costs were too great and he wanted to offer a simpler cuisine that would make his restaurant affordable for more of the people in his town. Sébastien Bras, a three-star chef in Laguiole, asked to be left out of the Michelin guide; instead, his restaurant was knocked down to two stars in 2019 (Rioux 2019).

Dining at a Michelin-starred restaurant requires reservations well in advance, and it is expected that diners will dress formally and observe impeccable table manners. Restaurants serving three-star cuisine approach cooking as an art, and chefs take great care to create subtle and unusual flavors and to assemble dishes that are as beautiful as they are delicious.

Fine-dining restaurants are also very expensive, averaging about $300 per person for dinner: Le Pré Catalan, a three-star restaurant in Paris run by chef Frédéric Anton offers an eight-course prix fixe menu for €290 (about $324), not including wine; a four-course lunch menu for €140 ($156), or €180 ($201) with wine; and à la carte desserts for €40 ($45). Two-star restaurants average about $165 per person and have a wider range of cuisine, some specializing only in seafood, some vegetarian, and some following classic French cooking. One-star restaurants average less than $110 per meal and are often owned by newer or younger chefs. They represent regional and creative cuisine and are scattered across the country, although a great many are found in Paris, near Lyon, and on the Mediterranean coast. To accommodate more modest budgets, the Michelin guide also lists restaurants with the label *Bib gourmande* that offer refined cooking at an average per-meal price under €37 ($42).

Since the nineteenth century, Paris has been home to celebrity chefs who carry on the tradition of fine dining from generation to generation. Three-star chef Alain Senderens ran his Paris restaurant, L'Archestrate, until 2005 when his protégé, Alain Passard, took over the restaurant and renamed it Arpège, and the restaurant maintained its three Michelin stars. Passard also shocked the French food world when he decided to make Arpège a vegetarian restaurant. At the time, one critic called this decision "a crime against French cuisine" since the great dishes of classic French cooking are based on meat. After several years of give-and-take, Passard adapted his menu to offer mostly vegetarian cuisine with some meat. To supply his restaurant with the best, freshest produce, he owns three organic vegetable farms in western France. Lyon and the Burgundy region are home to equally famous chefs and restaurants. Eugénie Brazier opened her own restaurant in Lyon in 1921 and was the first person to win three Michelin stars at two different restaurants, in 1933. She had been trained by another female chef, Françoise Fillioux, who transformed a wine shop into a restaurant in 1890 and served an unchanging menu of Lyon sausages, quenelles (fish dumplings), artichokes with truffled foie gras, and chicken *demi-deuil* (lined with truffles) until her death in 1925. Women had owned restaurants in Lyon since the eighteenth century, but the *bouchons* (traditional restaurants) in Lyon came of age with the so-called *mères lyonnaises* (mothers of Lyon) in the twentieth century. Four other French women have earned three Michelin stars, all for restaurants outside of Paris: Marie Bourgeois in 1933, from the Ain region in eastern France; Marguerite Bise in 1951, from Haute-Savoie in the southeast; Anne-Sophie Pic in 2007, from Valence in the southeast, and Dominique Crenn in 2018, for her restaurant in San Francisco.

Hollandaise Sauce

Yield: Makes 1 cup

Ingredients
1 tsp vinegar
2 egg yolks, room temperature
Salt
8 Tbsp (one stick) butter, melted
2 Tbsp lemon juice

1. In a small pan, whisk the vinegar and egg yolks together until smooth. Add a sprinkle of salt. Place over low heat and whisk constantly until it begins to warm, then add the butter in a slow drizzle, stirring constantly.
2. Once the butter has been incorporated, add the lemon juice slowly and continue whisking. Heat until thick enough to coat the spoon. Taste before serving to see if you would like more salt or lemon juice. Keep warm until ready to use. Serve over steamed asparagus.

Adapted from Paul Bocuse, *Paul Bocuse in Your Kitchen* (New York: Pantheon, 1982), 117.

The legendary French chef Paul Bocuse trained under Eugénie Brazier in Lyon and went on to become one of the greatest stars of French gastronomy.

Although Bocuse died in 2018, his restaurant (named Paul Bocuse) remains open near Lyon and is run by his protegés. It maintains a very high standard for classic French cuisine, serving Bocuse's signature dishes like black truffle soup, named for former president Valéry Giscard d'Estaing, red snapper with "scales" made of sliced potatoes, and Bresse chicken in the style of la Mère Fillioux, one of the eminent female chefs of Lyon. The Bocuse restaurant practices discipline in its cuisine and its service: lunch is served only from noon to 1:15 p.m. and dinner from 8:00 to 9:15 p.m. As with most temples of gastronomy in France, the emphasis is not on serving as many patrons as possible but on giving patrons a memorable experience.

In the Rhone Valley in southeast France, brothers Jean and Pierre Troisgros followed in their father's footsteps to run a restaurant called Les Frères Troisgros (Troisgros Brothers), dedicated to nouvelle cuisine with lighter cooking and simpler sauces. In 1962 they created their most famous dish, salmon poached with sorrel sauce. Emblematic of the new kind of cooking taking hold in France, the salmon was barely cooked and the sauce accompanying it had subtle flavor and a light texture. Pierre's son, Michel Troisgros, took over the restaurant in 1996 and modernized the menu, removing the famous salmon dish and adding seasonality and new dishes with influences from Japan. Starting in the 1970s, Michel Guérard also followed the tenets of nouvelle cuisine in his spa-restaurant in southwest France that featured salads and vegetable dishes. One of his most famous creations was the *confit byaldi*, a version of ratatouille with sliced vegetables that was invented in 1976. It was later featured in the animated film *Ratatouille* as adapted by the American chef Thomas Keller. Whether in Paris or the provinces, high-end restaurants in France are divided between those that serve French classics—traditional dishes with sauces and wine—and those that offer fusion cuisine that merges French cooking and some other influence, often inspired by Japanese, Chinese, and Vietnamese cuisine. Chefs at top restaurants seek to bring in a new clientele, one that is familiar with world cuisine and unafraid of bold flavors. Adeline Grattard, chef-owner of Yam'Tcha, in Paris, for example, has successfully created a menu of French ingredients prepared with Chinese techniques, such as steamed buns filled with blue cheese. The "temples of gastronomy" hold firm to French traditions, but younger chefs are free to be playful with cuisine.

Less Formal Dining

Beyond gastronomic, fine-cuisine restaurants, France has a long tradition of more casual, less expensive eateries that serve local diners. The *bouchons* (traditional restaurants) in Lyon, begun by the "mothers of Lyon," served rustic, filling food that took advantage of local products. Early *bouchons* set the tradition of "nose-to-tail" eating so as not to waste anything, serving less prestigious cuts like pigs' feet and beef shins in savory sauces and stews. The restaurants are still decorated with homey touches like copper pots and hanging baskets, and they often feature communal tables so that diners can get to know each other, all part of the convivial atmosphere built into French dining. Menus at Lyonnais *bouchons* have their own vocabulary for classic dishes, and the most famous one is *quenelles de brochet*, or pike dumplings served blanketed with a lobster sauce that uses lobster shells as its base.

Of course, excellent local wines accompany a proper meal at a *bouchon*. Meanwhile, a brasserie is the equivalent of a wine bar but for beer since

Quenelles de Brochet, Sauce Nantua (Pike Dumplings with Nantua Sauce)

Yield: Serves 4

Ingredients
1 ½ pound pike fillets, or any mild white fish (haddock, sole, or tilapia are good substitutes)
4 eggs
2 cups heavy cream
½ tsp Old Bay seasoning
Salt
½ cup water
1 pound shrimp in shells
2 Tbsp olive oil
1 cup cremini or white mushrooms, chopped
1 cup baby carrots, chopped
1 cup celery, chopped, plus the leaves from the bunch of celery
3 Tbsp tomato paste
4 cups whole milk
Pepper

Be sure to remove any bones from the fish before starting.

1. Chop the fish into small (about 1 inch) pieces and then process in a food processor until smooth. In a large bowl, beat the eggs lightly. Add the fish purée and stir in 2 cups heavy cream, Old Bay Seasoning and ½ teaspoon salt. Cover and refrigerate, at least 4 hours or overnight.
2. In a large saucepan, bring ½ cup of water to a boil. Add the shrimp, cover, and steam until the shrimp is pinkish and opaque, stirring once. Place the shrimp in a bowl and shell them, reserving the shells. Refrigerate the cooked shrimp until ready to use.
3. In a large frying pan, heat the oil over medium high heat and add the shrimp shells, pressing down on them to release any juices. Cook for 5 minutes. Add the mushrooms, carrots, celery and celery leaves to the pan and cook until the vegetables are soft, about 10 minutes. Add the tomato paste and cooked until the paste is lightly browned. Stir in 4 cups whole milk and reduce the heat to medium. Simmer, stirring occasionally, for about 20 minutes or until thickened. Strain through a fine mesh colander and discard solids. Return the sauce to the pan, add a pinch of salt and a sprinkle of pepper to the sauce and keep warm on the stove.

> 4. Divide the fish mousse into 8 portions. Shape each portion into a log with spoons. Dip the spoons in water to keep the mousse from sticking. Place the logs on a plate and refrigerate until firm, about 20 minutes. Meanwhile, fill a wide saucepan with water about a ½-inch deep. Bring the water to a simmer and add ½ teaspoon of salt. Carefully add the quenelles with a slotted spoon and poach them in the water, spooning the water over the quenelles occasionally. When the quenelles are puffed and firm (about 15 minutes), place them in buttered individual baking dishes (2 per dish) or one large, buttered baking dish.
> 5. Pour the sauce over the quenelles and bake at 375 degrees for 10–15 minutes or until bubbling. Remove the baking dish(es), and add a few shrimp to each dish. Raise the oven temperature to 450 degrees, and bake until golden brown on top, about 5–10 minutes more.
>
> Adapted from Daniel Boulud, "Pike Cakes with Crayfish Sauce," *Saveur*, April 26, 2016.

these establishments originally sold beer brewed on the premises and offered very simple food to accompany it. Similar to the microbreweries we know today, brasseries sprang up in Paris when beer became a popular drink in the nineteenth century, and they are open all day long. Traditionally, brasseries do not serve full meals (of the French three-course variety) but are a place to stop for a drink and a snack. Many brasseries specialize in raw bars of fresh oysters and some, especially in Paris, have more extensive menus. Classic examples of brasserie cuisine include *choucroute garnie*, the Alsatian dish of sausages and sauerkraut; *steak-frites* (steak with French fries); or steak tartare (raw, seasoned ground beef topped with a raw egg). Halfway between a brasserie and a fine cuisine restaurant, bistros are another more casual option for typical French cuisine. Bistros began in the nineteenth century as working-class bars or cafés, but in the 1960s the word came to mean a small but elegantly decorated restaurant serving middle-class cooking at reasonable prices. Menus at bistros often include snails cooked in garlic and butter, beef burgundy, *croque-monsieurs* (grilled ham and cheese topped with creamy béchamel sauce), omelets, and other regional specialties.

At bistros and cafés, the French have a custom of standing at the bar to take their glass of wine or coffee since it is cheaper to stand than to sit at a table, where there will be a small charge for the service. Restaurant service in France in general is less hurried than in, for example, the United States. Waitstaff do not interrupt patrons to ask if they are finished or would like

Croque Monsieur ou Madame (Grilled Cheese and Ham Sandwich)

Yield: Serves 2

Ingredients
2–3 Tbsp butter, divided
1 Tbsp flour
⅔ cup whole milk
Salt, pepper, nutmeg
4 slices of bread
1–2 Tbsp Dijon mustard
4 slices Gruyère or Swiss cheese
4 slices cooked ham
2 eggs, optional

1. For the béchamel sauce: melt 1 tablespoon of butter in a small saucepan over medium heat. When the foaming subsides, add 1 tablespoon of flour and stir constantly until butter is absorbed (about one minute). Add ⅔ cup milk and whisk constantly until thickened. Add salt, pepper, and a sprinkle of nutmeg. Keep warm.
2. For the sandwiches: spread two slices of bread with Dijon mustard. Layer one slice of Gruyère cheese on each slice of bread. Divide the cooked ham between the two slices of bread, and then add another slice of cheese. Top with the last slices of bread.
3. Melt 1 tablespoon of butter in a skillet over medium heat; when the foam subsides, carefully place the sandwiches in the skillet and cook gently until browned on one side. Using two spatulas, carefully turn the sandwiches to brown on the other side. Add more butter if needed.
4. Place toasted sandwiches on an ovenproof plate or cookie sheet. Top each sandwich with béchamel sauce and place under the heated broiler for 1–2 minutes or until spotty brown. Serve with extra Dijon mustard.

Note: to make this sandwich a *croque-madame*, add a sunny-side-up fried egg to the top of each sandwich.

the check (*l'addition*); diners take the time they want to enjoy their meals, and it is up to the diner to ask the waitstaff for the check. It is customary in France to spend an hour or more at a meal, even in a modest restaurant, and the French custom of conviviality at table means that waitstaff allow

Crêpes Bretonnes

Yield: Makes 8 crepes

Ingredients
2 eggs
1 cup milk
¼ cup water
2 Tbsp butter, melted, plus extra for cooking
½ cup buckwheat flour (optional)
½–1 cup all-purpose flour
Salt
Various fillings of your choice

1. Put 2 large eggs, 1 cup of whole milk, ¼ cup of water, and 2 tablespoons melted butter in a blender. Pulse to blend for a few seconds. Add ½ cup of buckwheat flour and ½ cup of all-purpose flour (or 1 cup all-purpose flour if not using buckwheat flour) and ¼ teaspoon salt. Blend until flour is mixed in, scraping down the blender every 5 seconds or so, until smooth. Refrigerate for at least 2 hours or overnight.
2. When ready to use, stir the batter to reincorporate the ingredients. Heat a nonstick crepe pan or small skillet on medium heat; add a small piece of butter (¼ teaspoon) to the pan. When the butter has melted, lift the pan and swirl the butter to coat the pan. Add about ¼ cup of batter to the pan and swirl to coat the bottom of the pan. Return to the heat for 30 seconds to a minute, until the top is set and the edges look dry. Lift an edge of the crepe to see if the bottom is cooked and lightly brown. If so, flip the crepe and cook for another 30 seconds, until the crepe moves when the pan is shaken.
3. Place the cooked crepe on a plate, cover with foil, and keep warm in a 200-degree oven. Repeat with the remaining crepe batter, adding more butter to the pan after every third crepe or as needed. Remember to add just enough batter to coat the pan. French crepes are much thinner than American pancakes.
4. Fill the crepes with cooked eggs, cheese, ham, or other savory cooked fillings. Roll the crepes around the filling or fold them into triangles or squares. For sweet crepes, fill with honey, jam, fresh fruit and whipped cream, Nutella or chocolate sauce, or the classic combination of melted butter, granulated sugar, and a squeeze of lemon juice.

Adapted from Lou Seibert Pappas, "Savory Crêpes," in *Crêpes* (San Francisco: Chronicle Books, 1998).

Dining Out

patrons to take their time. In most cases, the tip (*service*) is included in the price of the meal, but diners who had an especially enjoyable time may leave a few extra euros for the server.

In some parts of France, specialty restaurants serve one kind of food that represents that region. In Brittany and northeastern France, *crêperies* are dedicated to full meals of savory galettes (buckwheat crepes) as a main course and sweet crepes for dessert, sometimes accompanied by a salad and traditionally with hard cider to drink. Apple cider made in Brittany matches the flavor of earthy galettes and is not too sweet to enjoy with dessert crepes. Buckwheat galettes served in *crêperies* across France but especially in Brittany contain any number of savory fillings, like the classic *complet* of ham, cheese, and a fried egg. Variations are almost unlimited, and galettes can include smoked salmon, sausages, or even snails. Sweet crepes come filled with fruit jam, chocolate, Nutella, or ice cream, often topped with *chantilly*, or vanilla-flavored whipped cream.

The most traditional crepe filling is simply sugar and lemon juice. Near the coast of the South of France, where families of Tunisian or Moroccan heritage have introduced their eating customs, diners can find restaurants serving couscous, a stew of meat and vegetables served with a grain-like pasta. Couscous has become very popular in France since it was introduced in the 1930s.

Midmorning or midafternoon, the French can very often be found at a café enjoying a drink on the patio or inside the warm space. Cafés might serve pastries or croissants in the morning, but their purpose is not to serve food as much as to provide a pause in the workday to enjoy a hot drink and perhaps meet with friends or read quietly at a table. Before these institutions served coffee, they existed in the 1660s as shops where *limonadiers* (sellers of nonalcoholic drinks) sold hot and cold beverages, including hot chocolate and fruit juices. When drink sellers like Francesco Procopio, a Sicilian who is credited with the first successful café, added coffee to the menu and began to improve their shops by adding marble and mirrors to the interiors in the 1680s and 1690s, the shops began to stand out as fashionable establishments and earned the name "café" (Landweber 2015, 208).

A century later, there were nearly 2,000 cafés in Paris. Working-class cafés, on the other hand, served only wine until the eighteenth century, when they expanded their menu to include coffee, beer, and absinthe (Haine 1999, 15). Parisian cafés are now a photogenic tourist mecca and are historically famous as the gathering place for Enlightenment philosophers like Voltaire and radical revolutionaries like Danton. French cafés serve coffee and tea, of course, and the French enjoy cappuccino and café au lait in the morning, but espresso is popular all day. Cafés also offer soft drinks, wine, and beer, and the French stop at a café for a before-dinner drink (aperitif). A single espresso costs less than two dollars at most cafés, and a trip to a café can be a cheap outing for students who wish to spend time with friends. Traditional cafés are slipping away in France, however, and an alarming number have closed. More young people prefer to spend time in fast-food restaurants offering free Wi-Fi and cheap food than linger over a coffee on a café terrace.

Fast-food and quick-service restaurants have become more and more popular in France in recent years. McDonald's arrived in France in 1972, and a rival Belgian chain called Quick set up shop in France in 1980. The first McDonald's restaurants met with success, and the chain expanded quickly to 14 sites, but when the home company wanted to buy back the franchises from Raymond Dayan, the French businessman running the restaurants, he refused. McDonald's accused Dayan of poor sanitation at his restaurants and revoked his license, resulting in a closure of all French McDonald's for more than a year. But by 1988 the French had taken to American-influenced fast food, and McDonald's in France, with 1,200 locations, is the second-largest market for the company, after the United States (Wile 2014). It was first suggested that the French embraced McDonald's because they love all things American, but in fact McDonald's in France caters to French culture and the French approach to food. The chain buys local French beef and potatoes for its menu items and has added the McBaguette for breakfast and macarons for dessert. Even the sauces and cheeses on the hamburgers reflect French tastes, from blue cheese to harissa (a spicy Tunisian condiment). Fast-food restaurants,

Absinthe

When the phylloxera outbreak in the late nineteenth century destroyed numerous vineyards, the price of wine increased and consumption dropped, especially among the workers. In the 1880s, as a replacement, the working class started to drink absinthe, a spirit made from wormwood that was thought to cause hallucinations. Absinthe soon displaced brandy and beer as the second most popular drink in Paris. Authorities who wanted to discourage consumption of absinthe to deter alcoholism called wine a "hygienic drink" and abolished taxes on wine so that it cost the same as absinthe (Haine 1999, 95–98).

including Pizza Hut and Starbucks, have invaded French cities. New entries in the fast-food marketplace include American chains Steak & Shake and Five Guys, and there is a new interest among French consumers in eating breakfast at a restaurant, a foreign concept for a country that has traditionally consumed only coffee and bread as a morning meal.

Young people adore fast-food restaurants for their cheap food and casual atmosphere, while the older generation worries that classic French cuisine and the café may disappear. For as much as France has a remarkable restaurant tradition as the birthplace of the restaurant, as a people the French do not spend a large part of their household budget on eating out. The French spent only 5.9 percent of their household budget in 2005 on restaurants, cafés, and cafeterias, as compared to 5.1 percent in 1960. The amount spent at restaurants has grown, while spending at cafés has declined (Insee 2009, 96). Dining together at home as a family, particularly for important celebrations, is clearly more important to the French than eating out.

Further Reading

Ariès, Paul. 2016. *Une histoire politique de l'alimentation: Du paléolithique à nos jours.* Paris: Max Milo.

Bruegel, Martin. 2015. "Workers' Lunch Away from Home in the Paris of the Belle Epoque: The French Model of Meals as Norm and Practice." *French Historical Studies* 38, no. 2 (April): 253–80.

Courtin, Antoine de. 1681. *Nouveau traité de la civilité qui se pratique en France parmi les honnestes gens.* Paris: Hélie Josset.

David, Elizabeth. 1999. *French Provincial Cooking.* New York: Penguin.

Davis, Jennifer J. 2013. *Defining Culinary Authority: The Transformation of Cooking in France, 1650–1830.* Baton Rouge: Louisiana State University Press.

Haine, W. Scott. 1999. *The World of the Paris Café: Sociability among the French Working Class, 1789–1914.* Baltimore, MD: Johns Hopkins University Press.

Hesse, Jean-Pascal. 2011. *Maxim's: Miroir de la vie parisienne.* Paris: Assouline.

Insee. 2009. "Fiches Thématiques sur l'alimentation et le Tabac: Cinquante Ans de Consommation en France." Insee. https://www.insee.fr/fr/statistiques/1372380?sommaire=1372388.

Landweber, Julia. 2015. "'This Marvelous Bean': Adopting Coffee into Old Regime French Culture and Diet." *French Historical Studies* 38, no. 2 (April): 193–223.

Laurioux, Bruno. 2013. *Manger Au Moyen Age: Pratiques et Discours Alimentaires en Europe aux Xive et Xve Siècles.* Paris: Hachette.

Lazareff, Alexandre. 1998. *L'Exception culinaire française: Un patrimoine gastronomique en péril?* Paris: Albin Michel.

Mennell, Stephen. 2006. *All Manners of Food: Eating and Taste in England and France from the Middle Ages to the Present*. Urbana: University of Illinois Press.

"Menus du Restaurant Scolaire." 2017. *Commune de Villedieu sur Indre* (blog), October 2, 2017. http://www.villedieu-sur-indre.fr/menus-du-restaurant-scolaire.

Michelin Guide. n.d. Accessed May 31, 2019. https://guide.michelin.com/fr/fr/restaurants.

Pinkard, Susan. 2010. *A Revolution in Taste: The Rise of French Cuisine, 1650–1800*. Cambridge: Cambridge University Press.

Rioux, Philippe. 2019. "Guide Michelin 2019: La guerre des étoiles." *La Dépêche*, January 22, 2019. https://www.ladepeche.fr/article/2019/01/22/2944709-guide-michelin-2019-la-guerre-des-etoiles.html.

Spang, Rebecca L. 2001. *The Invention of the Restaurant: Paris and Modern Gastronomic Culture*. Cambridge, MA: Harvard University Press.

Trubek, Amy B. 2001. *Haute Cuisine: How the French Invented the Culinary Profession*. Philadelphia: University of Pennsylvania Press.

Wile, Rob. 2014. "The True Story of How McDonald's Conquered France." *Business Insider*, August 22, 2014.

CHAPTER TEN

Food Issues and Dietary Concerns

France stands, arguably, at the top of the world in culinary prestige. French cuisine remains the model for fine dining that it has been since the nineteenth century. The French see themselves as guardians of gastronomy, with an obligation to maintain culinary standards. They imagine France as an island of excellent cuisine, with a population trained to appreciate good food and wine. This effort to hold onto the title of "finest world cuisine" has resulted in challenges for the French, as classic French cuisine has come to be seen as elitist and outdated, accused of being unhealthy or even unethical (as in the case of foie gras). The French nation has done a poor job of integrating immigrant cuisines from North Africa and other former colonies, and it strains mightily against the invasion of the food from the United States. Inside France, authorities worry that cooking at home will slowly disappear in favor of frozen meals and fast food. To survive, France must overcome these growing pains without letting go of the foundation that made it the world's most famous cuisine.

Foie Gras and Cruelty

Perhaps the most recognizable food associated with France, foie gras (*foie* means "liver" and *gras* means "fat") belongs to the highest echelons of fine cuisine, alongside truffles and champagne. This elegant reputation covers the reality of foie gras production, which is seen by many as cruel and unethical. Foie gras comes from geese or ducks forcibly fattened on corn so that their livers and their meat become fatty and succulent. Farms in southwestern France (Périgord) and eastern France (Alsace), have produced foie gras and other goose and duck products for centuries. The practice of *gavage* (force-feeding) with corn likely began in the eighteenth century after corn, imported from the Americas, began to be grown in Europe. Prior to the use of corn for *gavage*, farmers in southwest France fattened geese with wheat or rye and dried figs (Clairacq 1980, 441). On farms and in factory productions, geese are force-fed with corn up to three times per day and ducks twice per day for up to a month, either by hand or through the use of a mechanical feeder attached to a sort of funnel filled with corn. Those in the business of making foie gras emphasize that the animals must be treated gently during *gavage* and kept calm so that all of the energy from their food goes to producing fat rather than muscle (Cazalet 1980, 283). Farms keep strict standards for hygiene because geese and ducks are susceptible to disease and the foie gras industry requires producers to meet specifications for quality.

In 1998 the European Union issued a directive explicitly banning *gavage* as well as all methods of feeding animals that bring unnecessary suffering. As a result, Poland and Israel, at the time two of the top producers of foie gras, stopped using *gavage* in 1999 and in 2003, respectively. Without *gavage*, production in Poland and Israel dropped off precipitously, and France benefited since French producers increased production in response to the reduced supply on the market. In 2017 France produced 70 percent of the foie gras in the world (11,000 tons), with a revenue of more than €100 million (Blaquière 2019). Five countries, including France, refuse to adhere to the European directive against *gavage*, likely due to the economic importance of foie gras for France and because the question of whether *gavage* causes pain or suffering to the geese remains unanswered.

Foie gras producers maintain that geese do not feel pain from the forced feedings because their esophagi are lined with gristly tissue. They insist that if given unlimited rations of corn, geese would stuff themselves voluntarily to arrive at the same result. Those who oppose *gavage* point out that it is possible to produce foie gras naturally by providing extra rations to geese without the need to force-feed them. However, this natural process takes much longer and produces smaller livers of lower quality. New techniques aimed at "natural" foie gras use environmental factors to induce geese to overeat (such as low lights and cool temperatures that imitate the coming of winter when geese ingest more food before migrating) but have achieved little success. In January 2019 the U.S. Supreme Court upheld a law in California banning the production, import, and sale of foie gras that the state had passed in 2004, followed by lawsuits and battles between fine-food purveyors and animal-rights activists. Other parts of the world have levied similar restrictions on foie gras: Sao Paulo, Brazil, banned the sale of the product in 2015, India banned the import of foie gras in 2014, and Amazon in the UK stopped selling foie gras in 2013. Chicago, Illinois, attempted to ban foie gras from restaurants and stores in 2006 but reversed the decision two years later (Blaquière 2019).

Faux Gras (Vegan Foie Gras)

Yield: Serves 8

Ingredients
½ cup apple juice
3 Tbsp olive oil
1 shallot, peeled and diced
4 garlic cloves, peeled and minced
1 tsp each dried rosemary, thyme, and sage
2 10-oz. packages of white mushrooms, diced
2 Tbsp soy sauce
3 cups cooked lentils
1 cup roasted walnuts
½ cup cooked beets or sweet potato
Pepper

1. Heat apple juice in a small saucepan over medium heat until reduced by half. Set aside to cool.
2. Heat 1 tablespoon olive oil over medium-high heat. Add shallot and cook until soft, 3–4 minutes. Add garlic and dried herbs and cook until fragrant, about 30 seconds. Add diced mushrooms and stir well. Add 2 tablespoons reduced apple juice and bring to a simmer. Add soy sauce and reduce temperature to low. Let simmer for 10 minutes, stirring occasionally, until the mushrooms are very soft. Add water if the mushrooms look too dry. Remove from heat and let cool.
3. In a food processor or blender, process the mushrooms with the remaining olive oil, lentils, walnuts, beets or sweet potato and ¼ teaspoon black pepper until smooth. Add more reduced apple juice to taste or if the mixture seems dry. Spoon into a jar with a lid. Refrigerate for several hours before serving.

Serve on toasted bread.

Adapted from Alexis Gauthier, "Foie gras vegan ou Faux gras," 750g, accessed May 10, 2020, https://www.750g.com/foie-gras-vegan-ou-faux-gras-r204778.htm.

Foie gras remains an essential ingredient on holiday tables, and the French have proven unwilling to forgo it, no matter the ethical questions. Recent controversies over foie gras in France have less to do with animal cruelty and more to do with national pride, as foie gras (and snails for the classic bistro dish *escargots à la bourguignonne*) imported from Hungary and Bulgaria appears more often than do French products in markets. Spain and Belgium are the remaining European producers of foie gras, along with China and Canada overseas. In 2012 news reports of the increased export of foie gras from French producers to Middle Eastern countries, avid consumers of the luxury product, met with criticism by the French public. Those who commented accused French producers of betraying their homeland and levied anti-Islamic insults against the foreign buyers who, it was suggested, should not eat foie gras because they do not celebrate Christmas (Reuters 2012).

Colonial Influences

Beginning with Saint-Domingue (now Haiti) in the seventeenth century and extending to Asia and Africa through much of the twentieth century, France's colonial empire implicated France in the slave trade and in direct exploitation of native populations. In terms of food, the French intended to use their territories overseas to extend trade routes and to expand agricultural output. Following poor grain harvests in metropolitan France in the nineteenth century, officials planned to develop grain fields in Algeria and Indochina (now Vietnam, Cambodia, and Laos). In French West Africa (occupied by the French from 1895 to 1958), colonial managers aimed to expand cultivation of bananas for export as well as peanuts and palm trees for oil. By the nineteenth century, peanut plantations had been established in Senegal, and in the twentieth century the French turned to cultivation of bananas in French Guinea (now Guinea[-Conakry]). By 1930 bananas exported from plantations in Guinea represented one-third of French consumption of the fruit, and by 1937 the French colonial empire provided all of the bananas imported into France (Chevalier 1944, 127). In Guinea, export of bananas reached 53,000 tons in 1938, and the first oil-processing plants for peanuts opened in Senegal in 1939 (Coquery-Vidrovitch and Goerg 1992, 131). In the French Caribbean, Martinique exported 37,000 tons of bananas in 1938, and Guadeloupe 50,000 tons. Later development of Ivory Coast focused on cultivation of coffee and cacao. The industry grew steadily throughout the 1930s, surpassing palm oil exports, and by 1954 Ivory Coast by itself provided 48 percent of the total agricultural exports from French West Africa (Coquery-Vidrovitch and Goerg 1992, 140).

The French established sugarcane plantations on Saint-Domingue in the late seventeenth century, having taken possession of the island in 1626. Sugar production expanded there over the course of the eighteenth

Crops from the Caribbean

The Caribbean territories still provide tropical fruit, particularly bananas, to France. In 2018, Guadeloupe produced 35,000 tons of bananas for export, compared to 143,000 tons in Martinique for a total of nearly 200,000 tons in all of the French overseas territories (Agreste 2019, 144). Guadeloupe and Martinique are now departments of France, and their residents enjoy voting rights as French citizens. Peanuts are no longer an important export crop for Senegal, but in Ivory Coast, coffee and cacao exports still represent a significant income source for the now independent country.

Carottes Vichy (Vichy-Style Carrots)

Yield: Serves 4

Ingredients
2 Tbsp unsalted butter, plus 1 tsp butter for serving
1 Tbsp granulated sugar
4 large whole carrots, peeled and sliced thin
1 can low-sodium chicken broth

1. In a large skillet, melt the butter over medium heat. Add the sugar and cook for one minute, stirring well. Add the sliced carrots. Stir to coat with butter mixture.
2. Pour the chicken broth into the pan. If the liquid does not cover the carrots, add water so that the liquid just covers the carrots. Bring to a simmer, and then reduce heat to low and simmer uncovered for 20 minutes or until carrots are tender and liquid is almost evaporated. Stir occasionally.
3. Add remaining 1 teaspoon butter and stir to coat. Serve warm.

Adapted from Cassiopée, "Carottes Vichy," Marmiton, accessed May 12, 2020, https://www.marmiton.org/recettes/recette_carottes-vichy_17717.aspx.

---

century until the successful slave-led revolution in 1794 ended France's claim on the island. Ironically, France consumed relatively little sugar domestically compared to the rest of Europe. Only about one-fifth of the sugar produced on Saint-Domingue and in other territories returned to

France, and the remainder was exported around the world. In 1791 France controlled 65 percent of the world sugar market, and sugar plantations in Saint-Domingue provided half of this total (Tomich 2016, 56). With the loss of Haiti as a source for sugar, the French increased sugar production in Martinique and attempted to develop other crops there, including coffee, with little success. In 1813 a hurricane destroyed much of the crop in Martinique, and the French nearly abandoned sugar production in its colonies. To sustain its people, Martinique depended on imports from mainland France and never reached self-subsistence in terms of agriculture. During the Vichy government in Nazi-occupied France during World War II, the French halted exports of food to Martinique, resulting in a devastating famine between 1940 and 1943. In 2010 Martinique received subsidies from France that provided for 42 percent of its agricultural budget.

In Algeria, first annexed as a French department in 1848, colonial managers established test gardens for sugarcane, vanilla, coffee, and cacao, but these experiments were largely unsuccessful. When the French mainland suffered a grain crisis in 1870, officials planned to turn the vast plains of Algeria into grain fields to provide France with wheat for bread and animal feed (Bonneuil and Kleiche 1993, 18). In addition to wheat, French colonists established vineyards in Algeria that eventually produced enough wine to make up for shortages in France when the phylloxera infestation destroyed French vineyards in the 1870s and 1880s. Wine became so profitable in Algeria that the French converted wheat fields to vineyards on a massive scale at the end of the nineteenth century. The French were so proud of Algerian wines that promotional materials for the Algerian pavilion at the 1931 Colonial Exhibition in Paris, a showcase of France's overseas colonies, described the country as "an immense vineyard, a giant wine-press" and declared that "wine is the future of Algeria" (Hodeir and Pierre 1991, 51). When Algeria gained its independence from France in 1962, France no longer acknowledged Algerian wine as a French product. After more than 100 years of production, Algerian wines, for the French, "did not exist within the French wine narrative" (Guy 2010, 156).

The experiments in colonial agriculture of the nineteenth and early twentieth centuries generally failed, leaving the countries in question significantly worse off than before the colonial occupation. French exploitation of the colonial lands led to food crises in Algeria in 1920 since France and other European countries exported most of the available grain, and colonial policies led to famine in much of Francophone Africa between 1917 and 1921 (Janes 2017, 14). French overseas departments (Guadeloupe, Guyane, Martinique, and Réunion) supply only a tiny percentage of the overall production of fruit and vegetables for France and its territories, and they are the sole source for a few products. In 2010 the overseas territories produced a minuscule amount of the total grain and vegetables grown in France and its departments, but 100 percent of the French production of sugarcane, bananas, pineapple, and "tropical" root vegetables, although France imports far more of these products from other sources (Agreste 2019, 144).

During the colonial period, the relationship between France and its overseas territories influenced the French diet on the mainland but only in a limited way. To create a market in France for products from colonial agriculture, the Agence Générale des Colonies (founded in 1919) offered tastings of "exotic" products like cocoa, bananas, and rice in order to familiarize the French with these products. The "Rice Committee," established in 1931, created propaganda to convince the French to adopt the ingredient, but it had little success. Banana products became popular in Europe in the 1920s, like the well-known breakfast drink Banania and its competitors, Bananavic and Superbanane. Advertisements for these products reproduced stereotypes of Africans as childlike. The Senegalese soldier famously featured on Banania packages honored the troops of soldiers from Senegal who fought for France in World War I, and these images became prevalent on Banania packaging around 1915. However, the invented Banania slogan, *Y'a bon!* ("Dat's good!") suggested that these soldiers spoke pidgin French. An advertisement for Bananavic in 1923 showed a black infant in a diaper, and one for Superbanane in 1929 featured three young, smiling black girls (Hale 2008, 97).

During and after World War I, a bread shortage in France prompted the colonial lobby in Indochina to promote rice flour as a substitute for wheat flour for French bread. France occupied Indochina (an area that is now Vietnam, Cambodia, Laos, and part of China) from 1887 to 1954, most productively in terms of agriculture in the 1920s. The French public resisted rice-flour bread wholeheartedly, in part because of its association with the foreign "other" in Asia and in part because the nation pined for a return to the days of prewar French prosperity and fine bread. In June 1926, influenced by the Indochinese lobby, the French government mandated that bread in France be made from at least 10 percent nonwheat flour. The Parisian Bakers Federation subsequently asked the Academy of Medicine to study the nutrition of bread made from rice flour, and the resulting report declared that rice, corn, and cassava flours were not suitable for bread (Janes 2013, 194). Clearly, French nationalist sentiment outweighed scientific reasoning or economic exigencies, and the French attitude indicated that they preferred no bread at all to bread they saw as threateningly foreign.

Poulet au Curry et Lait de Coco (Chicken Curry with Coconut Milk)

Yield: Serves 4

Ingredients
2 Tbsp olive oil
1 onion, cut in small dice
Salt
1 inch fresh ginger root, peeled and grated
¼ tsp ground cinnamon
1 ½ Tbsp curry powder
4 boneless, skinless chicken breasts cut in ½-inch cubes
1 can (15 oz.) of diced tomatoes
1 ½ cups coconut milk
1 lime
Pepper
2 Tbsp fresh parsley, chopped

1. In a large skillet, heat 1 tablespoon olive oil over medium-high heat. Add the onions and ½ teaspoon salt and cook until soft, about 4–5 minutes. Add grated ginger, cinnamon, and curry powder. Stir well and cook until fragrant, about 1 minute.
2. Add chicken to pan and sauté for 3–4 minutes, until lightly browned. Add more oil if needed. Add canned tomatoes and coconut milk. Bring to a simmer, then reduce heat to low and simmer for 20 minutes, stirring occasionally.
3. Before serving, add the juice of one lime and add salt and pepper to taste. Sprinkle with chopped parsley. Serve with cooked white rice.

Adapted from Jeanne Néant, "Poulet au curry et lait de coco: La meilleure recette," Le Journal des Femmes: Cuisine, accessed May 12, 2020, https://cuisine.journaldesfemmes.fr/recette/313926-curry-de-poulet-au-lait-de-coco.

The colonial lobby from Indochina and elsewhere made a concerted effort in the 1920s to sell "the idea of the colonies as a food source for metropolitan France as a motivation for investing in colonial development" (Janes 2013, 195). The French public generally rejected the idea that France needed food from the colonies, and as a consequence, colonial foods did not gain a significant foothold in metropolitan France. The only acceptable way to incorporate colonial influence in French food was on

---

Brochettes de Kefta (Skewers of Ground Meat with Moroccan Spices)

Yield: Serves 4

Ingredients
1 pound ground beef or lamb
1 small onion, minced
1 tsp each of cumin and ground cinnamon
½ tsp salt
¼ tsp of cayenne pepper
¼ tsp black pepper
2 Tbsp cilantro leaves, coarsely chopped
1 tsp vegetable oil
¼ cup ketchup
1 Tbsp harissa (hot pepper sauce)

1. Mix all ingredients except ketchup and harissa together until incorporated. Divide into eight equal portions. Shape the meat into logs and mold them around eight wooden or metal kebab skewers.
2. Heat oil in a large skillet over high heat. Cook the skewers, turning frequently, until well browned on all sides, 5–7 minutes. Alternatively, grill them on a gas or charcoal grill until well browned.
3. Mix the ketchup and harissa until blended. Serve the keftas hot with the prepared sauce.

---

the margins, as an extra touch of exoticism in sauces with curry powder or banana crepes, for example. Most recipes in cooking magazines in the 1920s and 1930s using colonial ingredients were for desserts, dishes that were outside the main part of the meal and more easily accepted. Colonial cuisine as it was presented in the 1920s and 1930s in Paris represented a homogenized image of the foreign peoples it represented, not an individualized representation of each colonized land (Janes 2017, 163). Inside the colonies as well, French citizens generally abstained from local specialties, preferring to import foods from home, mainly in jars and cans. The only non-French foods that most French colonizers in Indochina would eat were local tropical fruits. They particularly prized leg of lamb, a meat that was hard to obtain and not part of culinary traditions in this part of the world, making it essential as a mark of Frenchness and prosperity (Peters 1999, 151–54). Foods that made the transition to French cuisine from the colonial period include curry, tropical fruit (mainly in desserts), and exotic flavors added to standard French dishes (such as braised lamb with cumin and coriander or mussels in coconut milk).

Meat as a Symbol of France

French food is deeply connected to French cultural beliefs, and the changing face of the French nation due to waves of immigration from former colonies in Africa has had an effect on food traditions that must adapt to the new reality of the French population. Halal meat (meat butchered according to Islamic traditions) provoked a controversy in Paris during the 2012 presidential elections when Marine le Pen, head of the conservative Front National party, claimed that unlabeled halal beef had been sold in supermarkets without the knowledge of French consumers. There was no evidence that halal beef had been sold unlabeled, and Le Pen's accusation was part of a larger xenophobic trend aimed at recent immigrants, particularly those who practice Islam.

Because observant Muslims do not eat pork, some participants in anti-Islamic protests in France waved pork products like ham and salami as a confrontational gesture. Reports showed that 12 percent of racist acts in France in 2012 were associated with pork, such as leaving the head of a pig outside a mosque (Durmelat 2017, 394). School lunches in public schools were part of a related debate in 2018, when the mayor of a small town in southeast France eliminated the option of lunches without pork products. This option had earlier been made available for students who did not eat pork due to religious beliefs, such as practicing Muslims or Jewish students who keep kosher. The French government strictly enforces the separation between church and state, a deeply held tenet established after the French Revolution. Those who opposed a pork-free meal option for schools and prisons argued that those who asked for a special meal were imposing their religion on a public space. Ultimately an appeals court ruled that a substitute meal did not violate the separation between church and state even if it allowed students or prisoners in jails to adhere to their religious or moral principles. These alternative meals had been offered in schools for more than 30 years without any issues. The court's decision reversed the mayor's order and returned pork-free options to the menu.

In 1996 French beef became suspect under the threat of *la vache folle* ("mad cow"), a disease in cattle thought to have originated in England. Contaminated beef had the potential to infect humans with Creutzfeldt-Jakob's disease, a neurological disorder that attacks the brain and nervous system. After the first cases appeared in March 1996, French consumers rapidly cut down on their consumption of beef. By May of that year, government surveys showed that nearly 10 percent of the French had stopped eating beef altogether, and more than 50 percent had stopped eating beef imported from outside of France. Nearly a year later, 22 percent of those surveyed said they had cut down their consumption of beef due to concerns over contamination, even though fewer than thirty deaths from the disease had been reported by January 1997 (Peretti-Watel 2001, 7–8). In response to concerns that the disease might infect U.S. cattle, the U.S. government banned imports of French beef in 1996, a ban that would remain until 2017. Partially in response to health concerns and partially in response to consumer demands fueled by fear, the European Union passed regulations in 2015 requiring that all fresh meat products carry a label with the country of origin and slaughter.

In France the consumption of meat in general and beef in particular has dropped since the late 1990s. Experts attribute the change to the increasing popularity of frozen meals and snack foods that have replaced the customary family meal centered around a roasted or braised meat dish. More French consumers are also concerned about the environmental impact of meat production and the health effects of eating meat. In 1995, before mad cow contamination threatened French meat, a French governmental study found that 53 percent of French worried that the food supply posed a risk to their health; the number jumped to 74 percent in 2018, after a new outbreak of mad cow in 2000 and other incidents related to food safety (Hébel 2019, 79). Between 2000 and 2016, meat consumption overall in France dropped 12 percent, with beef showing the greatest decline (Tavoularis and Sauvage 2018, 2). Researchers attribute the reduction to generational differences. Younger French people consume the most meat but in the form of burgers, sandwiches containing ground meat, or other prepared foods with meat as an ingredient, and older populations enjoy whole cuts of butcher's meat, like beef roasts, veal, and lamb, but eat it less often. When the French eat meat, they often choose smaller cuts such as chicken breasts or pork chops rather than whole roasts.

Malbouffe (Junk Food)

Worries about the future of French food take two tracks: invasion by foreign influences and globalization, and the loss of interest in gastronomy by the younger generations. The slowly braised stews and delicate pastries of classic French cuisine require time in the kitchen and deserve hours at the table to be properly enjoyed. Younger generations have shown less interest in cooking and are more connected to food cultures outside of France as seen in films and on social media. Global companies like McDonald's and Starbucks continue to make inroads in France, helped by the youth market's desire to imitate American culture and the appeal of eating (and drinking) on the go. France is McDonald's second-largest market in the world, after the United States, and pizzas and hamburgers dominate casual food in France, having pushed aside baguette sandwiches and crepes. Older generations and those who hold French gastronomy dear lament these changes and fear the loss of France's most important cultural product: good food.

France has proven itself immune to some global food trends, compared to many countries. Unlike most Western countries, the majority of French people still eat three meals at regular times, usually with other people. Surveys taken between 1986 and 2010 showed little change in French mealtimes: half of all French people sit down to lunch at 1:00 p.m., and nearly 40 percent eat dinner at 8:00 p.m. (De Saint Pol and Ricroch 2012, 2). Most full meals still consist of three courses using the codified *entrée*-main dish-dessert model, and the French on average spend an hour eating together at lunch and at dinner (De Saint Pol and Ricroch 2012, 4). Snacking between meals does not occur with regularity in France, except for the rituals of the *goûter* (afternoon snack) and the aperitif (before-dinner drink), but the practice is growing in popularity in the younger generation. Among those over 60, only 20 percent eat between meals compared to 41 percent of people under 25 (De Saint Pol and Ricroch 2012, 2). Obesity is on the rise around the world, but the percentage of obese adults has stabilized in France: 17 percent of adults in France in 2016 fit the medical definition for obesity, approximately the same number measured in 2006 ("Esteban" 2017). In the overseas territories of Martinique and Guadeloupe, obesity rates ranged from 21 percent to 33 percent for adults (Yacou 2015, 7).

Nevertheless, in 2017 France developed the Nutri-Score nutritional labeling system for foods, a colorful label on the front of packaged food that rates food on a scale from A to E. Products with an A rating have the best nutritional quality, and those with an E have less fiber, protein, and vitamins and more saturated fat, salt, and sugar. Use of the Nutri-Score label is voluntary in France, but a number of major manufacturers have agreed to include the nutritional label on their products, including major supermarket chains and McCain, maker of frozen potato products. Danone-France adopted the label for its yogurt and dairy products in 2018. In 2019 the French health ministry published recommendations for diet and health that included a new focus on the importance of eating unsalted nuts and whole grains. The guidelines encouraged consumers to take note of the Nutri-Score rating on foods and for the first time took environmental factors into account, recommending seasonal fruits and vegetables, local produce, and organic produce ("Santé publique" 2019). The new guidelines also addressed physical activity, encouraging French people to increase physical activity but specifically to reduce the amount of time they spend sitting during the day.

Worries about obesity have a smaller role in France than concerns about the quality of food available. The term *malbouffe* appears regularly in the French media, meaning "poor quality food" in general but more often specifically targeting fast food and industrial food. McDonald's is a favorite target for the enemies of *malbouffe*, but the French people continue to patronize McDonald's and other fast-food restaurants like Pizza Hut and Domino's Pizza. French authorities warn against *malbouffe* not solely for the nutritional dangers of fast and processed food but also for the threat to French national pride. José Bové, an activist and cofounder of a rural farmer's union, gained national and international fame for his protests against genetically modified food in the 1980s in France. He became famous for his attention-grabbing act of vandalizing a McDonald's restaurant under construction in Millau in 1999. Bové's outspoken activism against the World Trade Organization and genetically modified organisms in French agriculture caught the public's attention, but his efforts had more to do with the effect of globalization on French food than with GMOs. Bové and his supporters feared that prized French agricultural products like Roquefort cheese might be erased by industrial cheese made

GMO Restrictions

Although the French public has expressed concern about GMO foods, the European Union permits only one genetically modified crop to be farmed on European soil: a strain of corn called MON810, mainly used for animal feed. As part of the European Union, France forbids cultivation of all other genetically modified crops, and in 2008 it banned MON810 as well. Before the ban, GMO corn and experimental plots of GMO plants constituted only a tiny portion of France's agricultural output. Since 2013 no GMO crops have been permitted on French soil. However, imported GMO crops remain a concern. France and Europe import most of the grain fed to animals, and some figures estimate that 80 percent of these crops are genetically modified (Ministère 2019).

cheaply and without integrity. The French AOC system and the subsequent European AOP label offer legal protections to such products, preventing imitators from using registered names (e.g., Roquefort, champagne, Menton lemons) for lesser-quality products. Such protections indicate a defensiveness among French producers that requires them to seek government intervention to maintain their business, but they also have kept Roquefort and other artisanal French products from disappearing in an increasingly global, industrial food landscape.

In line with worries about the loss of French traditions, there is a general concern that the younger generation does not cook at home and does not know basic cooking techniques. In 2014 a study revealed that French households spent half as much of their total budget on food as they did in the 1960s (from 25 percent of the household budget to less than 14 percent), and that people over 60 years of age spent 20 percent of their budget on food, while those 20–30 years old spent only 8 percent (Lejeune et al. 2014, 12). Many people in the 20–30 age bracket choose takeout food or prepared foods. Younger people have begun to abandon the sacrosanct three-part French meal in favor of a single main dish and a dessert (Hébel 2019, 87). Nevertheless, the popularity of shows like *Top Chef* and *MasterChef France* among the younger generation demonstrates that this generation has an interest in cooking at home. New services offering interactive cooking classes and meal kits are popular in France, targeted at the millennial generation. Kweezine, a "culinary discovery platform" based in Bordeaux, offers culinary experiences that range from communal cooking classes to wine and food tastings, with an emphasis on French cuisine. QuiToque offers meal kits for easy-to-prepare dishes selected by subscribers, with new options each week, and the service claims to prioritize ingredients sourced in France as much as possible. The company is based in Paris and owned by Carrefour, one of the largest *hypermarché* (hypermarket or giant supermarket) chains in France. Recipes favor world cuisine and young tastes over classic French dishes, offering one-pot pasta and rice dishes and simple salads, with a few recognizably French recipes: to cite two examples, fish with cream sauce and stuffed tomatoes.

Maintaining the French Legacy

In answer to the threat of *malbouffe* and the perception that the French tradition of gastronomy is slipping away, a committee of French academics and Michelin-starred chefs, supported by then president Nicolas Sarkozy, applied to have French cuisine recognized by UNESCO. The French team applied to add French gastronomy to the World Intangible Cultural

> **Tomates Farcies (Stuffed Tomatoes)**
>
> *Yield:* Serves 4
>
> *Ingredients*
> 4 large ripe tomatoes
> Salt
> 1 Tbsp olive oil
> 1 small onion, diced
> 1 garlic clove, minced
> 2 cups of chopped cooked beef (traditionally, leftovers from pot-au-feu) or sausage
> Pepper
> 1 cup dried bread crumbs
> ¼ cup shredded Gruyère or Parmesan cheese
>
> 1. Cut the top off of each tomato, about ¼ inch from the top. Reserve tops. Scoop the tomato out with a small spoon, leaving about ¼ inch of flesh inside the tomato. Be careful not to pierce the skin. Reserve tomato pulp. Sprinkle the insides of the tomatoes with ½ teaspoon salt and turn upside down on paper towels to drain.
> 2. Heat oil in a skillet over medium heat. Add onion and cook until softened, about 3–4 minutes. Add garlic and cook until fragrant, about 1 minute. Add tomato pulp, cutting up larger pieces if needed. Let reduce for 5 minutes uncovered. Add the cooked beef or sausage and salt and pepper to taste. Cook for 5 minutes until warmed through. Turn off heat and add ½ cup bread crumbs. Stir well.
> 3. Heat oven to 350 degrees. Stuff each tomato with one-fourth of the stuffing mixture. Top with remaining breadcrumbs and sprinkle with shredded cheese. Place reserved tomato tops on the stuffing. Bake tomatoes in a lightly greased baking dish for 30 minutes or until hot and the cheese starts to brown. Let cool for 10 minutes. Serve warm or at room temperature.

Heritage list that includes capoeira dancing in Brazil and Kabuki theater in Japan, among others. In 2008 the original application was rejected because, according to UNESCO judges, gastronomy does not belong unilaterally to the French and because fine dining of this kind is generally reserved for elites. The French mistakenly approached the proposal with the intent of proving that France had the best cuisine in the world (in fact, Sarkozy declared this belief openly in a press conference), a misunderstanding of the goal of the UNESCO list to recognize equally all cultural forms in danger of disappearing. Other countries immediately objected to France's claim of culinary superiority. The Italian farmers' union pointed out that the European Union recognized 166 specialties in Italy compared to 156 in France and that, unlike French escargots and foie gras, Italian dishes like pizza and pasta had conquered the world (Naulin 2012, 18).

The motivation behind such a proposal, seen by many as exemplary of French arrogance, has deep roots in French intellectual circles. In fact, the restaurant was born in France during the Revolution, and some argue that the restaurant meal can be seen as the democratic evolution of aristocratic cuisine. Before the advent of the public restaurant, only wealthy aristocrats with a private cook and a well-appointed kitchen could dine on finely crafted dishes at a private table. With the development of the restaurant in the late eighteenth century, those with a few extra francs had access to a private table and a menu from which they could compose a meal to be prepared especially for them. The range of restaurants, from bouillon shops and cafés to work cafeterias to palaces of gastronomy offered access to good food across nearly all economic classes. The French devotion to quality food at every price point ensured that even simple meals in restaurants were prepared with French know-how, and the French public learned to recognize and appreciate fine food.

From his perspective that the French culinary heritage is "in peril," Alexandre Lazareff expresses the belief shared by many French in the democratic notion of the gastronomic meal: "Nothing is more democratic than culinary practices" (1998, 17, my translation). Gastronomy open to all is not limited to fine dining because the essential democracy of French cuisine is embedded in French cooking technique, independent of where it is served. The patriotic, nationalistic belief in the superiority of its cuisine raises France above its neighbors. France has perhaps been less successful in military endeavors or in industry, but the French nation, some believe, rises far above all others in aesthetics and in good (culinary) taste. France has successfully preserved traditional mealtimes and the structure of the meal in three courses, even in school cafeterias and on airplanes. According to Lazareff, the French meal includes a "supplément d'âme" (extra-special something) that leads to conviviality. For the French, eating is a social activity that requires the mise en scène (setting of the stage) of a table set with care, proper manners, and conversation (Lazareff 1998, 18). Outspoken defenders of French cuisine, like those who prepared the first UNESCO application, believe that French culinary traditions must be preserved against the threat of global food and industrial food so that future generations do not lose their sense of taste for well-prepared cuisine. In French schools, the effort takes the form of "taste weeks," introducing students to new foods and classic flavors, teaching an appreciation for heritage cheeses and authentic French recipes. At school cafeterias, students sit attentively for meals that include an *entrée*, main dish, and dessert, and cafeteria staff teach table manners, prompting students to eat at least some of each dish.

After the rejection of France's application in 2008, a new application in 2010 requested Intangible Cultural Heritage status for the "gastronomic meal of the French," including both the recipes of French gastronomy and the practice of gathering together to share conviviality. The successful application recognized that gastronomy in France cannot be separated from the people who create and embody it and that the shared experience of French meals is as important as the dishes on the table. The revision of the UNESCO application took into account a survey of French households from 2009 that revealed that for the French people, gastronomy did not belong solely to famous chefs but to all French citizens. Of those surveyed, 95 percent claimed the gastronomic meal as part of their French national identity, and 99 percent believed that French gastronomic traditions must be preserved, valued, and passed on to future generations (Csergo 2011, 16). In the end, the UNESCO designation recognizes the French practice of celebrating a special occasion with a meal of at least four courses (including a cheese platter) prepared from traditional recipes with excellent ingredients, matched with carefully selected wines, served on an elegant table, and shared in a spirit of warm conviviality with family and friends who recognize and celebrate fine food.

In France, current food issues relate to food safety and nutrition, but fundamentally these issues inevitably return to the heritage of French cuisine. In an effort to preserve their gastronomic legacy, the French people have gone to great lengths, sometimes arrogantly and often with prejudice toward those who are not French (or who are not considered French even if they live in France or in a French territory). The French generally maintain healthy eating practices based on their traditions of sitting together for meals created from quality ingredients. But French arrogance and closed-mindedness about food has also led to violence toward immigrants and a reputation for snobbery. The future of French food depends on the young people of France, many of whom are more concerned with food safety and health than with maintaining classical French cooking. French people more and more seek out organic foods, local produce, meat from France, and foods without artificial ingredients. The French eat less meat than in the past and more prepared foods, but they haven't yet abandoned gastronomy, especially on special occasions. If gastronomy remains flexible and connected to the changing desires of the French people, future generations will certainly keep the French tradition alive.

Further Reading

Agreste. 2019. "Produits agroalimentaires." *GraphAgri 2019*, Ministère de l'Agriculture et de l'Alimentation. https://agreste.agriculture.gouv.fr/agreste-web/disaron/GraFraChap12.3/detail.

Blanchard, Pascal, Sandrine Lemaire, Nicolas Bancel, and Dominic Richard, and David Thomas. 2013. *Colonial Culture in France since the Revolution*. Translated by Alexis Pernsteiner. Bloomington: Indiana University Press.

Blaquière, Jean. 2019. "Où en est la fronde anti-foie gras dans le monde?" *Le Figaro*, January 11, 2019.

Bonneuil, Christophe, and Mina Kleiche. 1993. *Du Jardin d'essais Colonial à la Station Expérimentale: 1880–1930: Éléments pour une Histoire du Cirad*. Paris: CIRAD.

Cazalet, Catherine. 1980. "La production du foie gras. Exemple d'un marché: Pau." *Études rurales* 78–80: 277–88.

Chevalier, Auguste. 1944. "Contribution à l'histoire de l'introduction des bananes en France et à l'historique de la culture bananière dans les Colonies françaises." *Revue de botanique appliquée et d'agriculture coloniale* 24 (272–274): 116–27.

Clairacq, Jean. 1980. "Gavage des oies et canards et production de gras dans les exploitations agricoles en polyculture de Chalosse (Landes)." *Revue géographique des Pyrénées et du Sud-Ouest* 51 (4): 441–63.

Coquery-Vidrovitch, Catherine, and Odile Goerg. 1992. *L'Afrique occidentale au temps des Français: Colonisateurs et colonisés, 1860–1960*. Paris: La Découverte.

Csergo, Julia. 2011. "Le 'Repas gastronomique des Français' inscrit au Patrimoine Culturel Immatériel de l'Unesco." Le Mangeur-OCHA, September 19, 2011.

De Saint Pol, Thibaut, and Layla Ricroch. 2012. "Le temps de l'alimentation en France." *INSEE Première* 1417 (October). https://www.insee.fr/fr/statistiques/1281016.

Durmelat, Sylvie. 2017. "Making Couscous French? Digesting the Loss of Empire." *Contemporary French Civilization* 42, no. 3–4 (December): 391–407.

"Esteban (Étude de santé sur l'environnement, la biosurveillance, l'activité physique et la nutrition) 2014–2016." 2017. Santé publique France. https://www.santepubliquefrance.fr/determinants-de-sante/nutrition-et-activite-physique/documents/rapport-synthese/etude-de-sante-sur-l-environnement-la-biosurveillance-l-activite-physique-et-la-nutrition-esteban-2014-2016-.-chapitre-activite-physique-et-sede.

Ferguson, Priscilla Parkhurst. 2006. *Accounting for Taste: The Triumph of French Cuisine*. Chicago: University of Chicago Press.

Guy, Kolleen. 2010. "Imperial Feedback: Food and the French Culinary Legacy of Empire." *Contemporary French & Francophone Studies* 14, no. 2 (March): 149–57.

Hale, Dana S. 2008. *Races on Display: French Representations of Colonized People, 1886–1940*. Bloomington: Indiana University Press.

Hébel, Pascale. 2019. "Entre représentations et pratiques, l'alimentation santé au coeur du débat." *Cahiers français* 412 (September–October): 78–87.

Hodeir, Catherine, and Michel Pierre. 1991. *L'Exposition coloniale*. Paris: Complexe.

Janes, Lauren. 2013. "Selling Rice to Wheat Eaters: The Colonial Lobby and the Promotion of Pain de Riz during and after the First World War." *Contemporary French Civilization* 38, no. 2 (January): 179–200.

Janes, Lauren. 2017. *Colonial Food in Interwar Paris: The Taste of Empire*. London: Bloomsbury Academic.

Lazareff, Alexandre. 1998. *L'Exception culinaire française: Un patrimoine gastronomique en péril?* Paris: Albin Michel.

Lejeune, H., P. Balny, J. J. Bénézit, C. Dereix, M. de Galbert, F. Geiger, M. L. Madignier, et al. 2014. "On mangeait mieux avant." Ministre de l'agriculture et de l'alimentation, October 2014, https://agriculture.gouv.fr/mangeait-mieux-avant.

Ministère de la Transition Écologique Solidaire. 2019. "Les organismes génétiquement modifiés (OGM)." Ecologique-Solidaire, March 20, 2019. https://www.ecologique-solidaire.gouv.fr/organismes-genetiquement-modifies-ogm-0.

Naulin, Sidonie. 2012. "Le repas gastronomique des Français: Génèse d'un nouvel objet culturel." *Sciences de la société* 87 (December 1): 8–25.

Peretti-Watel, Patrick. 2001. "La crise de la vache folle: Une épidémie fantôme?" *Sciences sociales et santé* 19 (1): 5–38.

Peters, Erica J. 1999. "National Preferences and Colonial Cuisine: Seeking the Familiar in French Vietnam." *Proceedings of the Western Society for French History* 27:150–59.

Reuters. 2012. "Le foie gras halal, un marché en plein essor," *Le Point*, December 24, 2012.

"Santé publique France présente les nouvelles recommandations sur l'alimentation, l'activité physique et la sédentarité." 2019. Santé publique France, January 22, 2019. https://www.santepubliquefrance.fr/presse/2019/sante-publique-france-presente-les-nouvelles-recommandations-sur-l-alimentation-l-activite-physique-et-la-sedentarite.

Tavoularis, Gabriel, and Éléna Sauvage. 2018. "Les nouvelles générations transforment la consommation de viande." *Consommation et modes de vie*. CRÉDOC no. 300 (September). https://www.credoc.fr/publications/les-nouvelles-generations-transforment-la-consommation-de-viande.

Tomich, Dale W. 2016. *Slavery in the Circuit of Sugar: Martinique and the World Economy, 1830–1848*. Albany: State University of New York Press.

Trubek, Amy B. 2008. *The Taste of Place: A Cultural Journey into Terroir*. Berkeley: University of California Press.

Yacou, C., V. Cornely, et al. 2015. "Surcharge pondérale en Guadeloupe et Martinique." Orsag (Observatoire Régional de la Santé de Guadeloupe), November 6, 2015. https://www.orsag.fr/wp-content/uploads/2019/04/ORSAG_Surcharge_ponderale_en_Guadeloupe_et_Martinique_CO_2015.pdf.

Glossary

Absinthe
Green liquor derived from wormwood that triggered hallucinations in some drinkers.

Accras (or Akras) de Morue
Salt-cod fritters common in the French Caribbean islands; also known as *marinades*.

Andouillette
Pork sausage made from pork stomach and intestines stuffed into pork intestines. From the Champagne region but enjoyed all over France.

Aperitif
Before-dinner drink; *apéritif* comes from the Latin word for "opening."

Beignets
Fried dough lightly sweetened with sugar, served at Carnival for Mardi Gras.

Blanquette de Veau
Veal in a cream sauce with mushrooms and pearl onions.

Boeuf Bourguignon
Beef cooked in Burgundy wine.

Boudin Blanc
Sausage made from chicken or pork, combined with milk for a pale color, from the Champagne region. Served at Christmas.

Boudin Noir
Blood sausage made with pig's blood, served at Christmas in France and in Guadeloupe as an aperitif.

Bouillabaisse
Fish soup from Marseille.

Boulanger
Bread baker.

Boulangerie
Bread shop, separate from the pâtisserie, or pastry shop.

Brandade de Morue
Salt cod hash with potatoes.

Brasserie
The equivalent of a wine bar, but for beer.

Brick
Called *bourek* in Arabic, the thin, flaky pastry that originated in North Africa and is used for a number of warm savory pastries.

Brioche
Rich bread made with egg and milk, traditional at Easter.

Bûche de Noël (Yule Log)
Christmas cake made of sponge cake rolled around a soft filling, decorated to look like a log, complete with meringue mushrooms.

Café au Lait
Coffee blended with milk and sugar.

Cassoulet
A casserole of beans, sausages, and pork, duck or goose meat; a specialty of southwestern France.

Choucroute Garnie
Sauerkraut with sausages and many cuts of pork, from Alsace in eastern France.

Clafoutis
A sort of flan with cherries in an egg-rich, custardy batter from Limousin, in south-central France.

Colombo de Cabri
Goat curry, the national dish of Guadeloupe.

Coq au Vin
Chicken cooked in wine.

Coquilles Saint-Jacques
Scallops served in a cream sauce topped with toasted bread crumbs.

Cornichons
Tiny sour pickles.

Couscous
Both the tiny, pasta-like grains of semolina, steamed until fluffy, and the main dish consisting of a stew of vegetables or meats with warm spices such as cumin and

cinnamon served on the couscous grains; an important dish brought from immigrants from North Africa.

Crème Anglaise
Thin custard sauce for desserts.

Crème Brûlée
Literally "burnt cream," a custard dessert with a layer of caramelized sugar on top.

Croque-Monsieur
A grilled ham-and-cheese sandwich with a creamy sauce.

Croquembouche
Tower of cream puffs glued together with caramel, a must-have at French weddings and baptisms.

Digestif
After-dinner drink.

Entrée
Appetizer or first course.

Entremets
Side dishes or "between courses", dishes served at a large banquet between the roast course and fish courses; later, a sweet dish that will become the dessert course.

Escargot
Snails; snails à la bourguignonne (in the Burgundy style) are served in the shell with butter, garlic, and parsley.

Flammekueche
Alsatian specialty (*tarte flambée* in French, or "flamed tart," because it is cooked over a wood fire) similar to a thin-crust pizza, topped with cream, onions, and ham and served as an appetizer.

Flan
A custard pie made with eggs, milk, flour, and a little vanilla.

Foie Gras
Fattened goose or duck liver, a delicacy enjoyed on holidays.

Fraisier
A cake with fresh strawberries and strawberry mousse, often served at summer parties.

Galettes
Main-dish crepes made of buckwheat, originally from Brittany, in Northern France.

Garbure
A thick soup of bread and cooked cabbage, originally from Béarn, in southwestern France, in the Pyrenees.

Gâteau de Savoie
Savoy cake, sponge cake baked in a decorative mold.

Gougères
Cheese puffs made of choux (cream puff) dough.

Goûter
Afternoon snack.

Gratin
Any vegetable (usually potatoes) baked with cream and grated cheese.

Halal
Regulations for butchering meat according to Islamic religion; Muslim immigrants in France seek out halal meat.

Haricots Verts
Slender green beans.

Harissa
A spicy Tunisian condiment of chilis and sun-dried tomatoes.

Herbes de Provence
A mixture of marjoram, thyme, oregano, basil, and lavender originally from Provence, in the South of France; used as a flavoring for ratatouille and on grilled fish.

Hors d'Oeuvre
Literally "outside the work," first used in the late seventeenth century as a pre-first course; now a small bite served before the meal.

Kebab
Marinated meat cooked on a spit, shaved onto bread, and then topped with fries and sauce.

Lardons
Strips of uncured pork belly.

Limonade
A lightly flavored lemon-lime soda.

Macaron
A cookie made of almond flour with a ganache filling.

Malbouffe
French term generally meaning "junk food" and usually referring to industrial food or fast food.

Marzipan
Almond paste used as a filling for the Epiphany king cake.

Meringue
Whipped egg whites sweetened with sugar that are the key to a number of French desserts and are also baked on their own as a sort of light cookie.

Glossary

Meunière
Fillet of any light white fish served with a lemon and butter sauce.

Millefeuilles
Literally "a thousand layers," a dessert pastry featuring thin layers of flaky pastry and pastry cream.

Moules-Frites
Steamed mussels with French fries.

Navarin d'Agneau
A light stew of lamb and spring vegetables.

Nouvelle Cuisine
In the eighteenth century the trend leaving behind the stews and thick sauces of the previous generation in favor of flour-butter thickeners for sauces, and shallots, fresh herbs, and lighter flavors.

Nouvelle Cuisine
In the 1970s the trend that embraced lighter cooking with fish and steamed vegetables and eliminated strong marinades and rich sauces.

Oeufs à la Neige
Floating islands, or literally "eggs in the snow," a dessert of meringues on thin custard sauce.

Pain Bis
Dark, heavy bread made from mixed flours, starting in the Middle Ages and running through the eighteenth century.

Pain Complet
Whole grain loaves of bread.

Pain Mollet
Fine white bread made from soft wheat, first popular in the eighteenth century.

Pain Perdu
French toast of leftover bread soaked in egg and fried in butter.

Pains de Fantaisie
Soft white breads in different shapes, popular in the eighteenth century.

Pâté
Cooked meat made into smooth mousse or rustic spread, often made from duck or goose but also made of rabbit or pork. *Pâté en croûte* is pâté wrapped in pastry. In the Middle Ages, pâté was a baked pie of pastry filled with minced, cooked meat.

Pâte Feuilletée
Flaky dough with equal quantities of butter and flour and a little water and salt; very brittle and flaky, it is difficult to make and use.

Pâte Sablée
Sandy dough with lots of butter and sugar to make it crumbly; used for fresh fruit tarts.

Pâte Sucrée
Sugared dough containing only flour, butter, salt, sugar, and water to make a flaky base for apple tarts.

Pâtisserie
Pastry shop.

Pâtissier
Pastry chef.

Phylloxera Aphid
An invasive pest that feasted on grapevine roots and caused widespread destruction in French winemaking regions in the late nineteenth century.

Pièces Montées
Large decorative displays made of pastry and icing, now most commonly the *croquembouche*.

Plat Principal
Main dish.

Pommes Soufflées
Potato puffs made of sliced potatoes fried twice until they puff up; an elegant hors-d'oeuvre.

Pot-au-Feu
Beef boiled with vegetables, considered by some the national dish of France.

Potage
Vegetable soup from the French word *potager*, "vegetable garden."

Quenelles
Fish dumplings popular in Lyonnaise cuisine.

Quiche
A tart made of egg custard with vegetables or other fillings.

Ragoût
A dish of meat in sauce, introduced in the seventeenth century.

Ratatouille
A dish of cooked eggplant, zucchini, tomatoes, and peppers with herbs and plenty of olive oil.

Raw Milk
Unpasteurized milk used for artisanal cheeses, popular in France but banned in the United States unless aged for more than 60 days.

Glossary

Réveillon
Vigil, name for the holiday feasts on Christmas Eve and New Year's Eve.

Roux
A mixture of butter and flour used for thickening a sauce, introduced by the French chef La Varenne in 1651.

Service à la Française
French style of banquet service, in which all of the dishes for each course arrived at the table at once; popular until the end of the eighteenth century.

Service à la Russe
Russian style of service, in which individual plates are served to each guest; became popular in the nineteenth century.

Soupe
Originally broth thickened with bread.

Steak-Frites
Grilled hanger steak with French fries.

Steak Tartare
Raw, seasoned ground beef topped with a raw egg.

Tagine
Pyramid-shaped cooking vessel for making couscous (the stew).

Tartines
Toast with toppings: butter and jam at breakfast, Nutella for the after-school *goûter*.

Traiteur
In the eighteenth-century, a shop for cooked food, one of the few establishments selling food before the advent of the restaurant; in modern French, akin to a caterer.

Tripe
Cow stomach.

Vinaigrette
From the French word *vinaigre*, "vinegar," a sauce for green salads.

Selected Bibliography

Adams, Stephen. 2007. "Sèvres Porcelain and the Articulation of Imperial Identity in Napoleonic France." *Journal of Design History* 20 (3): 183–204.
Agreste. 2019."Produits agroalimentaires." *GraphAgri 2019*, Ministère de l'Agriculture et de l'Alimentation. https://agreste.agriculture.gouv.fr/agreste-web/disaron/GraFraChap12.3/detail/.
Agreste. 2018. "Equidés." *GraphAgri*, Ministère de l'Agriculture et de l'Alimentation. https://agreste.agriculture.gouv.fr/agreste-web/disaron/GraFraChap12.8/detail/.
Anthimus. 1996. *De Observatione Ciborum* [On the observance of foods; c. 511 CE]. Translated by Mark Grant. Devon, UK: Prospect Books.
APCM (*Association pour la Promotion du Citron de Menton*). n.d. "Le Citron de Menton." Accessed May 6, 2020. https://www.lecitrondementon.org.Ariès, Paul. 2016. *Une histoire politique de l'alimentation: Du paléolithique à nos jours*. Paris: Max Milo.
Armengaud, Christine. 2000. *Le Diable sucré*. Paris: La Martinière.
Bertrand, Michèle. 1992. "20 ans de consommation alimentaire 1969–1989." *Insee Données*, no. 188 (April): 1–4.
Besson, D. 2006. "Quinze Ans d'achats de Produits Sucrés: Moins de Sucre, Davantage de Produits Transformés." *Insée Première*, no. 1088. http://www.epsilon.insee.fr/jspui/bitstream/1/174/1/ip1088.pdf.
Biollay, Léon. 1877. *Les anciennes halles de Paris*. Vol. III. Paris: Société de l'histoire de Paris.
Blanchard, Pascal, Sandrine Lemaire, Nicolas Bancel, Dominic Richard, and David Thomas, eds. 2013. *Colonial Culture in France since the Revolution*. Translated by Alexis Pernsteiner. Bloomington: Indiana University Press.
Blaquière, Jean. 2019. "Où en est la fronde anti-foie gras dans le monde?" *Le Figaro*, January 11, 2019.
Boisard, Pierre. 2003. *Camembert: A National Myth*. Berkeley: University of California Press.
Boizot, Christine. 1999. "La demande de boissons des ménages : Une estimation de la consommation à domicile." *Economie et Statistique* 324 (1): 143–56.

Bonnefons, Nicolas de. 1654. *Délices de la campagne*. Paris: Pierre-des-Hayes.
Bonneuil, Christophe, and Mina Kleiche. 1993. *Du Jardin d'essais Colonial à La Station Expérimentale: 1880–1930: Éléments pour une Histoire du Cirad*. Paris: CIRAD.
Bonora, Tancrède. 2013. "Le goûter, c'est sacré . . ." *Le Parisien*, March 13, 2013.
Boudon, Jacques-Olivier. 2016. "A la recherche d'un héritier. Le mariage de Napoléon Ier avec Marie-Louise d'Autriche. 1er et 2 avril 1810." In *A la Table des diplomates*, edited by Laurent Stefanini, 71–79. Paris: Iconoclaste.
Bouillon, Florence. 2000. "Des escales dans la nuit: Les snacks égyptiens à Marseille." *Les Annales de la Recherche Urbaine* 87 (1): 43–51.
Bouton, Cynthia A. 1993. *The Flour War: Gender, Class, and Community in Late Ancien Régime French Society*. University Park: Pennsylvania State University Press.
Brégeon-Poli, Brigitte. 1995. "'Va pour treize!' La 'tradition' des desserts de Noël en Provence." *Terrain*, no. 24, 145–52.
Brennan, Thomas. 1989. "Towards the Cultural History of Alcohol in France." *Journal of Social History* 23 (1): 71–92.
Brennan, Thomas. 1997. *Burgundy to Champagne: The Wine Trade in Early Modern France*. Baltimore, MD: Johns Hopkins University Press.
Briffault, Eugène. 1846. *Paris à table*. Paris: Hetzel.
Brillat-Savarin, Jean-Anthelme. (1825) 1982. *Physiologie du goût*. Paris: Flammarion.
Bruegel, Martin. 2015. "Workers' Lunch Away from Home in the Paris of the Belle Epoque: The French Model of Meals as Norm and Practice." *French Historical Studies* 38, no. 2 (April): 253–80.
Camporesi, Piero. 1992. *Le goût du chocolat*. Paris: Grasset.
Carême Marie-Antoine. 1828. *Le Cuisinier Parisien: Ou l'art de la Cuisine Française au Dix-Neuvième Siècle*. Paris: Bossange.
Carême, Marie-Antoine. 1833. *L'art de la cuisine française au XIXe siècle : traité élémentaire et pratique*, Vol. 1. Paris: Chez l'auteur.
Carême, Marie-Antoine. (1815) 1834. *Le pâtissier royal parisien*. London: Mason.
Carlos, Marjon. 2015. "A French Caribbean Chef Talks Fashion and Vegetarian Cuisine." *Vogue*, September 30, 2015.
Cassely, Jean-Laurent, Jérôme Fourquet, and Sylvain Manternach. 2019. "Des Dimensions politique, socioculturelle et territoriale du kebab en France." Fondation Jean-Jaurès, October 5, 2019. https://jean-jaures.org/nos-productions/des-dimensions-politique-socioculturelle-et-territoriale-du-kebab-en-france.
Castelot, André. 1972. *L'histoire à table: Si la cuisine m'était contée*. Paris: Éditions Perrin.
Cazalet, Catherine. 1980. "La production du foie gras. Exemple d'un marché: Pau." *Études rurales* 78–80:277–88.
Chan, Kaling. 2016. "Les Entrées Préférées des Français." *Cuisine Actuelle*, February 22, 2016. https://www.cuisineactuelle.fr/dossiers-gourmands/tendance-cuisine/les-entrees-preferees-des-francais-283753.

Selected Bibliography

Chesnel, Adolphe de la. 1846. *Coutumes, mythes et traditions des provinces de France*. Paris: Périsse.
Chevalier, Auguste. 1944. "Contribution à l'histoire de l'introduction des bananes en France et à l'historique de la culture bananière dans les Colonies françaises." *Revue de botanique appliquée et d'agriculture coloniale* 24 (272–274): 116–27.
Clairacq, Jean. 1980. "Gavage des oies et canards et production de gras dans les exploitations agricoles en polyculture de Chalosse (Landes)." *Revue géographique des Pyrénées et du Sud-Ouest* 51 (4): 441–63.
Claudian, Jean, and Yvonne Serville. 1970. "Aspects de l'évolution récente du comportement alimentaire en France: Composition des repas et 'urbanisation.'" In *Pour une Histoire de l'alimentation*, edited by Jean-Jacques Hémardinquer. 174–87. Paris: Armand Colin.
CNC (Centre National du Cinéma). 2019. "Géographie du cinéma 2018." *Dossiers du CNC* 341 (September): 1–178.
Coe, Sophie, and Michael Coe. 2000. *The True History of Chocolate*. London: Thames & Hudson.
Coquery-Vidrovitch, Catherine, and Odile Goerg. 1992. *L'Afrique occidentale au temps des Français: Colonisateurs et colonisés, 1860–1960*. Paris: La Découverte.
Coquery-Vidrovitch, Catherine, and Henri Moniot. 2005. *L'Afrique noire de 1800 à nos jours*. Paris: Presses universitaires de France.
Courtin, Antoine de. 1681. *Nouveau traité de la civilité qui se pratique en France parmi les honnestes gens*. Paris: Hélie Josset.
Csergo, Julia. 2011. "Le 'Repas gastronomique des Français' inscrit au Patrimoine Culturel Immatériel de l'Unesco." OCHA, September 19, 2011. https://www.lemangeur-ocha.com/wp-content/uploads/2012/04/CSERGO-repas-gastronomique-francais-patrimoine-unesco2.pdf.
Day, Ivan. 1999. "Sculpture for the Eighteenth-Century Garden Dessert." In *Food in the Arts: Proceedings of the Oxford Symposium on Food and Cookery 1998*, edited by Harlan Walker, 57–66. Devon, England: Prospect Books.
Denjean, Claude, and Laurent Feller. 2013. *Expertise et valeur des choses au Moyen Âge I: Le besoin d'expertise*. Madrid: Casa de Velazquez.
De Saint Pol, Thibaut, and Layla Ricroch. 2012. "Le temps de l'alimentation en France." *Insee Première* 1417 (October). https://www.insee.fr/fr/statistiques/1281016.
Desportes, Françoise. 1987. *Le Pain Au Moyen Âge*. Paris: Orban.
Dictionnaire de l'Académie Française. 1694. Paris: Académie Française.
Dictionnaire portatif de cuisine. 1767. Paris: Vincent.
Dion, Roger. 1959. *Histoire de la vigne et du vin en France: Des origines au XIXe siècle*. Paris: Roger Dion.
Durmelat, Sylvie. 2017. "Making Couscous French? Digesting the Loss of Empire." *Contemporary French Civilization* 42, no. 3–4 (December): 391–407.
Escoffier, Auguste. 1903. *Le guide culinaire*. Paris: Flammarion.

Escoffier, Auguste. 1969. *The Escoffier Cookbook*. New York: Crown Publishers. Originally published as *Le guide culinaire* (Paris: Flammarion, 1903).

"Esteban (Étude de santé sur l'environnement, la biosurveillance, l'activité physique et la nutrition) 2014–2016." 2017. Santé publique France. https://www.santepubliquefrance.fr/determinants-de-sante/nutrition-et-activite-physique/documents/rapport-synthese/etude-de-sante-sur-l-environnement-la-biosurveillance-l-activite-physique-et-la-nutrition-esteban-2014-2016-.-chapitre-activite-physique-et-sede.

Fête du Citron. n.d. "87ème Fête Du Citron Menton." Accessed July 24, 2020. https://www.fete-du-citron.com.

Flandrin, Jean Louis. 2007. *Arranging the Meal: A History of Table Service in France*. Berkeley: University of California Press.

Flaubert, Gustave. (1857) 1945. *Madame Bovary*. Edited by R. Dumesnil. Paris: Belles Lettres.

France Nassain. n.d. "The History of the Oyster." Accessed July 24, 2020. https://www.francenaissain.com/en/the-oyster/the-oyster-and-its-origins/the-history-of-the-oyster.

"France Rapide." 2019. *Snacking: Le magazine de l'alimentation rapide et fast casual* 53 (April–May): 42–53.

Freidberg, Susanne Elizabeth. 2004. *French Beans and Food Scares: Culture and Commerce in an Anxious Age*. New York: Oxford University Press.

Fumey, Gilles. 2006. "Manger sur l'autoroute en France: Les pratiques alimentaires des touristes." *Collection EDYTEM. Cahiers de géographie* 4 (1): 231–38.

Garrigues, Jean. 1991. *Banania: Histoire d'une passion française*. Paris: Editions du May.

Gira Conseil. 2019. "Sandwich, Burger et Pizza, les stars du snacking en pleine forme en 2019." Snacking, September 19, 2019. https://www.snacking.fr/actualites/tendances/4440-Sandwich-Burger-et-Pizza-les-stars-du-snacking-en-pleine-forme-en-2019.

Girard, Alain. 1977. "Le Triomphe de 'La cuisinière bourgeoise': Livres culinaires, cuisine et société en France aux XVIIe et XVIIIe Siècles." *Revue d'histoire moderne et contemporaine* 24 (4): 497–523.

Goody, Jack. 2011. *Cooking, Cuisine, and Class: A Study in Comparative Sociology*. 2nd ed. Cambridge: Cambridge University Press.

Gouffé, Jules. 1867. *Le livre de cuisine*. Paris: Hachette.

Gouffé, Jules. 1873. *Le Livre de Pâtisserie*. Paris: Hachette.

Grignon, Claude. 1993. "La Règle, La Mode et Le Travail: La Genèse Sociale du Modèle des Repas Français Contemporain." In *Le Temps de Manger: Alimentation, Emploi Du Temps et Rythmes Sociaux*, edited by Maurice Aymard and Françoise Sabban, 276–323. Paris: Éditions de la Maison des sciences de l'homme.

Guy, Kolleen M. 2002. "Rituals of Pleasure in the Land of Treasures: Wine Consumption and the Making of French Identity in the late 19th c." In *Food Nations: Selling Taste in Consumer Societies*, edited by Warren James Belasco and Philip Scranton, 34–47. New York: Routledge.

Selected Bibliography

Guy, Kolleen M. 2003. *When Champagne Became French: Wine and the Making of a National Identity*. Baltimore, MD: Johns Hopkins University Press.

Guy, Kolleen M. 2010. "Imperial Feedback: Food and the French Culinary Legacy of Empire." *Contemporary French & Francophone Studies* 14, no. 2 (March): 149–57.

Haine, W. Scott. 1999. *The World of the Paris Café: Sociability among the French Working Class, 1789–1914*. Baltimore, MD: Johns Hopkins University Press.

Hale, Dana S. 2008. *Races on Display: French Representations of Colonized Peoples, 1886–1940*. Bloomington: Indiana University Press.

Hautcoeur, Pierre-Cyrille. 2005. "Was the Great War a Watershed? The Economics of World War I in France." In *The Economics of World War I*, edited by Stephen Broadberry and Mark Harrison, 169–205. Cambridge: Cambridge University Press.

Hébel, Pascale. 2019. "Entre représentations et pratiques, l'alimentation santé au coeur du débat." *Cahiers français* 412 (September–October): 78–87.

Hémardinquer, Jean-Jacques. 1970a. "Les graisses de cuisine en France: Essais de cartes." In *Pour une Histoire de l'alimentation*, edited by Jean-Jacques Hémardinquer, 254–71. Paris: Armand Colin.

Hémardinquer, Jean-Jacques. 1970b. *Pour une Histoire de l'alimentation*. Paris: Armand Colin.

Herpin, Nicolas. 1988. "Le repas comme institution. Compte rendu d'une enquête exploratoire." *Revue française de sociologie* 29 (3): 503–21.

Hess, Karen. 1998. *The Carolina Rice Kitchen: The African Connection*. Columbia: University of South Carolina Press.

Hesse, Jean-Pascal. 2011. *Maxim's: Miroir de la vie parisienne*. Paris: Assouline.

Hocquet, Jean-Claude. 1985. "Le pain, le vin et la juste mesure à la table des moines carolingiens." *Annales* 40:661–86.

Hodeir, Catherine, and Michel Pierre. 1991. *L'Exposition coloniale*. Paris: Complexe.

Hugo, Victor. (1832) 1959. *Notre Dame de Paris*. Paris: Garnier.

Hunt, Lynn. 2004. *Politics, Culture, and Class in the French Revolution*. Berkeley: University of California Press.

Husson, Armand. 1875. *Les consommations de Paris*. Paris: Hachette.

Hyman, Philip. 1986. "L'art d'accommoder les escargots." *L'Histoire* 85:41–44.

Insee. 2009. "Fiches Thématiques sur l'alimentation et Le Tabac: Cinquante Ans de Consommation En France." *Insée Statistiques*. https://www.insee.fr/fr/statistiques/1372380?sommaire=1372388.

Insee. 2019. "Consommation des Ménages En 2018." *Insée Statistiques*, May 29, 2019. https://www.insee.fr/fr/statistiques/4131372?sommaire=4131436.

"Jambon-beurre: Le roi des sandwichs menacé par la concurrence." 2017. *Les Echos*, March 2, 2017. https://www.lesechos.fr/2017/03/jambon-beurre-le-roi-des-sandwichs-menace-par-la-concurrence-164087.

Janes, Lauren. 2013. "Selling Rice to Wheat Eaters: The Colonial Lobby and the Promotion of Pain de Riz during and after the First World War." *Contemporary French Civilization* 38, no. 2 (January): 179–200.

Janes, Lauren. 2017. *Colonial Food in Interwar Paris: The Taste of Empire*. London: Bloomsbury Academic.

Kaplan, Steven L. 1984. *Provisioning Paris Merchants and Millers in the Grain and Flour Trade during the Eighteenth Century*. Ithaca, NY: Cornell University Press.

Kaplan, Steven L. 1996. *The Bakers of Paris and the Bread Question, 1700–1775*. Durham, NC: Duke University Press.

Khosrova, Elaine. 2016. *Butter: A Rich History*. Chapel Hill, NC: Algonquin.

Kindermans, Marion, and Lea Delpont. 2017. "Food-trucks: Malgré l'effet de mode, un business pas si facile à tenir." *Les Echos*, February 8, 2017. https://www.lesechos.fr/2017/02/food-trucks-malgre-leffet-de-mode-un-business-pas-si-facile-a-tenir-154607.

Kindstedt, Paul S. 2012. *Cheese and Culture: A History of Cheese and Its Place in Western Civilization*. White River Junction, VT: Chelsea Green.

La Chapelle, Vincent. 1742. *Le cuisinier moderne*. Paris: V. La Chapelle.

"La Maison Angelina." n.d. Angelina. Accessed June 21, 2019. https://www.angelina-paris.fr.

Landweber, Julia. 2015. "'This Marvelous Bean': Adopting Coffee into Old Regime French Culture and Diet." *French Historical Studies* 38, no. 2 (April): pp. 193–223.

Laurioux, Bruno. 1999. "Les repas en France et en Angleterre aux XIVe et XVe siècles." In *Tables D'hier, Tables D'ailleurs: Histoire Et Ethnologie Du Repas*, edited by Jean-Louis Flandrin, 87–113. Paris: Jacob.

Laurioux, Bruno. 2013. *Manger au Moyen Age: Pratiques et discours alimentaires en Europe aux XIVe et XVe siècles*. Paris: Hachette.

La Varenne, François. 1651. *Le cuisinier français*. Paris: David.

Lazareff, Alexandre. 1998. *L'Exception culinaire française: Un patrimoine gastronomique en péril?* Paris: Albin Michel.

Lebelle, Aurélie. 2018. "Tacos, bagels, pad thaï. . . . Les nouvelles recettes street food qui cartonnent." *Le Parisien*, August 26, 2018.

Lejeune, H., P. Balny, J. J. Bénézit, C. Dereix, M. de Galbert, F. Geiger, M. L. Madignier, et al. 2014. "On mangeait mieux avant." Ministère de l'Agriculture et de l'Alimentation, October 24, 2014. https://agriculture.gouv.fr/mangeait-mieux-avant.

Lentschner, Keren. 2014. "Les chips Vico partent à l'assaut de la forteresse Lay's." *Le Figaro* 15 March 15, 2014.

Lespinasse, René de. 1886. *Les métiers et corporations de la ville de Paris: XIVe-XVIIIe siècles*. Paris: Imprimerie nationale.

Levy, Armelle. 2019. "Chandeleur: Les Français mangent de plus en plus de crêpes industrielles." RTL, February 2, 2019. https://www.rtl.fr/actu/conso/chandeleur-les-francais-mangent-de-plus-en-plus-de-crepes-industrielles-7796418658.

Lippmann, Marion. 2010. "Orangina: Une histoire à rebondissements." *20 Minutes*, October 9, 2010. https://www.20minutes.fr/economie/559143-20090910-economie-orangina-une-histoire-agrave-rebondissements.

Selected Bibliography

L.S.R. [Le sieur Robert]. (1674) 1693. *L'art de bien traiter.* Lyon, France: Claude Bachelu.
Malouin, Paul-Jacques. 1779. *Description et Détails des Arts du Meunier, du Vermicelier et du Boulenger, avec Une Histoire Abrégée de La Boulengerie et Un Dictionnaire de Ces Arts.* Paris: n.p.
Marin, François. 1739. *Les Dons de Comus.* Paris: Prault.
Marrus, Michael R. 1974. "Social Drinking in the 'Belle Epoque.'" *Journal of Social History* 7 (2): 115–41.
Marty, Nicolas. 2008. "L'eau embouteillée: Histoire de la construction d'un marché." *Entreprises et Histoire* 50: 86–99.
Massialot, François. 1691. *Le cuisinier royal et bourgeois.* Paris: Charles de Sercy.
Massialot, François. 1692. *Nouvelle instruction pour les confitures, les liqueurs, et les fruits.* Paris: Saugrain.
Massialot, François. 1698. *Nouvelle instruction pour les confitures, les liqueurs, et les fruits.* Paris: Charles de Sercy.
McCabe, Ina Baghdiantz. 2014. *A History of Global Consumption: 1500–1800.* London; New York: Routledge.
Mennell, Stephen. 2006. *All Manners of Food: Eating and Taste in England and France from the Middle Ages to the Present.* Urbana; Chicago: University of Illinois Press.
Menon, François. 1753. *La cuisinière bourgeoise.* Brussels: Foppens.
"Menus du Restaurant Scolaire." 2017. *Commune de Villedieu sur Indre* (blog), October 2, 2017. http://www.villedieu-sur-indre.fr/menus-du-restaurant-scolaire.
Méreuze, Didier. 2015. "Les 'food trucks' envahissent Paris." *La Croix,* June 28, 2015. https://www.la-croix.com/Culture/Cuisine/Les-food-trucks-envahissent-Paris-2015-06-28-1328814.
Michelin Guide. n.d. Accessed May 31, 2019. https://guide.michelin.com/fr/fr/restaurants.
Miller, Judith A. 1999. *Mastering the Market: The State and the Grain Trade in Northern France, 1700–1860.* Cambridge: Cambridge University Press.
Ministère de la Transition Écologique Solidaire. 2019. "Les organismes génétiquement modifiés (OGM)." Ecologique-Solidaire, March 20, 2019. https://www.ecologique-solidaire.gouv.fr/organismes-genetiquement-modifies-ogm-0.
Mognard, Elise. 2011. "Les trois traditions du foie gras dans la gastronomie française." *Anthropology of Food* 8 (May 12). https://doi.org/10.4000/aof.6789.
Montorgueil, Georges. 1899. *Les Minutes Parisiennes: Midi.* Paris: Paul Ollendorff.
Mordor Intelligence. 2020. "Europe Food Spread Market, Growth, Trends and Forecast." https://www.mordorintelligence.com/industry-reports/europe-food-spreads-market-industry.
Mouthon, Fabrice. 1997. "Le pain en Bordelais médiéval, XIIIe-XVIe s." *Archéologie du Midi Médiéval* 15 (1): 205–13.
Naulin, Sidonie. 2012. "Le repas gastronomique des Français: Génèse d'un nouvel objet culturel." *Sciences de la société* 87 (December 1): 8–25.

"Orgeat." 2014. In *The Oxford Companion to Food*, edited by Alan Davidson and Tom Jaine. Oxford: Oxford University Press.

Papademas, Photis, and Thomas Bintsis. 2017. *Global Cheesemaking Technology: Cheese Quality and Characteristics*. Hoboken, NJ: John Wiley & Sons. Ebook.

Parmentier, Antoine Augustin. 1778. *Le parfait boulanger ou traité complet sur la fabrication & le commerce du pain*. Paris: De l'Imprimerie Royale.

Pépin, Pierre-Yves. 1963. "Le commerce extérieur de la France, analyse et commentaire (1950–1960)." *L'Actualité économique* 38 (4): 586–625.

Peretti-Watel, Patrick. 2001. "La crise de la vache folle: Une épidémie fantôme?" *Sciences sociales et santé* 19 (1): 5–38.

Peters, Erica J. 1999. "National Preferences and Colonial Cuisine: Seeking the Familiar in French Vietnam," *Proceedings of the Western Society for French History* 27:150–59.

Piponnier, Françoise. 2000. "From Hearth to Table: Late Medieval Cooking Equipment." In *Food: A Culinary History*, edited by Jean-Louis Flandrin, Massimo Montanari, and Albert Sonnenfeld, 339–48. New York: Columbia University Press.

Pliny the Elder. 1855. *Natural History*. Translated by John Bostock and H. T. Riley. London: Taylor and Francis.

Proust, Marcel. (1918) 1962. *A la recherche du temps perdu*. Edited by P. Clarac and A. Ferre. Paris: Gallimard.

Quellier, Florent. 2013. *La Table des Français: Une Histoire Culturelle, 15e–Début 19e Siècle*. Rennes: Presses universitaires de Rennes.

Raynal, Cécile. 2004. "La vente des eaux minérales par les pharmaciens." *Revue d'Histoire de la Pharmacie* 92 (344): 587–606.

Raynal, Cécile. 2005. "La vente des eaux minérales embouteillées [deuxième partie]." *Revue d'Histoire de la Pharmacie* 93 (345): 45–60.

Reuters. 2012. "Le foie gras halal, un marché en plein essor," *Le Point*, December 24, 2012.

Revel, Jean-François. 2007. *Un Festin en Paroles: Histoire Littéraire de la Sensibilité Gastronomique de L'antiquité à Nos Jours*. Paris: Tallandier.

Ribaut, Jean-Claude. 2010. "La galette des Rois, une tradition congelée" *Le Monde*, January 1, 2010. https://www.lemonde.fr/vous/article/2010/01/01/la-galette-des-rois-une-tradition-congelee_1286565_3238.html.

Rioux, Philippe. 2019. "Guide Michelin 2019: La guerre des étoiles." *La Dépêche*, January 22, 2019. https://www.ladepeche.fr/article/2019/01/22/2944709-guide-michelin-2019-la-guerre-des-etoiles.html.

Roche, Daniel. 2000. *A History of Everyday Things: The Birth of Consumption in France, 1600–1800*. Translated by Brian Pearce. Cambridge: Cambridge University Press.

Rondeau, Pierre. 2018. "Les émeutes pour du Nutella en promo en disent long sur l'état d'esprit des Français." Slate.fr, January 26, 2018.

Sanchez, Sylvie. 2005. "Pizzas, crêpes et autres galettes." *Communications* 77:127–48.

Sand, Georges. 1872. *Nanon.* Paris: Michel Levy.
"Santé publique France présente les nouvelles recommandations sur l'alimentation, l'activité physique et la sédentarité." 2019. Santé publique France, January 22, 2019. https://www.santepubliquefrance.fr/presse/2019/sante-publique-france-presente-les-nouvelles-recommandations-sur-l-alimentation-l-activite-physique-et-la-sedentarite.
Serres, Olivier de. 1600. *Le Théâtre d'Agriculture et Mesnage des champs.* Paris: Métayer.
Sévigné, Madame de. 1972. *Correspondance.* Vol. 1: 1646–1675. Paris: Gallimard.
Shephard, Sue. 2006. *Pickled, Potted, and Canned: How the Art and Science of Food Preserving Changed the World.* New York: Simon & Schuster Paperbacks.
Spang, Rebecca L. 2001. *The Invention of the Restaurant: Paris and Modern Gastronomic Culture.* Cambridge, MA: Harvard University Press.
Statista.com. 2015. "Préférences des français en matière de boissons chaudes au petit-déjeuner en 2015." https://fr.statista.com/statistiques/479234/boisson-chaude-preferee-petit-dejeuner-france.
Strabo. 1903. *Geography.* Translated by H. C. Hamilton. Edited by W. Falconer. London: George Bell & Sons.
Tavoularis, Gabriel, and Éléna Sauvage. 2018. "Les nouvelles générations transforment la consommation de viande." *Consommation et modes de vie.* CRÉDOC no. 300 (September). https://www.credoc.fr/publications/les-nouvelles-generations-transforment-la-consommation-de-viande.
Tebben, Maryann. 2014. *Sauces: A Global History.* London: Reaktion.
Tebben, Maryann. 2015. "Seeing and Tasting: The Evolution of Dessert in French Gastronomy." *Gastronomica* 15 (2): 10–25.
Teuteberg, Hans Jurgen and Jean-Louis Flandrin. 2013. "The Transformation of the European Diet." In *Food: A Culinary History*, edited by Jean-Louis Flandrin, Massimo Montanari, and Albert Sonnenfeld, 442–56. New York: Columbia University Press.
Tilly, Louise A. 1971. "The Food Riot as a Form of Political Conflict in France." *Journal of Interdisciplinary History* 2 (1): 23–57.
Tomich, Dale W. 2016. *Slavery in the Circuit of Sugar: Martinique and the World-Economy, 1830–1848.* Albany: State University of New York Press.
Toussaint-Samat, Maguelonne. 2004. *La très belle et très exquise histoire des gâteaux et des friandises.* Paris: Flammarion.
UNESCO. n.d. "Gastronomic Meal of the French." Accessed May 6, 2020. https://ich.unesco.org/en/RL/gastronomic-meal-of-the-french-00437.
Vastine, Clémence. 2017. "Les plats les plus commandés par les Parisiens au restaurant sont . . ." *Le Figaro Madame*, September 28, 2017. https://madame.lefigaro.fr/cuisine/commande-restaurant-les-parisiens-preferent-le-tartare-de-saumon-et-la-piece-de-boeuf-280917-134467.
Vovos, Joffrey. 2019. "Sur la route des kebabs." *Le Parisien*, May 4, 2019. https://www.leparisien.fr/societe/sur-la-route-des-kebabs-le-sandwich-dont-les-francais-raffolent-04-05-2019-8065452.php.

Wagda, Marin. 2005. "A l'origine était la crêpe." *Hommes et Migrations* 1254 (March–April): 130–33.

Watts, Sydney. 2006. *Meat Matters: Butchers, Politics, and Market Culture in Eighteenth-Century Paris*. Buffalo, NY: University of Rochester Press.

Wells, Patricia. 1985. "Fare of the Country: As French As Tarte Tatin," *New York Times*, March 24, 1985.

Wheaton, Barbara K. 2015. *Savoring the Past: The French Kitchen and Table from 1300 to 1789*. New York: Touchstone Books.

Wile, Rob. 2014. "The True Story of How McDonald's Conquered France." *Business Insider*, August 22, 2014.

Wright, Gordon. 1964. *Rural Revolution in France: The Peasantry in the Twentieth Century*. Stanford, CA: Stanford University Press.

Yacou, C., V. Cornely, et al. 2015. "Surcharge pondérale en Guadeloupe et Martinique." Orsag (Observatoire Régional de la Santé de Guadeloupe), November 6, 2015. https://www.orsag.fr/wp-content/uploads/2019/04/ORSAG_Surcharge_ponderale_en_Guadeloupe_et_Martinique_CO_2015.pdf.

Zola, Emile. (1877) 1961. *L'Assommoir*. Vol. 2. Edited by A. Lanoux and H. Mitterand. Paris: Gallimard.

Index

Absinthe, xxi, 99, 104, 172
Aperitif (before-dinner drink), 17, 142–143, 151, 172, 186
Appert, Nicolas, xix, 5, 13

Bakeries, 19, 35
Beef, 25–26, 66, 67–69, 160, 168, 184–185; halal, 16, 184; veal, 5, 43–44, 69
Beer, 22, 99–100, 104–105, 166, 168
Bouillabaisse (fish stew), 24, 72
Bread: medieval period, 2–3, 137, 156; modern era, 13, 16, 19, 22, 141, 181; regulations on, 6–7, 13, 21; revolutionary era, 5–8, 20–21, 37; shapes, 21–22; for soup, 55; types of grain for, 1, 19–20, 37, 180, 181
Brioche Rolls (Brioches de Pâques), 127
Brittany (region), 48, 72, 100, 108, 133; crepes from, 20, 150, 171; meat from, 122, 126
Brunch, 134
Burgundy (region), 24, 52, 126, 164; wines from, xvi, 69, 103–104
Butchers, 3, 8–10, 26; for horse meat, 26

Café au lait (coffee with milk), 111–112, 138
Cafés: beverages served in, 107, 108, 113–115; history of, xvii, 111, 171–172
Cake from Gascony (Cake de Gascogne), 128
Camembert (cheese), 14, 29
Carême, Marie-Antoine, xix, 44, 52, 68, 121; desserts, 84, 85; sauces, 67; soups, 54–55
Carrots, Vichy-Style (Carottes Vichy), 179
Cassoulet, 74–75
Champagne, region, xx, 10, 44, 101–102, 120
Champagne, wine, xx, 90, 99, 102–103, 120, 127–128
Cheese, 1, 28–29, 58, 78, 160, 187
Cheese Twists (Feuilletés au fromage), 143
Chicken Curry with Coconut Milk (Poulet au curry et lait de coco), 182
Chicken in a Pot (Poule au pot), 64
Chickpea Salad (Salade aux pois chiches), 58
Cider, 4, 38, 100–101, 129, 171
Coffee, 111–112, 138, 178–179, 180
Colonial agriculture, 14, 178–181

Colonies, foods from, 13, 20, 31, 34–35, 178–179, 182–184
Cookbooks: *Dons de comus* (Marin), 45, 58, 65, 66; *L'art de bientraiter* (L.S.R.), xvii, 42, 66–67; *L'art de la cuisine française* (Carême), xix, 11, 54–55, 85; *Le cuisinier français* (La Varenne), x, xvii, 4, 42–45, 56; *Le cuisinier français* (La Varenne): meats, 66, 68; *Le cuisinier français* (La Varenne): sauces, 28, 65–66, 201; *Le cuisinier français* (La Varenne): soups, 54; *Le cuisinier royal et bourgeois* (Massialot), 5, 12, 36, 48, 57, 67; *Le guide culinaire* (Escoffier), xxi, 67, 91–92; *Le livre de cuisine* (Gouffé), 68, 69; *Le livre de pâtisserie* (Gouffé), 84, 85, 88; *Le Ménagier de Paris*, 3, 20, 24, 32, 42, 62; *Le Viandier* (Taillevent), xvi, 3, 32, 74; *Nouvelle instruction pour les confitures* (Massialot), 81, 112
Couscous, 76, 171
Crab Stew with Dumplings (Dombrés aux crabes), 125
Crème brûlée, 93
Crepes, 129, 149–151, 171
Crêpes Bretonnes, 170
Croque Monsieur ou Madame (Grilled Cheese and Ham Sandwich), 169
Cured meats, 25, 59, 78, 128, 143
Custard, 27, 94, 95, 137; crème brûlée, 81, 93, 94, 96; flan, 141–142

Éclairs, 88, 96
Eggs, 2, 27, 42, 45, 59, 77, 126; in desserts, 17, 95, 135; meringues, 81, 82, 86
Escoffier, Auguste, xxi, 67, 91–92, 96

Fast food, xiii, 140, 148–149, 151, 172–173, 187; McDonald's in France, xxii, 16, 148, 172, 187
Female chefs, 15, 34, 138, 164–165
Fish, xvi, 22–24, 48, 59, 62, 66, 72–73; amount consumed, 62–63; in overseas territories, 50–51, 71, 73, 124–126; as part of Lenten "lean days," 23, 62, 63, 78; pike, 11, 51, 166–167; salt cod, 23, 24, 48–50; shellfish, 51, 66
Fish with Lemon-Butter Sauce (Tilapia Meunière), 23
Foie gras (goose liver), 34, 42, 44, 59, 121–122, 132–133; at celebrations, 26, 127, 133; production of, 175–178
French Caribbean, 31, 44, 52, 63, 96, 115, 130, 178–179; Creole dishes, 71, 73; Indian cultural influence on, 52, 70–71; seafood in, 50–51, 124
French Revolution, 8, 103, 123, 129–130, 157, 159, 184

Gastronomy, 10–11, 130, 159, 190; gastronomic meal of the French, 16–17, 130, 160, 188–189, 191
Gaul, 1–2, 22, 69, 99, 108, 155
Gougères (cheese puffs), 53
Grilled Cheese and Ham Sandwich (Croque Monsieur ou Madame), 169

Haiti, xviii, 34, 83, 115, 178–180
Halles, les (covered market), xix, xx, 11–12, 23, 138
Hen's Milk (Lait de poule), 109
Hollandaise Sauce, 165
Hot chocolate, 36, 108–110, 112, 138, 171
Hot Chocolate, French (Chocolat chaud), 110

Index

Immigration, 76, 111, 144–145, 148, 184
Industrial food, 29, 142, 143, 187–188

Kebab (sandwich), 144–145, 148, 151

Lamb (and mutton), 3, 63, 66, 126, 156; leg of lamb, 65, 66, 74, 78, 126, 134, 183; popularity of, 25, 65, 69, 185; stewed, 43, 69, 126
Lemonade (Citron pressé), 114
Lentils, 45, 69
Lentils with Vinegar and Coriander (Lenticula), 2

Macaron (cookie), 90, 172
Meat: amount consumed, 25–26, 185; game, 16, 24–25, 62, 63, 66; hierarchy of, 3, 8, 25, 62, 63, 122, 156; legal regulation of, 8, 9–10, 26, 67; Lenten abstinence from, 23, 28, 43, 54, 62–63, 124; offal (organ meats), 44, 69, 73, 138. *See also specific types of meat (e.g., beef, pork)*
Meringues, 82
Michelin Guide, xx, xxi, 15, 163–164
Mint-flavored Sparkling Water (Diabolo menthe), 114–115
Moroccan Meat Skewers (Brochettes de Kefta), 183
Moroccan Mint Tea (Thé à la menthe), 116

Napoleon I, xviii, 11, 84, 134
Normandy (region), 8, 10, 25, 28, 38
Nutella, xxiii, 36, 137, 141–142, 144; in crepes, 129, 149, 171

Occupation of France, 11; German, 14, 163; Prussian, xx, 13, 26, 104, 122

Omelet with Herbs (Omelette aux Fines Herbes), 27
Orangina, xxii, 107
Oysters, xviii, 23, 24, 45, 48, 121, 162, 168

Pastry shop (patisserie), 35, 86, 88, 90, 96, 123, 137
Pâté, 25, 42, 52–53, 121
Persillade (Parsley Sauce), 30
Phylloxera (vineyard infestation), xx, 12–13, 172, 180
Pike Dumplings with Nantua Sauce (Quenelles de Brochet, Sauce Nantua), 167–168
Pike in German Sauce (Brochet à la sausse allemande), 12
Pistou (French Pesto), 30
Pizza, 146–148, 187
Pizza, "French Style," 147
Pork, 3, 25, 53, 62, 63, 68, 75; pork fat, 2, 71, 72; and religious dietary rules, 151, 184; salt pork, 1, 58, 63, 69, 72
Pork Loin with Sauce Robert (Longe de porc à la sauce Robert), 4
Potatoes, 16, 36–37, 46, 69; chips, 151–152
Potato-Leek Soup (Potage poireaux-pommes de terre), 56
Potato Puffs (Pommes soufflées), 162
Poultry: amount consumed, xii, 16, 25–26, 63; chicken, 26, 34, 38, 63–65, 69, 71; duck, 36, 43, 45, 66, 74, 78, 162–163; goose, 66, 72, 74 (*see also* Foie gras [goose liver]); in pâtés or terrines, 26, 52, 53; status of, 62, 64–65, 72, 122; turkey, 64, 66, 122
Profiteroles (Cream Puffs with Chocolate Sauce), 89
Proust, Marcel, xxi, 68

Quiche, 77, 130
Quiche Lorraine, 77

Rabbit, xii, 26, 53, 68, 69
Ragout (meat in sauce), 42–43, 44, 66
Raspberry Charlotte dessert (Charlotte aux framboises), 87
Ratatouille, 47–48, 166
Ratatouille (Tian à la famille Louyot), 31–32
Rationing, xxii, 8, 9, 13–14
Regional cuisine, 10–11, 15, 31–32, 51, 68, 73–76
Restaurants: origin of, xvii, 10–11, 158–160; types of, 10, 172. *See also* Fast food
Rice, 13, 20, 46, 69, 181; rice pudding, 42, 85, 94, 95
Rice Pudding (Riz au lait), 94
Roquefort cheese, xxi, 28, 29
Rum, 52, 88, 115, 130

Salad, 37, 42, 56–58, 59, 83, 148
Salt Cod and Potato Purée (Brandade de morue), 50–51
Salt-Cod Fritters (Accras de morue), 49–50
Sandwiches: Ham-Butter (Jambon-beurre), 145; Pickle-Pâté (Pâté-cornichons), 139
Sauce Hollandaise, 165
Sauce Robert, 11
Sauces, 4, 11, 12, 32, 65, 66–67, 159
Sauerkraut with Sausages (Choucroute Garnie), 76
Sausages, 25, 44–45, 75, 85, 150, 164; boudin, 44, 122, 138; in cassoulet, 73–74

Scalloped Potatoes with Chicken Broth (Pommes boulangères), 47
Scallops with Cream Sauce (Coquilles St. Jacques), 121
School cafeterias, 160, 184, 190–191
Seasonal eating, x, 57, 59, 187
Shepherd's Pie (Hachis Parmentier), 70
Snails (escargot), 24, 42, 44, 51, 168, 171
Soup, 13, 54–56, 68, 71–73, 112, 133; Onion Soup with Cheese Croutons (Soupe à l'oignon gratinée), 161
Spices, 4, 29–30, 31–32, 132; in Caribbean cuisine, 71–72, 124
Strawberry Cake (Fraisier), 131
Stuffed Tomatoes (Tomates farcies), 189
Sugar production, 34–35, 73, 83, 130, 178–181
Sugar sculptures, 83–84, 85, 86, 134

Tacos, "French Style," 149
Tartine (After-School Snack), 142
Tea, xix, 112, 113, 115
Truffles, 33–34, 132, 165

UNESCO, xxiii, 16–17, 130, 188–191

Veal Shoulder Bourgeois-Style (Epaule de veau à la bourgeoise), 5
Vegan Foie Gras (Faux Gras), 177
Vegetarian cooking, 43, 69, 78, 141, 164
Vinaigrette for a Green Salad, 33
Vineyards, 12, 100–101, 103, 180

Yule log (bûche de Noël), 122–123

ABOUT THE AUTHOR

Maryann Tebben, PhD, is professor of French and head of the Center for Food Studies at Bard College at Simon's Rock, the country's first residential early college. She earned her BA in French from the University of Notre Dame and her doctorate in French literature from the University of Southern California. Dr. Tebben has taught French language and literature at Simon's Rock since 2000, including a course on French food culture and several hands-on food studies courses. Her research examines the relationship of food culture to national identity in France and Italy, and her publications include a book chapter on the naming of Italian pasta sauces in *Representing Italy through Food* (2017) and an article on the evolution of dessert in French gastronomy in *Gastronomica*. She appeared in two food documentaries on French television, one on sandwiches and the other on French fries. Her first book *Sauces: A Global History* was published in 2014; her new book *Savoir-Faire: A History of Food in France* was published in November 2020. When she is not reading or writing about food, she enjoys making *tarte Tatin*, eating French cheese, and traveling, usually with a food destination in mind. She lives in Massachusetts with her family.

www.ingramcontent.com/pod-product-compliance
Lightning Source LLC
Chambersburg PA
CBHW060949230426
43665CB00015B/2130